Taking Liberties

Chris Atkins would like to thank:
  Nicky Moss
  Tim Aldrich
  his parents

&

Harry, I promise I'll never do this again.
Until next time.

TAKING LIBERTIES

BY
CHRIS ATKINS, SARAH BEE
& FIONA BUTTON

Editor Becca Ellson
Additional Material by Christina Slater

REVOLVER BOOKS
Published by the Revolver Group

Revolver Books Ltd, 10 Lambton Place, Notting Hill Gate,
London W11 2SH

First published in Great Britain in 2007 by Revolver Books,
an imprint of Revolver Entertainment Ltd, registered offices:
Craven House, 16 Northumberland Avenue, London WC2N 5AP

Copyright © S2S Productions Ltd, 2007
Foreword copyright © Henry Porter, 2007
All rights reserved

The right of Chris Atkins to be identified as the author of this
work has been asserted in accordance with the Copyright,
Designs and Patents Act, 1988.

ISBN: 978-1-905978-03-8

Cover design © Freeform London

A CIP Catalogue record for this book is available from the
British Library

Text design and typesetting by Dexter Haven Associates, London
Printed in the UK by CPI Bookmarque, Croydon, CR0 4TD

www.revolverbooks.com

Contents

Foreword

Henry Porter

These days it's difficult to concentrate. Our attention is jerked from war in the Middle East to global warming to genocide to bird flu to terrorism and back again in a series of vivid freeze frames. There's no time to think. We're overloaded with bad news, or news that is simply too enormous or incomprehensible to absorb, and after a session with the newspapers or TV news, what we're left with is a keen sense of our own helplessness.

But concentrate we must on the subject Taking Liberties. The erosion of freedom in Britain, the manner of its theft and the combination of paralysis and fecklessness in the institutions that are meant to protect us is of compelling importance to each one of us. We have arrived at a moment in British history which most of us never thought would come. We took it for granted that we lived in a country where all but a few extremists shared a sense of miraculous good fortune about our system of rights and personal liberty. We used to lecture foreigners that Britain was a place where all men and women were born free and everyone could do what they wanted unless it was specifically outlawed by statute. Our freedoms were so ancient, so much part of the makeup of every Briton that we did not even require the insurance of a constitution or a bill of rights. Lesser nations might need these bits of paper because, well, they didn't have our history, their democratic systems were much younger, and they had to control the dark, authoritarian impulses of their characters. But we, on the other hand, had freedom in our blood.

I was just as guilty of this complacency as anyone else. Whatever George Orwell's speculations in *1984*, it seemed impossible to me to envisage a British government, as we have now, attacking so many rights at once and promoting a society in which individual privacy will be so thoroughly compromised. I never thought I would hear a British prime minister almost boast of his view that civil liberties arguments were made for another age. Much more important – and I suppose more depressing – I never imagined that my countrymen would meet such an onslaught with so little resistance, so little sense of what they were losing.

It sounds melodramatic, but we now face a choice that is as important for us as it is for our children and grandchildren. Either we let the slide continue, with successive governments paring down these rights and liberties until Britain can no longer be said to be a functioning democracy; or we begin to assert our own rights and stand up for those of others, which of course includes future generations who rely on us to defend the system we inherited.

It's a sign of the intellectual laziness of our times, as well as the atrophied standards of debate, that when faced with the evidence of the attack on liberty, which, incidentally, is not very hard to come by, so many people respond by saying, 'If you've done nothing wrong, you've got nothing to fear'. The first problem with this is that it hands everything to the state and sets each one of us in a position of servitude in relation to it. The second is that this response is almost always uttered by people who cannot think of society in terms other than of their own well-being, gratification and comfort.

Whenever someone says to me that they have nothing to fear because they've done nothing wrong, I ask them a few questions. How can you be sure you've done nothing wrong? When was the last time you looked at the statute book? Can you name just three of the three thousand new criminal offences that have been added to the law under New Labour? Are you certain you know the difference between what is wrong in your own mind and what is now illegal? After all, there are many activities that could never be described as wrong but which now may result in a criminal conviction. For instance, you may get yourself into trouble under the Harassment Act merely by sending an emailed complaint or protest to someone twice. You can be arrested for walking in Parliament Square with a placard without having first received the permission of a policeman. You may be fined under public-order laws for shouting a joke at a constable or wearing a T-shirt which he believes may insult the Prime Minister or US President. These actions are not wrong, but they are now illegal.

And what about the steady reduction in defendants' rights which has been one of New Labour's signature policies? Are you happy about the introduction of hearsay evidence in antisocial behaviour cases? What about control orders, where suspects who have not been found guilty of any crime are deprived of their liberty and ability to earn a living? They are not even allowed proper legal representation or to know the evidence against them. In the Union of Myanmar, the Burmese military junta would call this house arrest, for that is exactly what it is. The use of house arrest is one of the key indicators of a police state. We're not there yet, but we are building the requisite legal apparatus to create one, and we already have the sophisticated surveillance technology to enforce it. Yet there's hardly a whisper of complaint in parliament, and persistent concern is almost absent from the media.

The current Government's ambitions do not of course stop at the use of control orders as a counter-terrorist measure. There are new proposals to extend them to include serious criminals. International drug gangs and people smugglers are certainly a problem, but if we start punishing people without a court first deciding that the law has been broken, we surely abandon one of the principles of British law, indeed one of the greatest inventions of our culture. If these new laws are passed it will be enough for the authorities merely to suspect someone's criminal intent to take action against them. Politicians have argued that this is a regrettable but necessary measure to deal with one of the threats of the modern world. Yet once the practice is established there's no reason why a government should not begin to introduce other ways of controlling and disciplining the population without having to go to court. In times of crisis, these precedents for extrajudicial action might prove extremely tempting to a cabinet under pressure. We've already got people being arrested for carrying blank placards within a kilometre of Parliament Square, being hauled from Labour conferences for shouting at ministers and being prevented from taking part in legitimate protests, so new orders aimed at curbing, say, incitement, agitation and sedition wouldn't be a great leap.

The crucial tactic in a successful campaign against rights and liberties, such as has been waged by New Labour in the last decade, is to persuade the vast majority of people that the loss of liberty only affects those who are a menace – terrorists, serious criminals or people held to be guilty of antisocial behaviour. It's an easy argument to make in a society which believes that if you have done nothing wrong you have nothing to fear and which, as a result, has become far less scrupulous in the general application of rights. A system of rights only works if it is universal and if there is a general acceptance that when one person's rights are removed or infringed we all somehow suffer, because their rights are in fact our rights – even if we don't think we will ever need them. Nearly a hundred years ago Winston Churchill put it well when he said, 'The mood and temper of the public in regard to the treatment of crime and criminals is one of the most unfailing tests of the civilisation of any country. A calm dispassionate re-cognition of the rights of the accused, and even of the convicted criminal, against the State – a constant heart-searching by all charged with the duty of punishment... These are the symbols, which, in the treatment of crime and criminal, mark and measure the stored-up strength of a nation, and are sign and proof of the living virtue in it.'

As this campaign by the Government against out rights has proceeded, New Labour has sought to portray its actions as meeting the needs of the modern world, even though Britain has faced far greater threats in the past. The Government has asked us to trust its motives, yet at the same time it builds a vast and sinister apparatus of state surveillance. If things go as planned, it will eventually include a database on all children, the National Health database, the total surveillance of British roads and town centres by number recognition cameras, and the ID card system, which will track and record the movements of people as they identify themselves at banks, pharmacies, hospitals, hotels etc. The tentacles of these databases will naturally reach out to each other to form a surveillance network that would be the dream of every dictator. Of one thing we can be sure: privacy in Britain will very soon be a distant memory.

I happen to believe that it is right to regard every government of whatever political complexion with extreme wariness. But after ten years of New Labour, my suspicion has been replaced by fear. As this excellent book demonstrates on every page, all of us – whatever claims of innocence we make – have much to fear from a government that has shown such contempt for our liberty. *Taking Liberties* is the best argument I have yet seen for a new British constitution and bill of rights which enshrine our rights and place them beyond the reach of unscrupulous politicians.

Henry Porter
London, 2007

Introduction

Taking Liberties – what's it got to do with me?

This book is all about you. Liberties, freedoms, human rights – whatever you call them – are here for your protection. Things like freedom of speech and the right to a fair trial are here to defend you against injustice. Our democratic society has survived on the idea that no matter who you are – office worker, taxi driver, full-time parent, peace protestor, terror suspect or Labour Party fundraiser – we are all equal in the eyes of the law. Faced with the threat of terrorism, our current Government has told us that we must lay down our freedoms for our lives. Perhaps they've forgotten the millions of people from past generations who have laid down their lives for our freedom.

> *Sometimes we have to modify some of our own freedoms – in the short term – in order to prevent their misuse.*
>
> **JOHN REID, 9 AUGUST 2006'**

> *Well, I expect terrorists to attack my liberty – I don't expect my democratically elected government to do the same thing.*
>
> **RACHEL NORTH, WRITER AND 7/7 SURVIVOR**

We have spent over a year following the stories of normal people whose lives have been changed by New Labour's avalanche of authoritarian laws.

These stories of injustice are startling. Some are shocking, some are hilarious; some might make you cry and a few will definitely make you angry. All are true.

There are many reasons for this drain on our liberty, but whenever an ancient freedom is removed one phrase in particular is always heard: 'The War Against Terror' (TWAT).

> *Governments need people to be frightened in order to*
> *control them.*
>
> **TONY BENN, FORMER LABOUR MP AND CABINET MINISTER[2]**

> *'The vocabulary of war, and the War on Terror, is so useful*
> *for the Government because it does legitimate their*
> *intrusions into people's liberties. Or seems to legitimate it.*
>
> **BORIS JOHNSON, CONSERVATIVE MP[3]**

We'll also peer behind the spin and fear that emanates from our Government. We have spoken to dozens of experts and commentators from across the academic and political spectrum and the range of opinion could not be broader. It's not often that you hear Left and Right saying the same thing.

Our stories of injustice fall into six main chapters:
- Free speech and the right to protest;
- Surveillance, privacy and identity;
- Detention without trial;
- Respect;
- Extradition;
- Torture.

After this cheery subject we'll look at the reasons why this has happened (the enigmatically titled 'Why?' chapter), and then look at what we can do to turn the tide (daringly named 'What Next?'). When you've finished the book you'll have two choices:
1) You can chuckle at the jokes, feel sorry for the people whose lives have been ruined and then go back to watching *Celebrity Face Swap*.

2) You can actually do something about it, and we've made a few suggestions.

If enough people take the second option, we could make sure that democracy isn't just something our children will read about in textbooks.

THE ROAD TO HELL IS PAVED WITH GOOD INTENTIONS

Those readers expecting us to reveal a huge conspiracy per-petrated by shadowy figures in smoky rooms are going to be disappointed. The sad truth is that our leaders are restricting our rights and freedoms with the genuine desire to protect us.

> *Of all tyrannies, a tyranny exercised for the good of its victims may be the most oppressive.*
>
> **C.S. LEWIS**[4]

Neither will we be painting too rosy an image of the past. If we tried to convince you that Britain, until Tony Blair came along, was a land of peace and harmony with fairness and justice for all, you might start to regret buying this book. If we then denounced Blair for turning the country into a 'Big Brother' style totalitarian nightmare that's two steps away from Nazi Germany, you would be well within your rights (what remains of them) to demand your money back and buy a book by Gordon Ramsay instead. He does a great new one on pies by the way.

Clearly we are not in a fully fledged police state. And the previous 18 years of Conservative rule are rarely viewed as a golden age of freedom for the individual. Anyone who was in-volved in the miners' strike, poll-tax riots or the rave scene can testify to this. But the last ten years has seen an unprecedented shift of power from the individual towards the state. The freedoms and rights that we have had for hundreds of years have either been eroded or removed in the seemingly endless 'War Against Terror'. New Labour has dismantled protections for the indivi-dual in a way that no other government has even contemplated.

The reasons given for this relentless power shift are at best misguided and at worst dishonest.

WHY NOW?

At the time of writing, Tony Blair is currently shuffling off his political coil, and will doubt soon be pushing up the daisies on a well-earned lecture tour of the US. His legacy is a deluge of laws that have chipped away at every one of our basic rights and freedoms. As he flies first class to Washington, he'll be leaving a country that's taking its first steps towards a modern-day authoritarian state. Every leader from here on in will inherit the invisible grip over the public that was built up under Blair's rule. Even if you accept that the current Government will not use this power against you, there is no guarantee that a future one will not. If we want to stop the rot, now is the time to speak up.

Losing your rights is often a one-way street. Giving up your liberty to your government is not like lending your mate a fiver... Unless it's one of those mates who refuses to give it back to you, then denies they ever took it in the first place, then, if you stand outside their house demanding it back, calls the police and has you arrested. When Blair finally leaves office, the counter of liberty will not reset to zero. Control is always attractive to politicians, as it makes their job easier. It's like asking me if I'd rather write this book with a quill and ink, or with a PC. Free people are unruly, unpredictable and criticise governments when they screw up. People who are not free are far easier to govern. It is unlikely that any ruler will enter Downing Street and immediately reverse all these authoritarian laws. Unless their hand is forced.

JUST HOW BAD IS IT?

> *Well of course the erosion of civil liberties doesn't feel dangerous – unless you're a human-rights nerd like me – it doesn't feel dangerous to most people – until they experience injustice.*
>
> **SHAMI CHAKRABARTI, DIRECTOR OF LIBERTY**[5]

As a taste of what's to come, your government now has the power to:

- imprison you for peaceful protest;[6]
- demand to know every last detail about your private life;[7]
- have you tracked 24 hours a day;[8]
- place you under house arrest without charge;[9]
- have you extradited to America without evidence of any crime;[10]
- facilitate your torture overseas.[11]

As we'll explain, the restrictions on your freedom that are being imposed today are greater even than in times of war. Judging by the rhetoric that is emanating from politicians on both sides, things are about to get a whole lot worse.

Unless we do something.

But before the barricades come out, let's have a quick look back at how it all started...

Chapter 1

What were we thinking?

ONCE UPON A TIME...

Nineteen ninety-seven was the first time my generation voted. We had grown up with 18 years of Tory rule, and the country wanted a change. *Really* wanted a change. We'd have voted in Ozzy Osbourne to get rid of the Tories. It started to go badly for them on Black Wednesday. I didn't really understand what the ERM was, but I remember my dad telling me that John Major had dropped a bollock, interest rates had doubled, the mortgage had trebled ... and then he hit the scotch and cancelled Christmas. As the nineties wore on, the Tories became mired in sleaze. Every month there seemed to be another minister brought down by money, guns or ho's: Neil Hamilton (money), Jonathan Aitken (guns and money), David Mellor (ho's) ... and then there was Jeffery Archer. He couldn't have been more bent if he'd been tied in a knot. And it wasn't just that they were dodgy – they had to go and smear their corruption in our faces.[1] By the time we came to vote in 1997 we were itching to give the Tories their marching orders.

The only problem was that the country had a bit of a blind spot when it came to voting Labour. In 1992 everyone walked into the polling booth thinking 'Labour, Labour, Labour ...' and promptly put a cross in the blue box. At that point there was just something, well, smelly about the Labour Party that prevented them gaining the public's trust.

But just at the moment of despair, when people actually thought they might have to consider voting Liberal Democrat, Tony Blair appeared on the scene.

(Lights flash, fanfare plays, smoke billows.)

Wow. He wasn't a politician, he was a movie star! He quickly put a stake through the heart of 'Old' Labour (Socialism, high taxes, elbow patches, trade unions, Karl Marx) and forged 'New' Labour (Ford Mondeos, nice hair, catchy slogans, Islington) in the fires of Millbank.

Blair took the country by storm. Look at that smile, look at those teeth. You wouldn't catch him banging on about the redistribution of wealth, he'd be too busy playing squash with Chris Evans or giving out a Brit Award. Cool Britannia! He's got my vote alright...hell's teeth, even the *Sun* loved him! And he *sounded good*:

> *Tough on crime, tough on the causes of crime (Wallop!)[2]*
> *We will be whiter than white (Go for it Tony!)[3]*
> *Education, education, education! (You had me at*
> *'education')[4]*

Come 1 May '97 we were gagging to elect the man. And who can forget *that night*? The Tories didn't lose, they were *executed*... every hour of the night had another delicious casualty.

1 a.m. Michael Portillo (think Eton and Stasi) lost his true-blue Enfield seat! Huzzah!

2 a.m. Up comes a Cabinet Minister, Malcolm Rifkind (think Scottish Dalek). Bang! Right between the eyes.

3 a.m. David Mellor (think greasy hair and Chelsea shirt) bites the dust...Everyone chanting 'Out! Out! Out!' at the TV...

4 a.m. Neil Hamilton (think...you know) kicked in the goolies by Martin Bell. Ding dong the witch is dead![5]

And then...in rode the white knight. Tony Blair crowd-surfed from Sedgefield to London's Festival Hall to the sound of 'Things Can Only Get Better' which, interestingly, is a song written about the effects of the drug ecstasy. The similarities between voting

New Labour and taking E are striking – an expensive and totally synthetic feeling of manic euphoria that you later massively regret.

But that night, our Tony was on fire. Most of the country had been up all night, so recollections are hazy. A majority of 3478! Go Tony! He swept into Downing Street like a cross between Gandalf the White and the English football team in 1966. He kicked in the door of No 10 and chucked John Major and his odious henchmen into the gutter. Good riddance, and we all collapsed into a smug heap. Off you go Tony, we trust you.

FAST FORWARD TO 7 JULY 2005 ...

Rachel North:

> *I first thought I was blind and deaf. I couldn't hear or see anything and I thought I was dying. I realised I was still alive and I heard a scraping noise as the train came to a halt. It was very disorientating, it was like one minute you were on a train and the next you were night diving without a regulator and drowning. I couldn't breathe, there was no air anymore.*
>
> *I could hear this terrible, terrible screaming from the back of the train carriage. People were starting to scream with panic and fear, praying and saying that they were going to die, just horrifying noises. We struggled to our feet. I thought the tunnel was going to collapse on us. I thought we were all going to burn to death because all I could smell and taste was smoke.*
>
> *We decided that if we just kept calm and held each other's hands we could probably cope with the next few minutes. We gradually got off the front of the train, down a little ladder, and started to walk down the tracks. As we got to Russell Square we realised that we were all covered in black oily soot and blood. People were bleeding, they had glass in their feet, people were badly injured, they were crying. So I kept on saying 'Come on, we're nearly there, don't worry,' and 'Lets go and*

complain to London Underground, this has been a rubbish journey'.

When I got to Russell Square, I went outside and looked for ambulances, but there was nothing, just people trying to get on the train to go to work. They were saying 'Why can't we just get on the train?' and I was going 'Well you can't,' and they were going 'What the hell's the matter with you?' and I was thinking I don't know what the matter is with me. I just think I'm supposed to be dead and you're all here asking why you can't get on the train, it's ridiculous.

I got to hospital and said, 'I hope you are sending lots of ambulances, there are loads of people that are really hurt, there's been a bomb on my train.' That's when people started to come in and they'd had their legs blown off and were covered in blood, covered in soot, it was just the most extraordinary, extraordinary day.[6]

Ken Livingstone was on his way back from celebrating London winning the 2012 Olympic bid. Visibly shaken, he gave an off-the-cuff speech:

This was not a terrorist attack against the mighty and the powerful. It was not aimed at presidents or prime ministers. It was aimed at ordinary, working-class Londoners, black and white, Muslim and Christian, Hindu and Jew, young and old. It was an indiscriminate attempt to slaughter, irrespective of any considerations for age, for class, for religion, or whatever.[7]

Later that day Tony Blair made a speech that also seemed to capture the mood of the nation:

We will not allow violence to change our society and values.[8]

But a month after the attacks Blair summoned the media to Downing Street and made it clear that the exact opposite would be taking place:

The rules of the game have changed.[9]

He listed a '12-point terror plan' which signalled a dramatic acceleration in the rate of law-making that would change our society and values. The laws that followed the 7/7 bombings built on the authoritarian framework created in Blair's first eight years in office, and continued to attack every one of our basic civil liberties.

Freedom of speech

The 2000 Terrorism Act gave the police unlimited powers to stop and search. These have yet to catch a single terrorist, but are regularly used on protestors who disagree with the Government. It also gave the Home Secretary the power to 'proscribe' non-violent organisations, making joining or supporting them a criminal offence.[10] The 2005 Serious Organised Crime and Police Act banned protest in the square kilometre surrounding parliament without special police authorisation.[11] The 2006 Terrorism Act brought in the new offence of 'encouragement of terrorism', which means that you could theoretically be jailed for saying the phrase 'Nelson Mandela was a good bloke'.[12]

Privacy

ID cards will soon be a reality, as will the vast National Identity Register (NIR) behind them. The NIR will link together all the other databases so that in a few years any member of the government, any civil servant, or anyone they choose to share or sell your data to will be able to know every last detail about your life. Britain is already the most spied-on nation in the world, with 4.2 million surveillance cameras,[13] and this number will continue to rise.

The rule of law

'Innocent until proven guilty' is becoming a thing of the past. The 2001 Anti-Terrorism, Crime and Security Act gave the Home Secretary the power to detain foreign nationals indefinitely without charge.[14] The 2003 Extradition Act means that you can be extradited to the USA without evidence.[15] The 2005 Prevention of Terrorism Act has given the Home Secretary the power to place any British citizen under house arrest based only on a 'reasonable suspicion'.[16]

The 2006 Terrorism Act means that the police can now hold anyone for 28 days before charge. Fixed penalty notices are now applicable for dozens of different crimes, which means the police can decide your guilt on the spot.[17]

Ban on torture

New Labour backed the Bush Administration in setting up Guantanamo Bay, and in doing so facilitated the torture of British citizens and residents. The Home Office fought to bring torture evidence into British courts, and still gives value to information extracted under torture.[18] They have prevented British citizens seeking damages after years of torture abroad. New Labour is clearly implicated in the American process of 'Extraordinary Rendition' that involves outsourcing torture to other countries using British airports.[19]

All of this has been done in the name of reducing the risk of terrorism, but the evidence will show that oppressive legislation usually has the opposite effect. The victims of the 7 July bombings are frequently used as a reasoning for this increase in government power. Rachel North has been horrified at the way the victims and survivors of the bombings have been used to further the Government's agenda.

> What did you think of the Government response to the
>   attacks?
> *Rachel: There was the 12-point anti-terrorism plan, 'let's*
>   *bang people up without charging them for 90 days',*
>   *and lots of headline-grabbing stuff. Done often, it must*
>   *be said, in the name of the victim. This did amuse me*
>   *in a slightly bitter way, because I don't remember them*
>   *asking any of the victims whether this would make*
>   *them feel any safer.*
> And ID cards and the database?

Rachel: I don't think that having a national identification database would have stopped the bombers, and I don't think the bombers would have felt remotely put off by the fact that their details were known. I think they would have welcomed it.

Do you think that increase in police powers will help?

Rachel: It's important when you look at trying to prevent things like terrorism that you don't throw the baby out with the bathwater. It you're instigating stop-and-search, locking people up without trial, putting people under house arrest simply under suspicion of being a bit dodgy, and the people who you are locking up tend to be generally brown-skinned Muslims, then everybody who falls under that category is going to have a certain amount of edginess about them.

The restriction of protest around Westminster is apparently for security as well.

Rachel: You have to remember that people who tell us not to panic about these things are driving to work in bulletproof cars, sitting behind concrete bollards, surrounded by armed police. They've got less reason to worry than me getting on the Piccadilly Line in the morning.

Do you think 'the rules of the game have changed' now that there's a 'War Against Terror'?

Rachel: I didn't get off that train saying the rules of the game had changed, I got on that train a civilised person – I got blown up with civilised people. I do not want to throw away my decency in order to continue a war that I never called, that I never bought into, that I never believed in. This isn't a war so don't make it into one, it dignifies it. If you have war you can divide everything into us and them, goodies and baddies. It's a story, and at the end of the story the goodies always have to win. Well, it doesn't work like that; this is a nuanced world with shades of grey.

We're told that these things are necessary to stop this happening again.

Rachel: It's horrible what happened, dreadful, evil, atrocious suffering, and yes we should learn every possible lesson we can from it, but it doesn't mean that we should live our lives as if every train we get on is going to blow up and every day is going to be another 7 July. Let's try and calm the hell down a bit; this is not the end of the world. Even if I had died, I wouldn't want the constitution to be shredded on my behalf.[20]

Chapter 2

Free speech and the right to protest

SILENCE IS GOLDEN

> *You have the right to free speech as long as you're not*
> *dumb enough to actually try it.*

THE CLASH, 'KNOW YOUR RIGHTS'

'*I'm arresting you for conducting an unauthor– er, demonstration,*
outside of 10 Downi– er, outside of Downing Street without, er,
giving ... given authorisation ...'

Steve Jago wasn't entirely surprised to be hearing his rights
haltingly read to him by a young policeman in June 2006. He
was standing alone by the imposing gates of Downing Street,
holding a rather tasteful and understated placard bearing a quote
from George Orwell's *1984*: 'In a time of universal deceit, telling
the truth is a revolutionary act'. It was a pretty polite protest, but
nevertheless changes in the law had made his action illegal in and
of itself. So he was obliged to submit to being handcuffed and
removed from the scene in a police car.

What did surprise Steve was what happened next. The police
search of his possessions turned up three copies of a *Vanity Fair*
article entitled 'Blair's Big Brother Britain'. He was told these
items constituted 'politically motivated material' – a subversive
stash, in effect – and would be used as evidence against him. The
article was by the novelist and *Observer* columnist Henry Porter,

and was a scathing assault on the Government's efforts to erode civil liberties in the UK. Someone told Henry that his article was being used as a tool by the very forces to which it was in such vehement opposition. Henry was cross – although he doubtless keenly appreciated the irony.[1]

While Steve waited for a court date to be set for his case, the *Independent* newspaper reprinted 'Blair's Big Brother Britain' on its front page under the prominent warning: 'Reading this article can get you arrested'. A friend of Steve's tested this a few days later by sitting down opposite Downing Street and reading that day's *Independent*. She wasn't arrested, but she was questioned at some length. Still, you couldn't say she wasn't warned. What George Orwell would have thought is anyone's guess.[2]

In Britain today, such absurdities are becoming more commonplace. In fact – and we'd have to check this with our legal people, but it's certainly possible – the book you are currently reading may well amount to a subversive document, evidence pointing towards your criminal intent if found on your person. It does contain at least one quote from Henry Porter's incendiary article. If you do not want to be arrested, look away now:

> *What is remarkable – in fact almost a historic phenomenon – is the harm [Blair's] Government has done to the unwritten British constitution in … nine years, without anyone really noticing, without the press objecting or the public mounting mass protests. At the inception of Cool Britannia, British democracy became subject to a silent takeover.[3]*

Freedom of speech is what allows Henry Porter to say that, and what allows you to read it, and quote from it if you like. It's what allows us to write this book and make the film that it's the book of. Free speech really exemplifies the concept of freedom itself. What luxury to be able to say whatever you like, whenever you want, without fear of arrest or official censure. It's the bread and butter of human rights, perhaps the most fundamental, inviolable right in a democracy, and it has some pretty stiff competition for that sacred place. The right to protest, which goes hand in hand with it, is also guaranteed as part of any decent democracy package – it is the direct means by which you use your right to freedom of speech to tell your elected government your grievances. Both of these rights, which go together like a horse and something a horse really gets on with, are presently under threat. Through the Government's restriction of the right to protest, we can gauge its desire to infringe upon the right of all of us to free speech, and as things stand at the moment, it seems the Government would really rather we all piped down. And they aren't afraid to change the law to make sure we do.

It's a quiet, insidious threat, which you may not have noticed yourself. It's one of those incremental things, nothing so self-evident and alarming as a giant concrete wall or a tank stationed where you used to park your car. But as an increasing number of people who've fallen foul of new legal restrictions on this most breezeblock-basic right can tell you, it's gaining ground. Given the current climate, in fact, we should probably stop here and write something else. Just in case. Something about kittens.

~~KITTENS AND THEIR CUTE LITTLE STRIPEY KITTEN PAWS: A SOCIAL HISTORY~~

Oh well, in for a penny.

FREE SPEECH – NOT JUST FOR LOUDMOUTHS

> *If people do not have free speech, the right to assemble, the right of belief, the right of travel, as was the case say in East Germany, they don't have the right to examine their government. The government becomes unaccountable – and a democracy can only work if the government is accountable to the people.*
>
> **HENRY PORTER**[4]

> *The so called War on Terror has had an impact on human rights in general ... Freedom of expression is*

*going to be shrunk because the government and
militaries and people in positions of power will try to
protect what is being said… in the name of security.
So globally for the last three or four years, the security
agenda has had a fairly negative impact on freedom
of expression.*

DR AGNES CALLAMARD, EXECUTIVE DIRECTOR, ARTICLE 19, FREE SPEECH NGO[5]

It almost goes without saying that the right to free speech has
been fought for throughout history, all over the world, and
remains an ongoing struggle. Whether over political convictions or
porn, individuals and groups are constantly striving to be allowed
to voice their beliefs in the face of censure. Many bold steps have
been taken to define and secure the right to free speech, chipping
away at the intimidation, intolerance and ignorance that smother
it. The 1689 Bill of Rights granted freedom of speech in parliament, and in 1770 Voltaire is thought to have been first to express
the sentiment that would become a mainstay of believers in free
speech no matter how infuriating the opposition's view might be:
'*Monsieur… I detest what you write, but I would give my life to
make it possible for you to continue to write.*'[6]

John Wilkes is credited with establishing the principle of free
press in England. He ran a satirical anti-government magazine
called the *North Briton* and was prosecuted and subsequently
outlawed for an issue that vehemently criticised George III and
his ministers. There was a mini-uprising in reaction to this,
and the Government backed down. Wilkes remained unloved
by the ruling classes, and was once accosted by the Earl of
Sandwich:

> *Sandwich: You shall die of the pox or on the gallows.*
> *Wilkes: That, Sir, depends on whether I embrace your*
> *mistress or your politics.*[7]

It's not just about ink, of course – plenty of blood has been
shed in the pursuit of the freedom to voice or even hold opinions.
In what became known as the Peterloo Massacre, the cavalry

charged a peaceful public meeting at St Peter's Fields in Manchester in August 1819. Eleven were killed and hundreds injured. Magistrates had ordered the arrest of the leaders of the Manchester Patriotic Union Society, which advocated radical parliamentary reform, because they feared the meeting would end in rebellion. The press were outraged, but the Government praised the actions of the Yeomanry, and followed it up with the restrictive 'Six Laws' legislation which suppressed radical meetings and publications.[8]

Naturally, the massacre and the following legislative crackdown only fuelled anger and further dissent, and in the late 1830s the Chartists emerged with their own set of demands. They wanted, fairly reasonably, the vote for all men over 21 (at the time, the working class weren't quite eligible, being a bit working class and all), voting by secret ballot and annual election to parliament. This time when a Chartist-driven workers' strike occurred, the Duke of Wellington sent in the troops and one thousand five hundred Chartists were arrested. Eventually, all the Chartists' wishes were fulfilled.[9] With the exception of that fiddly annual election one.

One of Britain's most significant moves in favour of free speech came courtesy of the relentless pressure of the Suffragettes. The network of women who would stop at nothing to gain the right to vote took serious direct action, smashing windows and chaining themselves to railings. When taken into custody, they would go on hunger strike. Herbert Henry Asquith's Government passed the crafty Prisoners Act in 1913 to attempt to derail the sympathy the public had for the women, by allowing them to be released until they recovered. Unfortunately, they found it difficult to re-arrest the hunger strikers later, and the Act became known as the 'Cat and Mouse Act'. The Suffragettes kept up the demonstrations, and finally political movement followed, granting partial suffrage in 1918 and granting all women the right to vote in 1928. Women were quite chuffed.[10]

In 1948 the UN General Assembly adopted the Universal Declaration of Human Rights, intended to safeguard among

other crucial rights the prerogative of everyone to freedom of
expression. We've been pretty good at keeping to that since, on
the whole – and have built a good reputation for ourselves in the
world on the basis of it. But in recent years things have taken a
distinct slither towards the kind of suppression of free speech
you'd never expect from a modern democracy, especially one that
prides itself so highly on its freedom of speech. That might be
why people haven't noticed it happening.

> *Many of the rights and freedoms that were
> agreed by people after the war actually
> grew in this country over hundreds of
> years. The sad irony seems to be that
> whilst people all over the world have
> fought to have these basic rights, we in
> Britain who have enjoyed them for so
> long are a little bit too complacent as they
> are hampered, diluted, sometimes
> formally taken away.*
>
> **SHAMI CHAKRABARTI, DIRECTOR OF LIBERTY**[11]

*Shami Chakrabarti is
Director of NGO
Liberty and defends
civil liberties across
the media.
Affectionately
described by Henry
Porter as a 'Petite
Whirlwind', she has
quite a cult
following.*

New Labour has sought to attack freedom of speech from the
base up; and it has mostly got away with it, in a way our ancestors
would never have believed possible. Britain has always been
staunchly pro-free speech, and has an international reputation as
a proudly outspoken nation. Now terrorism is achieving what two
world wars couldn't, and is stifling us. Except, wait, it's not
terrorism, it's the *threat* of terrorism, which is an entity unto
itself – a sort of wibbly, all-powerful phantasm that's become
available to the Government to use to control the population with
fear. The beauty of it is that we generate the fear *ourselves*, taking
our cue from the solemn pronouncements of ministers about
the danger we are in and the vigilance we must maintain, and
gradually begin to oppress ourselves as a result. The Government
hardly needs to lift a finger. You could call it the ultimate Labour-
saving device. If you were going to go there.

Nestling among the sprawling package of new laws brought in since 9/11 is the Serious Organised Crime and Police Act of 2005. Buried in there, beside regulations about money laundering and other terror-related transgressions, is a section outlawing unauthorised demonstration within a kilometre of parliament. This part of the act is ostensibly intended to protect the country and its citizens from terrorism. Terrorists, naturally, are known to congregate in Parliament Square to protest their agenda in an orderly manner before committing their planned acts of terrorism, necessitating restricted access of the public to the area for their own safety. The fact that the UK has suffered from terrorism before without feeling compelled to take such action – in a patriotic, for-the-sake-of-the-children sort of way – doesn't seem to register. This is all-new super-terrorism, from strange and terrifying and unexpected and unpredictable places, and everything needs to change in order to deal with it. Everything. And we just need to get used to it.

Simply, the Blair Government has suppressed even mild dissent in the name of security.[12]

Of course, if you criminalise criticism then that's just one more reason for the people of your country to criticise you ... er, but since you'll be suppressing the criticism of your criticism-suppression anyway, it kind of doesn't matter.

WALTER WOLFGANG – THE ART OF NONSENSE

Tony Benn is a permanent thorn in the side of New Labour. Although he is well into his eighties, he shows no signs of slowing down – he left parliament in 2001 to 'devote more time to politics'.

Walter made the best speech of the conference.

TONY BENN[13]

I saw Wolfgang ... surrounded by the press as he got out of the taxi, there were an absolute army of them swarming around this taxi and this elderly man got out. He was menaced by all these cameras and the

sound equipment, and standing by were police armed to
the teeth with machine guns. I mean that is a black day,
an elderly man who was coming to assert his rights to
go to the Labour Conference after being thrown out, and
to see armed police right there...this elderly man – it's a
picture I'll never forget.

JOHN CATT[14]

Walter Wolfgang is, by anyone's standards, an old man. He has bad eyes and dodgy ears, and a couple of stubborn wisps of white hair drifting across his shiny head. He occasionally, politely but loudly exclaims 'Sorry?' when a question is asked. However, there's no doubt about the sharpness of his mind. He is well-informed and impeccably erudite, his precise sentences delivered with crisp remnants of a German accent. This is the bloke who was bodily thrown out of the Labour Party Conference in 2005.

Walter was born in Frankfurt in 1923. As a Jew he was obliged to leave Germany in 1937, having grown up aware of his own oppressed status, but also inspired by the values of the country that adopted him and his family. Settled in London, Walter joined the Labour Party in 1948, joining the Victory for Socialism group within it. He attended his first party conference in 1951, and has devoted himself to intelligent campaigning against aggressive foreign policy and unjust military action ever since.

But by 2005, with Iraq in chaos and the Government in denial, his faith had started to slip a teensy bit. He had become seriously concerned and angered by the craven shift in the actions and philosophy of the party he had devoted much of his life to supporting.

'I think Britain unfortunately has conformed to a United States policy,' Walter says. 'What's happened under Bush makes the United States a global threat.'[15]

It's this rampant superpower muscle which Walter saw as leading Britain meekly into the mire of Iraq. Blair's statement that 'The rules of the game have changed' had the ring of empty confidence; and according to Walter, it's no longer a game so much as a pantomime. 'The trouble now is that you have got a theatrical idiot as prime minister, I mean, to be perfectly blunt about it,' he says, bluntly. 'Being theatrically minded he thought the Americans were on the side of right and God. And therefore thought it was right to present the facts as he saw them. I don't think the distinction…was very clear to him, because he's too theatrical. All life is a theatre.'

Walter had settled into his seat on the fourth day of the conference, and listened patiently to Foreign Secretary Jack Straw tiptoe around the sleeping beast of Iraq.[16] No debate of the issue had been allowed to occur so far, to Walter's frustration. He had little patience with the very idea of the 'War Against Terror' anyway – 'You cannot have a war against a noun'. Iraq had been kept off the agenda. 'Do we ignore Iraq? Do we ignore nuclear weapons? Do we ignore the flashpoints in the world? For a political party, it's ostrich-like and it's going to damage it. They think that if they can control a conference, they control public opinion. They don't. And of course the effect was exactly the reverse.'

Straw came to sum up, and in so doing 'sent me off. He came to Iraq and said, "Well, the only reason why we are in Iraq is that we wanted to bring democracy to Iraq". It was too much for me and I burst out and shouted, "Nonsense".'

Walter figured that he would be shushed by a steward for his outburst. 'Instead of that, two heavies came and tried to lift me out of my seat. I said, "Now look. I'm 82. I'm not very well. If you want me to leave the conference I will, but don't lift me out of my seat." And then somebody shouted out, "Leave the old man alone"…and they set on him.'

Several of these 'toughs' descended on Walter. A man who shouted support, NEC union official Steve Forest, was 'actually pummelled'. Forest's credentials were removed and he was physically ejected. Outside the auditorium, Walter was also told to leave. 'I had an immense shock, you see. I mean, I wasn't very well, that's number one. Secondly, I never believed for one minute that they would, of all people, throw me out of the conference. I had far too many friends, and I didn't think they would be that crazy.'

After Walter left, the press pounced. The staunch Labour supporter, fascist regime escapee and frail geriatric was all over the media within hours, with most of the coverage sympathetic, and in places even celebratory. The news had also travelled quickly within the conference, from the many astonished and appalled witnesses, and Walter was applauded and invited to speak when he attended a Labour Representation Committee meeting in the evening. He was suddenly a hero, the latest distinguished embarrassment to Labour. Imagine the scene.

> Party minion: Sir, that chap that was forcibly removed
>   from the conference today... well...
> Blair: What about him?
> Minion: (whispers to Blair for some moments)...Nazi
>   Germany... party membership... not very
>   well... 'There's No One Quite Like Grandpa'...
> Blair: Oh, balls.

When Walter attempted to re-enter the conference, he found his way barred. He then discovered first-hand what confusion the slew of new laws which have cascaded from parliament in the last few years can cause – and how broadly the definition of 'act of terror' can be stretched. He was detained by a police officer, who told him he was stopping him under the Terrorism Act.

'A policeman who was standing there mumbled something at enormous speed and gave me a slip of paper... for that period I was under arrest. Under detention if being accurate.'

Section 44 of the Terrorism Act of 2000 gives the police powers to stop and search anyone they please without needing to justify it. The police used this relatively new ability six hundred times in Brighton in the week of the conference, mainly against peace protestors. That year, they used it to stop and search more than thirty-five thousand individuals throughout the country. None of them was an actual terrorist, mind, but better safe than sorry.[17]

One man stopped under the new powers in Brighton that week was John Catt, a World War II veteran who had been in RAF intelligence. During the Brighton conference John had been wearing a T-shirt of his own design in the town centre, suggesting Tony Blair was a war criminal. He was stopped by police, questioned and searched, and then given a slip detailing the incident, in case he was questioned again. In 2006 he was also tailed by two police vehicles on his way to London, and again stopped and questioned. Well, you can't say they're not thorough.[18]

Walter believes it is shocking that today anti-terror laws are being used by the police 'to stifle freedom of dissent. They have misused all these acts in that way because they have a tendency to side with the establishment, whatever the establishment may be, when in actual fact they ought to protect the freedom of the subject.'

Fellow detainee John Catt echoes Walter's sentiments, believing these are small hints of worse to come. 'This is the dangerous thing now – unless there's enough people to come forward, politically and otherwise, to reverse some of these measures...then we're saddled with a society where we will be at the dictates of those who hold power as never before.'[19]

In early 2003, more people were alerted to the possibility of the erosion of free speech in the aftermath of the biggest expression of the right to protest that the country had ever seen. It had become apparent that Britain was sliding towards war in Iraq. Thousands of ordinary people were in a position to show their feelings and maybe have some small influence, so they got out on the streets to say no to the war.

THE DEMOCRATISATION OF PROTEST – NOT IN BLAIR'S BACK YARD

On 15 February 2003 no fewer than seven hundred and fifty thousand people – roughly six Glastonbury festivals' worth – but very probably quite a few more than a million marched on London. They all believed that invasion of Iraq would be illegal and immoral, that the British people were being conned into support, that innocent lives would be lost for an unjustifiable cause. The three-and-a-half mile march began around midday. The marchers had come from all over the country, their actions echoed by protestors in Glasgow and Belfast, as well as in up to sixty countries around the world. As the first marchers started on their route to Hyde Park in the biting cold, Blair was giving another urgent speech to that year's Labour Party Conference, insisting that there would be 'bloody consequences' if the Iraqi tyrant were not challenged. Of course there were extremely bloody consequences for sending in the troops. Tony would say that hindsight is a wonderful thing. It's just that there were a good million of us banging on about it on the streets, so it technically doesn't count as hindsight if you think about it.[20]

What made the protest different wasn't just its sheer size, but its diversity. Men, women and children, from all races and religions. Middle-class, staunchly law-abiding suburbanites, people with functional families and moderate views. *Voters*. Voters in clean boots who'd turned up in coaches, and when they were on the coaches, they'd made sure they tidied up all the rubbish from their packed breakfasts. They had foregone their usual Saturday activities – gardening, DIY, squash – to come out and show their vehement disagreement with the Government.

This was a grave development. Previously, protestors came in one or two varieties, easily identified by the Government and media. They had been easy to spot, sling in the back of vans and dismiss as work-shy loons and neo-hippies. There were always small single-issue demos attracting other specific groups, of course, but these were still clearly-defined

Typical protestor as seen by government and media, pre-2003 ('Smelly')
- *Dreadlocks*
- *Levellers T-shirt*
- *Large badge (slogan: 'If censorship is the answer, then it was a f***ing stupid question')*
- *Tattoos, especially on visible areas, suggesting unemployability*
- *Various bangles made of coloured plaited string*
- *Combat trousers (with designated king-size Rizla pocket)*
- *Scuffed/scarred knee (from resisting arrest)*
- *Doctor Marten's boots (RRP £29.99)*
- *Clenched fist.*

'types': unhappy teachers or nurses or firemen, disgruntled farmers, parents irate about 'paedos'. The 'career protestors', however, were the ones who were assumed to come out for a plethora of issues: vivisection, building on greenbelt, drug legalisation, eviction of squatters. They were easily profiled. They didn't vote or pay tax. If they worked at all, it was in some vague 'creative' role, part-time. They were primed to be arrested for any number of repeated misdemeanours, and so had little to lose by parading around in the streets about one thing or another.

Anti-war demonstrations, then, which occurred reliably every once in a while about one conflict or another, had hitherto been safely predictable as the province of those who may be delicately called 'the smellies'. (It hasn't turned up in any government documents yet, but the inference of fragrance is probably there somewhere. And it's probably somewhere in the annals of the *Sun*.)

Undoubtedly the smellies and their milder, less scary-looking derivatives were out in great numbers on the fifteenth. The Government could cope with the idea of those protestors – they could disregard them. But overwhelming these comfy stereotypes were the newly minted 'normies'. The sight of them struck a nameless fear into the heart of the Prime Minister, to whom popularity was still so important.

The normies, freezing their way through London, were people with coffee tables. They paid their mortgages and taxes and didn't look like they lived up a tree, or made a habit of jumping on bandwagons. It was clear to see that protesting had been completely demo-cratised. The usual social divisions didn't apply to the motley million on the streets of London – you only had to hear the number, even the lowest estimate, to know that this protest was a serious threat.

Typical protestor as seen by government and media 2003 onwards ('Normy')
- *Pleasant smile*
- *Clean clothes*
- *Photographs of children in wallet (also contains hard-earned cash and non-overdrawn credit cards)*
- *Brushed hair*
- *Unobtrusive jewellery*
- *What?*
- *No, seriously.*
- *Really?*
- *I think we might be in trouble.*

Party minion: Sir, latest estimates suggest there are a
   million people marching today.
Blair: A million?
Minion: A million, sir.
Blair: Oh, balls.

How to explain away this impassioned mass of humanity marching in protest at your mooted plans? Like a lawyer. And quickly. Divert focus, explode context, and passive-aggressively plea for proper perspective, with guilt-trip to taste (strategically targeting self-loathing middle-class marchers who secretly believe all the country's problems are their fault).

There will be no march for the victims of Saddam, no
protests about the thousands of children that die
needlessly every year under his rule, no righteous anger
over the torture chambers which if he is left in power,
will be left in being.
   I rejoice that we live in a country where peaceful
protest is a natural part of our democratic process... But
as you watch your TV pictures of the march, ponder this
– if there are five hundred thousand on that march, that
is still less than the number of people whose deaths
Saddam has been responsible for. If there are one
million, that is still less than the number of people who
died in the wars he started.[21]

And that was that. By the time the protestors had got home and put on the news, it was as if they'd never left the house.

There was a bitter irony in Blair's sensationalist brandishing of Saddam's war victims, as he stood on the brink of starting his own war. The argument was outrageous – a pseudo-mathematical equation in which marchers multiplied by square root of victim total equals moral justification for war – but it didn't matter. If you're going to dismiss a million, you don't have to worry about how they're going to take your dismissal. Not when you're a) confident they won't have any real alternative to vote for next time, and b) completely convinced that you're right, with a 45-minute margin of error.

> *Faced with the choice between changing one's mind and proving there is no need to do so, almost everyone gets busy on the proof.*
>
> **JOHN KENNETH GALBRAITH**[22]

Five weeks later, the Coalition of the Willing invaded Iraq, as it was probably always going to. On the day war began, 19 March, ten thousand schoolchildren across the country followed the example of the million who had gone before them. They deserted their classrooms and took to the streets. Many in London poured into Parliament Square, and as countless peaceful protestors have done throughout history (and as Jack Straw had done as a student), the children held a sit-in on the grass, refusing to budge in the traditional display of peaceful obstinacy.[23]

The protest caused a degree of confusion and conflict among teachers. The Secondary Heads Association asked its members to punish the students for truancy as they would under any other circumstances. Some teachers couldn't help but feel supportive of the action, knowing that they would have done just the same thing. They had to feel a bit proud, too – there had never been anything like this protest, with teenagers and children as young as 11 feeling compelled to demonstrate against what they felt to be an unjust war. The teachers had to be doing something right if the children were so aware of the world around them, and motivated by conscience in a way you don't usually expect of sulky, self-centred adolescents.[24]

> *I'm prepared to take my punishment. I've been given a Saturday two-hour detention. I'll probably get into more trouble if I keep missing school to protest, but we have to face the consequences.*
>
> *It's just what I believe in. War isn't right.*[25]

The sit-in was short-lived. Police broke it up and removed the children. Those who were hit in the face might have been discouraged from expressing their political opinion in future. Alternatively, they might have been galvanised to come back.[26]

With the dismissal of the march and the obscenely heavy-handed reaction to the schoolchildren's sit-in, protest in the UK had taken one of its biggest knocks; although no one anticipated the next one it would sustain. A year and a half later, in November 2004, the House of Commons saw the Serious Organised Crime and Police Act for the first time. Throughout, and long before the normies had taken to the streets, a lone figure had kept a vigil in Parliament Square, surrounded by pictures of the casualties of war. This was Brian Haw, who we'll meet shortly. SOCPA was brought in primarily to shut him up.

> *Democracy doesn't just mean voting once every five years.*
>
> **SHAMI CHAKRABARTI, DIRECTOR OF LIBERTY**[27]

It must be emphasised that this is still one of the better places to be in the world if you want to speak your mind. Restriction of freedom of speech is still mostly a problem for political activists. But as the Stop the War march showed, more and more people were becoming politically active, willing to demonstrate even if they'd never thought of it before. So it's a good idea to keep an eye on the people exercising their right to protest, because they are more than a noisy nuisance – in a very real sense, they are defending one of our most basic rights.

PLACARDS AT DAWN: THE RIGHT TO PROTEST

> *Never doubt that a small group of thoughtful, committed citizens can change the world; indeed, it's the only thing that ever has.*
>
> **MARGARET MEAD**[28]

The right to protest is the tiny needle with which you may publicly poke your employees in parliament. Direct action, which often involves going out in the cold toting a bit of board on a stick, has often been a nuisance to governments, but one tolerated, providing it is peaceful.

There's a fat file showing the historical successes of protest. Sometimes it influences history. The rest of the time, it's a resonant symbolic act; as a protestor, you're marking yourself out as a member of a democracy which allows you to go into the street and vocalise your strongly held views, however unpopular they may be to others or to the Government. And it is a sort of check on the Government – they may discount it, but public disapproval will always filter through, and while there are other ways to achieve that, direct action is…well, the most direct. It's the front line. And usually bloody cold too.[29]

It's sobering to remember that there are places in the world where having a little pop at the people who run the show is rather frowned upon. You could put yourself in real danger in North Korea or Saudi Arabia by suggesting that the president or head of state isn't your absolutely favourite person. In the UK, however, it's generally been quite different. Governments are obliged to be accountable, which means that their citizens have the right to criticise them however, whenever and wherever they see fit (short of blowing the place up).

So it's an important thing to be allowed to protest peacefully, and any restriction or curtailment of it by a government is a warning of what may be to come. Once the right to protest is quashed, free speech itself is knocked back; which means you can't speak up against detention without trial or torture, which means detention without trial and torture can go ahead; and you can't speak up against ID cards and surveillance, so they go ahead; and if you're imprisoned because of a cock-up, people can't speak up on your behalf. The whole house of cards which amounts to a democracy can collapse. And all because a few people with banners and whistles were stopped from standing somewhere.

Blair's immediate, audacious dismissal in 2003 of the biggest protest Britain had ever seen was quite something. Two years later, the Serious Organised Crime and Police Act was passed, preventing spontaneous protest within a kilometre of parliament. This was primarily because of a lone protestor in Parliament Square, who's probably quite flattered.

SOCPA – EXTREMELY SERIOUS AND INCREDIBLY ORGANISED

> *One of the things the Government is very, very good at is to smuggle measures that it wants through in the legislation that appear always to be in the public interest, protecting the public from crime, terrorism, antisocial behaviour. In this instance the Serious Organised Crime and Police Act introduced the idea that people could no longer demonstrate outside their parliament without the permission of the Metropolitan Commissioner.*
>
> **HENRY PORTER**[30]

The unsmilingly named Serious Organised Crime and Police Act was passed through parliament in April 2005. It was introduced in the name of security, in alignment with several others of a similar ostensible purpose. It begat the Serious Organised Crime Agency, whose job self-evidently was to tackle serious organised crime. This all seems quite straightforward, but SOCPA is in fact something of a mixed bag of disconnected measures. It has effectively relegated the phrase 'arrestable offence' to the history books, as it granted the police the power to arrest for *any* offence.[31]

Then there's Section 132 of SOCPA, which criminalises protest without permission.[32]

The 'designated area', the polite official term for what tends to be more harshly termed the

> **SOCPA 132 Demonstrating without authorisation in designated area**
>
> (1) Any person who (a) organises a demonstration in a public place in the designated area, or (b) takes part in a demonstration in a public place in the designated area, or (c) carries on a demonstration by himself in a public place in the designated area, is guilty of an offence if, when the demonstration starts, authorisation for the demonstration has not been given under section 134(2).

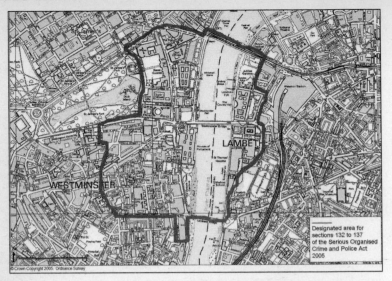

Designated area for sections 132 to 137 of the Serious Organised Crime and Police Act 2005

© Crown Copyright 2005. Ordnance Survey

'exclusion zone', covers an area of one kilometre from any point in Parliament Square. It goes on to state that authorisation must be applied for six days in advance of a demonstration, or if that's not possible, at least 24 hours in advance. The maximum penalty for conducting an unauthorised demonstration as stated in Section 136 is imprisonment for a period of up to 51 weeks. The exact nature of 'a demonstration'... isn't really defined anywhere. Tricksy.[33]

Whose fault is SOCPA? Yes, Mr Haw, we're all looking at you. Brian Haw, a shouty bloke camping on parliament's doorstep with only a beanie hat for company, was the catalyst for the new law. The million on the Stop the War march had alerted Tony Blair to the immense power of protest, and Brian Haw, with his megaphone, was reminding him every day. It figured that to bring protest under control, it was best to start at home – in Parliament Square, with one individual.

BRIAN HAW – OF NUTS AND SLEDGEHAMMERS

> *Every day I see protestors demonstrating at Downing Street…I may not like what they call me, but I thank God they can…That's freedom.*
>
> **TONY BLAIR, 2002**[34]

> *It is a sledgehammer to crack a nut, but he is a nut.*
>
> **DAVID BLUNKETT, 2005**[35]

After Blunkett was appointed Home Secretary in 2001 he removed the right to trial by jury in some cases, increased the police powers of surveillance and championed ID cards. His finest hour was during a prison riot at Lincoln Jail, when the governor called the Home Secretary for instructions. Blunkett became hysterical and shouted that 'he did not care about lives' and to 'call in the troops and machine-gun the prisoners'.

I don't think Brian is too offended if you call him a nut. A Great British Nut. He saw the world in his youth as a deck-hand in the merchant navy, and now he lives in Parliament Square with a megaphone. On 2 June 2001 the fifty-something father of seven pitched his tent on the immaculate grass, set up a couple of placards broadcasting displeasure with the Iraq sanctions which were in place, and sat on one of those collapsible fishing chairs to wait. Since then he's only left to attend court hearings or hospital. He has spent his many hundred days talking to passers-by and journalists about politics, the need for peace in the world and his determination to stay put 'as long as it takes'; collecting and setting up placards

Brian Haw

from those sympathetic to his cause; and berating parliament. This he's got quite good at, developing a sort of throaty hectoring bellow in which to deliver tirades about the iniquities of foreign policy and the tyranny of Tony Blair. He's like the Pavarotti of protest. Except skinnier.[36]

Haw's presence was a pain in the parliamentary arse. Having someone sit and shout outside your office is going to grate after a while, especially if they are accusing you of mass murder. The most staggering thing about Brian's story is not that New Labour has stopped at nothing to crush him and silence his protest, or the millions of pounds of taxpayers' money that they have spent taking him to court in a multitude of ways. It's that he's beaten them almost all of the time.

April 2002

Ten months after he had set up his unruly display accusing the Government of murder, Westminster City Council began legal proceedings under Section 149 of the Highways Act, deeming Brian to be a 'nuisance'. Brian won.[37]

September 2002

Westminster Council begin injunction proceedings to remove Brian's placards for 'obstruction' (of the pavement, although they were all on the grass) and 'unlawful advertising' (though advertising what they were unable to divulge). The case is heard in the High Court in October, with witnesses including the venerable Tony Benn. Brian wins. Next.[38]

January 2003

Brian is having a cup of coffee in Waterloo Station when he is rather brusquely and physically interrupted by four policemen. They arrest him for assault. Five months later the case is thrown out for abuse of court process.[39]

June 2003

An American working at the US Embassy attacks Brian and his display, breaking Brian's nose. The police stand by and watch. Brian goes to hospital, where he collapses.[40]

May 2004

Just before the visit of the Chinese premier, in a sudden midnight police operation, Brian is beaten and arrested and his display is trashed. He is charged with failing to leave a cordoned area that he knew nothing about. Maybe the police were trying to make the Chinese premier feel at home? All charges are dropped, and Brian successfully sues the police, winning substantial damages.[41]

In November 2004 Brian was bashed but unbowed. However many times it was contrived to remove him from his post, he kept going back. The Government decided to act. Brian was to have his own law. This was Section 132 of the Serious Organised Crime and Police Act, preventing unauthorised demonstration within a designated zone around parliament. It followed a small inquiry by the House of Commons Procedure Committee, which heard that terrorists concealing bombs would be able to mingle with protestors on the Square to get close to parliament. Honestly.[42]

August 2005

SOCPA comes into force. Bye bye Brian!

Or not.

The thing about SOCPA was that it states that you have to get police permission before the start of a demonstration. Brian's demonstration had started several years previously, so his protest predated the act which had been brought about to stop it. Brian Haw ended up being the only person in Britain allowed to protest in Parliament Square without permission.

Haw Haw.

In August 2005 the High Court made a ruling that Brian was exempt from SOCPA. Whoops. In order to try and ensure the whole thing hadn't been a ghastly waste of time and money, and to scrape the rapidly congealing egg from their faces, the Home Office went for an appeal.

A summary of the technical legal argument that the Home Office offered is: 'We have made a complete pig's ear out of the whole affair and we look like idiots, but as we're the Government and he's just a nut we can do what we want'.

In May 2006, the Appeal Court agreed that the Government had actually meant for the act to be applied to all demonstrations regardless of date of commencement, they just, er, didn't put it very well.[43]

Soon afterwards, 78 police mounted an operation at 3 a.m. to demolish Brian's display, publicly humiliating the man who had done the same to them. Officers in riot gear trashed the placards and banners and arrested Brian and the supporters staying with him. Sir Ian Blair, the Metropolitan Police Commissioner, told the Metropolitan Police Authority that the cost of the raid was only £7200. The next day Sir Ian was forced to admit that he had lied, as the true cost of the raid was revealed as £27,754.[44]

> It is daft that we should have to pass a law for the purpose, but that is what happens when people make a monkey of the existing law.
>
> **DAVID BLUNKETT (AGAIN)**[45]

Mark Thomas is a much loved comedian and political activist who has campaigned against the arms trade for many years. He was arrested for criminal damage at the DSEi arms fair in East London for chaining himself to the underside of a bus full of arms dealers, but got off on the technicality that he was innocent.

> I've talked to parliamentary PPSs who've said, 'Yeah, it was to get him out of Parliament Square. Why should he have all that space when other people can't protest?' Which is a pathetic argument, and I think it shows the Government as petty, vindictive, spiteful, bloody-minded control freaks.
>
> **MARK THOMAS**[46]

After the raid, the police arbitrarily gave Brian a one metre by three metre space to protest in. The ultimate symbol of state control

– you can protest but only within restrictions *we* give you. At the time of writing, Brian Haw is still in Parliament Square. Other protestors, as we'll see, have discovered that standing up to SOCPA can be a nasty business, however quietly you do it.[47]

In February 2007 Brian was nominated alongside Tony Blair for the Channel 4 Most Inspiring Political Figure of the Year Award! The public voted in their thousands and Brian beat Tony by a massive majority.

Since SOCPA's inception there have been dozens of arrests – the first conviction was a 25-year-old woman who read aloud the names of soldiers killed in Iraq at the Cenotaph, without permission.[48]

MILAN AND MAYA – RINGING OFF

> *I think essentially the reason why I didn't fill in the form was that it was asking me to request permission to remember people who'd been killed by this Government, and that was something in the end I wasn't prepared to do. What I think is going to happen is that probably I'm going to spend a little bit of time in prison, maybe a week or two, because I wouldn't fill in and sign a form asking the police for permission to remember the dead.*
>
> **MILAN RAI**[49]

> *I'm sure I've done many wrong things in my life, but being a serious organised criminal isn't one of them.*
>
> **MAYA EVANS**[50]

Milan and Maya

Another day, another arrest of a serious organised criminal with a placard and a bell. Maya Evans, a 25-year-old vegan chef, and veteran activist and writer Milan Rai are sitting quietly in the back of a unmarked police van on 25 October 2005. They have just been arrested for conducting an unauthorised demonstration by the Cenotaph in Whitehall, wherein they had both read out the names of people killed in Iraq – Milan reading the names of civilians, Maya soldiers. It's a short drive through some back streets to Charing Cross police station, where the police take their detainees out of the van and separate them.[51]

In the station, Maya gives her name and address to the custody sergeant, then quibbles over the necessity of adding her date of birth and other personal details (there isn't one). She and the custody sergeant have a brief conversation about Iraq and whether the troops should be withdrawn. Then, allowed to keep her David Attenborough book, Maya is led to a cell and her lace-up shoes are confiscated.

> *The door closed behind me. I was alone. Looking around the cell, I had a moment of panic. How would I cope with being confined in a stale, windowless room? I was also worried about the fluorescent lighting, because after a while that kind of light makes me queasy. I looked around for a CCTV camera in the cell but I couldn't see one.*
>
> *Then I calmed down. I wasn't being oppressed. The bed was covered in plastic, so it was probably quite clean. And I was on my own, not having to cope with other prisoners. I decided I had to be in strong survival mode. I lay down on the bed and started reading. The photographs of natural beauty were a real joy, taking me out of my surroundings.[52]*

After an adrenalin-washout period of sleep, some soggy lunch and a while trying not to look at the light, Maya is released, having spent just over five hours in the cell.

> *I was taken to the custody desk and charged with participating in an unauthorised demonstration. I said,*

> *'Today I took part in a ceremony to remember an*
> *estimated hundred thousand Iraqis and 97 British*
> *soldiers killed in the war with Iraq. The war was illegal*
> *and illegitimate. US and UK troops should be withdrawn*
> *immediately.*[53]

Maya leaves with Milan, who despite being arrested as the organiser had yet to be charged. Just over a month later Maya becomes the first person to be put on trial for the offence.[54]

It was a very understated demonstration: two people sombrely ringing little Tibetan bells, reading aloud a list of names without comment. The placards were expository, simply explaining the purpose of the event – not a bolshy permanent-markered exclamation mark in sight. It was a gentle and simple act of peaceful protest, free of any aggressive or even accusatory sentiment. And they did give notification – they just didn't ask for permission. This is what made them serious and organised criminals in the eyes of the law.[55]

> *People are allowed to protest all the time. You have*
> *always had to get permission to protest outside*
> *parliament. Protesting outside parliament is just the*
> *same as holding an event in a park where you would*
> *have to ask permission by parks police.*
>
> **GEOFF HOON, TALKING RUBBISH**[56]

Milan is a quiet and deeply committed, fiercely intelligent, jolly amiable bloke. He's also, like many serious activists, a smidgin eccentric. You probably need a healthy sense of the daft to be able to deal with the sheer amount of legislative and bureaucratic silliness you encounter if you tread on the law's toes on a regular basis. He has done his share of transgressing. He's broken into missile bases with a bunch of activists, all wearing Mickey Mouse ears, the rationale being that no US sniper could ever bring himself to take out Disney's finest. He's played frisbee with armed soldiers as they all waited for the police to show up. But he knows when it's necessary to play by the rules, and where protest is concerned, there are (or were) certain unwritten rules of courtesy. As the organiser of the British leg of '100,000 Rings for Iraq', he rang the police several weeks in advance to inform them of the demonstration.

> *I've organised a lot of this kind of event opposite Downing Street, and as usual I rang up the police … and told them the time and the date that we wanted to have the event and there'd probably just be less than five of us and so on. They told me that there was this new legislation and that there was this form to fill in, and at that moment I was kind of assuming that I would fill in the form and send it back. It was just so important to us to complete 250 rings outside Downing Street. But … when they actually emailed me the form and I started thinking about having to fill it in and sign it and send it back to them, I began to have doubts about it.*[57]

Milan checked around to see if there was a boycott of the new legislation among protestors. There wasn't. It was up to him and Maya to go along with it or defy it on their own.

> *The more I thought about it and the more I talked about it, the less I felt that I could co-operate with this erosion of our freedom to protest. In the end I decided that I just couldn't co-operate with this law, and that I couldn't fill in this form and send it back. So I rang up the police and said we're still intending to come, confirmed the date and time, and said that I'm not going to be sending in the form. They said, 'Well, if you don't do that then the maximum penalty is 51 weeks' imprisonment' … and the maximum penalty for anyone participating would be £1000 fine.*[58]

Milan warned Maya that she could be arrested, and told her she could pull out if she wanted to. Maya decided it was worth the risk. On 25 October, they made their way to Whitehall, armed with their boards and bells. They were greeted by the sight of several police officers waiting at the designated spot. An officer showed them a map of the designated area, informed them that they were in breach of SOCPA and had ten minutes to move on, or they would be arrested. Maya and Milan affirmed that they understood. Reluctantly they gave the bells to their friends for safekeeping, knowing they would be confiscated otherwise, and began to read the names. The protest, divested of one of its key elements, had taken on another – it was now a protest not just for peace, but for the right to protest for peace itself. Maya focused on her protest.

> *I said very little to the police. I concentrated on reading out the names of the British dead. I read each soldier's name, his rank, and his age…Whenever you read out the list of names, a shiver goes through you, and you feel sad for the people who've died. You feel so sad that they've lost their lives In such an unnecessary war.*
>
> *Somehow…reading the names in the presence of the police made the whole experience much more intense. And I felt almost as if the police were being affected by the reading more than I was.*[59]

After about a quarter of an hour, Maya and Milan were arrested. There were 14 police in attendance at the demonstration, almost two per participant's limb.

The demonstrators, in accordance with their protest ethos, went without any resistance. As the organiser, Milan faced the higher penalty, and so both of them expected that if there was going to be media attention it would fall on him. However, it was Maya who ended up being the focus of the nation after her conviction on 7 December.[60]

> *Journalists rang saying they really wanted to interview me in person, and I'd say,*

In the time it took to arrest and charge Milan and Maya, 14 police could:

1) give wrong directions to 1400 Japanese tourists for a laugh;

2) eat 280 Donuts (20 each – it's a cinch);

3) catch some real criminals. Crime in Westminster at that time was three times the national average. A total of 17,356 crimes were committed in the area in that three-month period, which is an average of 192 offences per day.[61]

> *'Well, I'm kind of at work today'. It didn't occur to me*
> *to take the day off…I rang work to tell them what was*
> *going on…I said, 'Seth, there's been this media*
> *coverage and it's been really huge and I'm going to be*
> *late for work. I'm really sorry.' He said, 'That's okay'. He*
> *paused, and then said, 'You do realise you're on the*
> *front page of the* Independent?'[62]

The day after her court appearance (at which she'd been besieged), she was amazed to have 11 missed calls on her mobile, all from journalists, before breakfast.[63] The unassuming nature of the pleasant and well-mannered girl from Hastings, arrested under ludicrous circumstances, helped to propel her into a media maelstrom. She was a nice, approachable sort of person who appeared about as inclined to violence as a templeful of Buddhists. This brought it into stark relief for the public that the Government really was criminalising the inoffensive and blameless. People who might never have sympathised with protestors before, even grumbled about them, were outraged that anyone could be arrested for holding what was in effect a war memorial service. It was rather a big deal. Maya ended up on *Newsnight*, sandwiched between an irate Jeremy Paxman and stumbling Government minister John Denham. It got a bit heated.

> *Paxman: What sort of society are we living in where you*
> *have to have police permission to demonstrate?*
> *Denham: We have to accept, Jeremy, that one of the*
> *things which has changed over the last twenty*
> *years…is that there were restraints on what you did [on*
> *a protest], many of which have now broken down.*
> *Pressure groups now have no compunction about*
> *breaking into parliament, about throwing things at the*
> *Prime Minister.*
> *Paxman: She wasn't doing that! She was reading the list*
> *of British soldiers who have perished in Iraq!*
> *Denham: Nobody wants to stop that, and I wouldn't.*
> *Paxman: But she* was *stopped!*

Denham: The reason…

Paxman: She was arrested for doing it.

Denham: The reason why parliament has legislated is that over the past few years other protest groups, the Countryside Alliance and others, have shown themselves willing to disrupt the way things operate. I regret the need to pass out that legislation. But the truth is, it has come in response to certain groups who have tried to disrupt the way in which parliament wants to operate. I think that somebody like Maya ought to be able to stand up…

Paxman: But she's not!

Denham:… and do that demonstration.

Paxman: She got prosecuted for it![64]

Debates along the same lines erupted across the media, and commentators and the public weighed in. Roy Hattersley wrote:

> *Miss Evans has done the nation a service by demonstrating how ridiculous the law has become. The Government should reciprocate by repealing it.*[65]

Milan Rai and Maya Evans were both found guilty and fined, and refused to pay. In all likelihood they will both spend a short time in prison for their crimes. Both continue to participate in peaceful demonstrations, attracting further arrests. Recently Maya had bail conditions imposed that forbade her from even entering the SOCPA zone.[66] On 13 November, 19 days after Milan and Maya had managed to read a few names of soldiers and civilians before being removed, a remembrance service for the fallen in all British wars took place in Whitehall, as it has every year for many decades. It was organised by Tony Blair and attended by the Queen. They laid wreaths and stood in silence at the Cenotaph, remembering the dead.[67]

THE SILLINESS OF SOCPA

You've got to laugh, really. A thousand years or so of freedom of speech in Britain, and in the space of a decade we've found ourselves having to watch what we say, what we read, what we do and where, in circumstances that are rarely less than ludicrous. So many grave things have led us to this point – a terrorist threat and an over-zealous Government, combining to put us back into a place we can't quite get our heads around. The thought that our freedom of speech is actually being curtailed, and that people are being harassed and intimidated and worse for expressing an opinion, is nothing less than appalling. But the British are awfully good at meeting the depressing with sarcastic grins. The surreal goofiness of SOCPA has naturally brought out the Python in many of the people who know what they stand to lose from it.

Paul Carr is a publisher and writer who lives in central London. With the advent of SOCPA, which he was planning to defy by attending an unauthorised Parliament Square carol service the following evening, Paul realised that his Westminster flat fell within the designated area. Did this mean that if he wanted to hold a protest on his own property, he could be arrested? What if it was on the balcony, in view of other members of the public, from their homes or passing planes? He thought he'd better find out. He wrote up his findings as accurately as possible for the weekly satirical newsletter, *The Friday Thing*.

> 'Hello, New Scotland Yard, how may I help you?'
> 'Hello … I've just been looking at the map of your protest exclusion zone around Parliament Square, and …'
> 'It's not an exclusion zone, sir.'
> 'Muh?'
> 'It's not an exclusion zone. If you want to protest, you need to get permission. We're not excluding protest. How exactly can I help you, sir?'
> 'Well, the funny thing is, I was looking at your exclusion …'
> 'Permission.'

'Permission zone around Parliament Square, and I
realised my new flat is right smack-bang in the middle
of it...'

'And?'

'Well, you see, I have a roof terrace which can be seen
from the road. I was just wondering whether I'd be
allowed to protest there if I wanted to? I'm just worried
about being arrested and having all my banners torn
up.'

'Who owns the property, sir?'

'I do.'

'And who are you planning on protesting against?'

'Does that matter? The point is whether it's now illegal
for me to protest on my own roof... Let's say I'm
protesting against myself.'

'Are you planning to protest against yourself?'

'Well, I don't like myself very much at the moment, so
let's say yes...'

'Let me look at my map. Well, as far as I know, as no
one would be likely to complain if you were to protest
against yourself...'

'They might.'

'It's unlikely.'

'OK. Forget me then. What about if I was protesting
against my neighbour?'

'On your roof?'

'Yes.'

'Well, then that would depend whether they were likely
to see it and be upset by it.'

'Not see it and not be upset? OK. Got it. Oh, only thing
is, my neighbour is the Home Office.'

'Well, if you're protesting against the Government and
they were likely to see the protest then you'd need to
come in and have a chat with us.'

'Oh, right, OK. But only if I'm likely to upset them.'

'What do you mean, sir?'

'Well, if I protested for the Government that would be
  OK?'

'For the Government? You mean protesting in favour of
  the Government?'

'Essentially, yes.'

'Then that wouldn't be a protest.'

'Got it. So it's only illegal if I'm protesting against the
  Government in a way that might upset them?'

'Yes – no. That's not what I actually said.'

'Oh, I'm terribly sorry. What did you actually say?'

'I said that if you wanted to protest against the
  Government on your roof terrace then you should
  come in and have a chat with us first.'

'But only if I'm protesting against the Government.'

'That's right.'

'In a way that might upset them.'

'That's right.'

'Otherwise I might be arrested?'

'It's possible, sir, yes.'

'OK. Thanks.'

'Thank you sir, is there anything else I can help you
  with?'

'Not today. Merry Christmas.'

'Thank you for your call, sir.'[68]

Paul's investigative efforts blew apart the public's perception of SOCPA. Far from being an anti-terror measure, or a targeted action to remove protestors from Parliament Square, it was just something to stop us from being mean to each other. Or ourselves. Because the Government cares.

A group who host tea parties in Parliament Square – still a public area – got into trouble because one of the cakes had subversive icing.

Mark Thomas explains, 'There's a nice woman called Sian, she does all the tea at protests, she brings out all the cakes. She had a picnic in Parliament Square and it had one word on one of the cakes, it had "Peace" on one of the cakes and the police threatened to arrest her. They deemed her cake to be a political cake and when you get to the stage where the police can threaten you with arrest because you've got "Peace" iced upon a fairy cake that's fairly nuts.'[69]

Activist and picnicker Mark Barrett was among those at the tea party. He returned the next day hoisting a blank placard, and succeeded in not getting arrested, for protesting against nothing. Parliament Square is now where protest meets existential philosophy. Or something.[70]

DOES SOCPA MATTER?

Of course, there is always the question of whether or not that grotty little section in SOCPA really, actually matters. Most demonstrations are organised a lot more than six days in advance anyway, and most people would probably want to inform the police even if they weren't obliged to – just to emphasise that they have only peaceful and law-abiding intentions. Does it really matter that we can't just run onto Parliament Square and fart in the seat of government's general direction on a whim?

There are several answers to this.

1) It's symbolic
Regardless of its relatively minor implications in purely practical terms, SOCPA has enormous symbolic significance. For the first time in centuries we risk arrest if we make a spontaneous protestation in a public space outside parliament. It's not overly dramatic to say that it's like the Government putting a hand over the mouth of its people, when it could just continue to put fingers in its ears instead.

2) What next?
The much over-used phrase 'the thin end of the wedge' would be extremely relevant about now. Free speech and the right to protest are always the first things to go. Once the public loses its

voice it can no longer bring the leaders to account, and they suddenly find it easier to get away with far more draconian restrictions on our lives.

Whatever you think of a bit of red tape popping up around parliament, and however tiresomely Orwellian and far-removed from daily life it might sound when you say it, you've got to keep asking – what next?

3) Betty Hunter

'We said, "We think we've made our protest. We think the British Government realises that, you know, they can't do this without some opposition. We think we should go peacefully." And we left. So at that point we weren't aware that we would be prosecuted.'[71]

Betty Hunter is a bit of a living refutation of the Government's assertion that six days' notice is no great shakes. Your archetypal favourite aunt, the leader of the Palestine Solidarity Campaign (PSC) is committed to peaceful demonstration. When SOCPA put its ugly mug into her business she was careful to fill in the forms and submit them on time every time she wanted to voice her views in central London. Breaking such a law does nothing but damage the reputation of protestors, she acknowledged, and so she scrupulously abided by it, despite her own conviction that it was a crock. The message was more important.

However, on 14 March 2006 Betty found herself in an extremely difficult position. The PSC was deluged with emails and phone calls telling them that three British peacekeeping monitors were about to withdraw from a Jericho prison. The withdrawal inevitably meant an Israeli attack would follow. The people in the prison feared for their lives. As far as Betty and her colleagues were concerned, they had to get to Downing Street and plead a reconsideration of the withdrawal. This was a problem. In six days, people would be dead – it was a mortal situation, and although Betty had been careful not to breach SOCPA and didn't want to now, it was more unthinkable to start buggering about with forms and pens and queues. So she phoned the police, told them her team would be demonstrating that afternoon, and made her preparations. The police told her she could be arrested. Betty accepted the risk.[72]

When the fifty members of the PSC arrived at Downing Street with their placards they found a welcoming committee of a dozen police.[73] Betty and her team were as distressed by this as any law-abiding people would be, but they went ahead and held the demonstration. When the police started asking for names and addresses, Betty decided to call it a day, and the demonstrators left. Later that day the Israeli army invaded the prison and demolished it, killing one and injuring and kidnapping several others.[74]

A week later the police invited Betty to Charing Cross police station to discuss the situation. Keen to continue to do the right thing as far as she was able, Betty went along for this free exchange of ideas and found herself, after a little light interrogation, charged with breaching SOCPA. A bad lot, that Betty.[75]

So, yes, there are times when spontaneous demonstration is necessary, and worth struggling for, and SOCPA is more than a minor legislative blip. It's worth noting at this point that planned demonstration isn't having the best time of it either. No one knows this better than Malcolm Carroll.

PLANE STUPID – FLYING OFF THE HANDLE

> I discovered so much had gone: my computer, my
> mobile, my PhD, complete four-drawer filing cabinet.
> Loads of maps, other personal documents, camera,
> GPS... They had been round while we were in custody.
>
> **MALCOLM CARROLL**[76]

More and more people are starting to become concerned about the effects of climate change. There aren't quite enough of them in government yet (and you could probably swallow the Bush Administration's file on the matter without needing a glass of water), but there are many who have been trying to raise awareness of the issue since long before it was fashionable. One of these is Malcolm Carroll, a Baptist minister, active member of

Greenpeace and fifteen-year veteran of peaceful protest. His perspective on climate change is in alignment with that of experts who now consider it a matter of damage control rather than solution. 'Even if we did everything we could possibly do to combat climate change now,' he says, 'it's inevitable, for example, that 10 million Bangladeshis already below the 1m line – they're really stuffed.' Climate change, for him, is simply the biggest issue we face today. Malcolm is especially concerned about the massive availability of short-haul flights, and their effect on the environment. So he formed a grass-roots action group, Plane Stupid. This move was to cost him under Blair's new laws.[77]

With airlines among the chief polluters, the group decided an airport was the logical place for a peaceful protest, 'as friendly and as calm as possible'. On 24 September 2006 a group of just over twenty demonstrators went to Nottingham East Midlands Airport, which specialises in short-haul flights and freights (many of which are 'simply unnecessary'), to make their point.[78]

'We designed something that was particularly fluffy, you know, really non-confrontational but still a real protest, actually taking it to the aviation industry. We did a service of remembrance for the 150–160,000 people who die each year through climate change – via extreme flooding, extreme droughts. That's 9/11 every week. So a two-minute silence, traditional sort of thing…me as a Baptist minister leading the service, and there was a congregation of 24 people chained together.'[79]

Having cut through a fence, the protestors sat quietly on a taxiway and listened to Malcolm speak. They were trespassing, but not obstructing or endangering themselves or others, as they were nowhere near the runways where the planes actually take off and land. The group was mostly composed of people in their late teens and early twenties, some students, representatives of a demographic that is supposedly politically apathetic. One of the group stayed behind and informed security, and the group expected either security or police to arrive shortly and escort them from the area. The hope was to make it to twenty minutes, and Malcolm had a 'wild dream that we might last an hour'.

They figured they might incur a caution for trespass. So it was something of a shock when the hostage negotiator arrived along with security and armed police.[80]

'There was this kind of security cordon, and they must have felt happy they had cordoned us off. And it was quite bizarre…I was trying to engage the head of security, he wouldn't make eye contact…We were saying "Excuse me, we have made our point now", and eventually one guy had to unchain himself and go over and say "What's going on?" And the police response was "We don't know, we're waiting for somebody to make a decision". So we were there for the best part of four hours. That was quite strange. "Can you arrest us please?" And that is a typical kind of English thing, that is how protests go. But then they hit us with a public nuisance charge because at that time we were causing nuisance to the public.'[81]

Planes were taking off and landing as normal, and the group's activity hadn't put any spanner in any works, as Malcolm had carefully planned that it shouldn't. The protestors sat meekly in their chains, getting pins and needles, waiting to be arrested. Instead, delicate negotiations were initiated.

'It was a bit like – absolutely no disrespect, but we didn't expect a social worker. There was all this kind of bargaining stuff. "We want to be friends here," and "Let's have these agreements". You know – just arrest us mate, that's what you're gonna do. And that whole process took about another hour, and it was really quite strange. They were treating us as if it was a kind of hostage situation and we were some dangerous group. We're not, we're citizens in our own country making an obvious protest about obvious issues.'[82]

Finally, the arrests happened. Then it was four hours in a cramped police van and equally cramped prison van, clinging to continence for dear life. 'I was desperate to, you know, relieve myself, but had nowhere to go in more senses than one. That wasn't fun.' The protestors were taken to separate stations and interrogated. Malcolm had already realised this wasn't the usual way a protest break-up went, and was braced for whatever was to come next. Ellen and Rose Rickford (aged 19 and 23) were on their first 'direct action' protest and were arrested along with everyone else. We met the sisters with their parents in North London, and hopefully they won't be too offended if I describe the family as 'completely normal'.

> Rose: I have been involved with a lot of different
> campaigns in politics, and I put a lot of energy into the
> Iraq anti-war movement. I felt like I just put my whole
> life into it for a year. And I mean wandering around the
> streets of London with placards, didn't seem to make
> any difference.
>
> Ellen: You can do all sorts of indirect action but until you
> have done a direct action to actually put the issues
> we're trying to campaign against on the map, no one is
> going to take any notice.

Doesn't sound like an apathetic generation. Even though he was worried to hear that both his daughters were arrested, their father, Brendan, is not ashamed of what they did: 'The climate change issue is really a very important issue for young people, for very clear reasons. Their grandchildren are not going to be living on a viable planet unless something is done about this. We shouldn't be surprised, and I am proud that they feel that much more viscerally than our generation has done. The problem is fantastically urgent and the fact that young people are taking urgent action to deal with it, I find it very encouraging, actually.' The girls were taken to a separate police station from the boys, and were locked up in their own cells. Neither had been in any trouble with the police before, but after a while Rose soon realised that this was not going to be a small slap on the wrist.

'Having been in the police station for about six hours, I was removed from my cell and taken to a police officer, who arrested me again for conspiracy to cause criminal damage. I think at that point I sort of thought "Oh...".'

Conspiracy is a very serious crime, and if proved can carry a substantial prison sentence.

Brendan: 'If the conspiracy laws are going to be used to criminalise political association then I think we're in big trouble.'

They were not allowed to make phone calls, and were held for 36 hours, the maximum possible without using the terrorist laws. They were then released one at a time onto the streets after midnight:

> Rose: When you have been held for 36 hours on your own, you are beginning to lose it a little bit. You have actually just been looking at the same walls for 36 hours and no one to talk to. We're probably not in the best psychological condition and then they released us, one by one in the middle of an area we didn't know. And told us our bail conditions were that we weren't allowed to associate with each other.
>
> Ellen: That was the worst bit for me actually; I didn't mind being in the cell, being released and finally like 'Oh god I am out,' and then they're like, 'You can't talk to anyone, we have got your phones'. She actually said, 'You've got a tenner you're not going to get far on a tenner, are you?'
>
> Rose: Someone asked, 'How are we supposed to get home?' Most of us didn't have any money, and certainly none of us had any change for a phone or anything. And she basically said, 'That's your problem,' and kind of laughed.

The police saw it as necessary to let several young women out onto the streets in a dangerous area, in half-hour intervals, without phones or the means to get home. They were told that they would be monitored by CCTV and were told that if they were seen talking to each other on the streets – even just to trying to get home – they would be re-arrested. The girls' mother, Frances, was appalled at this.

> The girls were told that they were going to be watched. I mean how can that not be vindictive, I mean, just horrifying really. And I don't know why they felt they

> had to be like that, I don't; they had already been in
> the cell on their own for 36 hours. Why did they feel
> they had to be so cruel?
>
> Malcolm: It's punishment policing. I also think it's pretty
> poor policing, because there was a duty of care not to
> put young people in harm's way.[83]

When they managed to return to their homes they found out
that while they had been under lock and key, their homes had
been raided.

> Malcolm: My son was woken by loud banging and the
> word 'Police' at 2.45 in the morning, and went
> downstairs. He thinks one of the officers had a
> gun…All the personal belongings were taken. My
> computer, my phone, my son's computer, his mobile,
> my filing cabinet. My PhD, which I had been trying to
> complete for six years, they took that. I am a Baptist
> minister of 51, just trying to do what I can to save the
> planet from destruction – it's what you might do on
> your day off.[84]
>
> Ellen: They raided my boyfriend's house; he's only 17,
> and they kicked in the door there. They kicked the lock
> in, they broke the door frame, they cracked the
> window on the door completely. They went through his
> stuff, took his computer.
>
> Brendan: What it suggests is that the police themselves
> at the front line are getting caught up in this
> atmosphere that says, that doesn't draw a clear
> distinction between peaceful protest and terrorism. So I
> think we have to be very worried about these small
> steps, and that people need to really be aware of how
> the erosion takes place. Funnily enough it's a bit like
> climate change. You don't see it from day to day. But
> take it over five years or ten years and you see – my
> God, things have changed! And then it's too late to do
> anything about it.

At one point the future was looking extremely bleak for the activists. They were looking at prosecutions in the Crown Court on charges that could attract a jail term. But the conspiracy charges were dropped. Seventeen activists got one-year conditional discharges (the minimum sentence available), and each was charged £70 in costs.

Malcolm is still angry, but still inspired. 'I don't know how determined that group of people was before the action, but we're bloody determined now. We will be citizens and we will define our own citizenship. We won't have it circumscribed by Mr Blair or his successor. You think you are just being a citizen, and all of a sudden you find it's been criminalised. That's what's been happening to protest.'[85]

Such dramatic heavy-handedness with protestors is on the increase. It has the same theatricality that Walter Wolfgang sees in Blair. In 2003, a few weeks after the Stop the War march, 120 activists on their way to a legally sanctioned anti-war demonstration found themselves in quite a production. It had the budget, it had the suspense... it was pure cinema.

THE GREAT FAIRFORD COACH-NAP – WHERE'S KEANU WHEN YOU NEED HIM?

> *Jack, nothing tricky now. You know I'm on top of you!*
> *DO NOT attempt to grow a brain!*
>
> **HOWARD PAYNE (DENNIS HOPPER), SPEED, 1994**[86]

Five thousand activists from all over the country were making their way to a US airforce base at Fairford, Gloucestershire, on 22 March 2003. Their plan was to protest against the week-old war in Iraq, and hear speakers including writer George Monbiot and comedian and activist Mark Thomas. Among them were a group of 120 people, from a wide assortment of groups, who were travelling from London on three coaches. They never made it.

A few miles from Fairford, the coaches were stopped. They were subjected to a meticulous search for weapons under the

Criminal Justice and Public Order Act of 1994. The passengers hung around by the coaches for an hour and a half, and made no objection to the search. The police had seized a frisbee and a bag of toy soldiers, just to be on the safe side, but were satisfied no weapons were on board. They allowed the passengers to re-board without making any arrests. But just to make absolutely sure, they forced the coaches to return to London under continuous police escort, against the will of everyone on board. There were between nine and twelve police vehicles alongside the coaches throughout. The coach-nappees were amazed to see that whole sections of the motorway were shut down, as well as helicopters covering their every move.

As Malcolm Carroll observed, you need a record-breaking bladder to be a protestor these days. The loo-less coaches, prevented from stopping at services under threat of arrest, had to keep going for the entire two-and-a-half hour journey back to London regardless of the discomfort of the passengers. They'd expected to spend the day protesting against the war; instead, they were protesting for their right to go for a wee. One described the experience as 'just like the movie *Speed*, except that it was the police who were stopping us from slowing down'. In the film, funnily enough, it's a terrorist who forces the bus to keep going.[87]

'The whim of a madman'. I like that!

HOWARD PAYNE[88]

This story has, for a change, a happy ending, and one with implications for the future of peaceful protest. The courts heard the judicial review case in early 2004. The judgement, a year later, claimed that the police acted unlawfully in detaining the passengers and preventing them from exercising their right to protest at a legal demonstration. But the High Court refuted this, saying that the police were right. The passengers pressed on with an appeal to the House of Lords, and on 13 December 2006, just in time for Christmas, they won. The Lords ruled that the police did act unlawfully in detaining the passengers, as well as violating the right to freedom of expression and lawful assembly.[89]

In giving judgement, Lord Bingham said the case 'raised important questions on the right of the private citizen to demonstrate against government policy, and the powers of the police to curtail exercise of that right'. Fairford Coach Action's rather pleased lawyer John Halford said:

> The House of Lords judgement is a wake-up call for democracy. The Lords have given a principled judgement on where the line should and must be drawn – peaceful protest can only be prevented in the most extreme circumstances, which are very far from this. These campaigners wanted to protest lawfully against an unlawful war. The Lords have unhesitatingly said they had that right.[90]

Fairford was, eventually, a bit of a triumph for the right to protest. It shows what a gaggle of people can do with a little legal knowledge and steadfast convictions.

THE POLICE – WHAT'S ALL THIS THEN?

> Q: How many police officers does it take to change a lightbulb?
> A: I wouldn't crack jokes if I were you. This is a very serious incident.

It's worth pausing for a moment to look at the people whose job it has become to prevent protestors from protesting under SOCPA, and who feature heavily in these first stories but don't have one of their own. When it comes to implementing law, from the moment it's passed, it's always the police who pass it on to the public. The police are the immediately answerable ones. The Government may make the law, but they are not the ones directly dishing it out. Just as army recruits don't get to opt out of wars they disagree with, the police don't have any choice but to arrest people who break the law. Although it's not quite that simple.

Police officers can use their own judgement up to a point when it comes to who needs to be bundled into a van and for what. No two situations are going to be the same – this is surely what many police officers enjoy about their work.

What many must hate about their work is having to apply those laws they personally do not believe are just. Of course the police who enjoy their job the most (or at least bear it with the least frustration; it's still a job, after all, and only a lucky few people really *love* their jobs) are bound to be the ones who don't think about it in that way at all. The police force has undergone something of a period of development under the Blair Government.

First, it's been given increased powers under SOCPA. (They're in the title and everything.) Henry Porter called the act 'a piece of legislation that will profoundly alter the relationship between the police and the public', and it's hard to argue with that assessment. The police can now arrest anyone for any offence, where before only certain offences carried the threat of arrest. Everything considered an offence – and there are considerably more of those today than there were ten years ago, with not even the Attorney General's office knowing exactly how many are on the statute book – you can now be arrested for if you are found doing it.[91]

The police can also now take your photo, your fingerprints and DNA, even if you have not been charged; if you are charged but later found not guilty, you can no longer request that this information about you is deleted from the system. (Lots more of this lovely stuff coming up when we get onto ID cards and surveillance.) They can stop and search you on a whim, without having to justify it to you or anyone else. The emphasis is more focused on minor transgression, arresting people for less, and obliging them to give up more. We have to answer to them in a way we've never had to do before in peacetime. (Ah, except we are at war. Kind of. Are we? Well yes. So sacrifices must be made.)[92]

> *They took my fingerprints, of my hands and thumbs and*
> *so on. They also wanted to film my eyes, the centre of*
> *my eyes, and also took a swab for DNA. I said, 'Look, I*

*haven't committed any crime, and I've never had this
before, what is this?' And I was told if I didn't volunteer
for this, they would take action, they would enforce it. I
felt that this is dreadful. This is criminalising you before
they can prove you're a criminal.*

JOHN CATT, PROTESTOR[93]

The number of purely guiltless people in Britain, in the face of the new police powers, has effectively shrunk.

Then there's the T-word. Despite insistences that terrorism would not alter life in this country, it is doing so by proxy, through a Government that has wheeled out new act after new act in its name. The Government is so fixated on anti-terror measures and legislation meant to combat terror that its ghoulish enthusiasm is contagious. The agenda of the Government filters down through the police, who become politicised.

> *There is always a danger with giving the
> police powers which are too broad. It's not
> even the police's fault. If you give them a
> power that's too broad, it's a recipe for
> disaster. Anti-terror powers are by
> definition exceptional powers; if they're
> too broad they become part of routine
> policing, and we've seen anti-terror laws
> used as public order powers which is bad
> enough), and then those powers used in a
> way which is … arbitrary, discriminatory
> and at times political.*

SHAMI CHAKRABARTI, DIRECTOR OF LIBERTY[94]

PhD student Kevin Gillam found this out for himself. On his way to the Edexcel centre

Giving offence
Between May 1997 and August 2006 Tony Blair's Government created 3023 new offences. Our favourite is the Polish Potatoes Order 2004, which states 'No person shall, in the course of business, import into England potatoes which he knows to be or has reasonable cause to suspect to be Polish potatoes.' (But they work ever so hard and never even take tea breaks.) It is also illegal to impersonate a traffic warden, which makes life difficult for some obscure strippograms, and you may no longer sell those grey squirrels you'd put aside as an investment. And if you didn't create a nuclear explosion before 1998, you've missed your chance.[95]

in London to demonstrate against the DSEi arms fair, a bi-yearly event that sees the world's biggest arms companies pitch up to ply their wares, he was stopped by the police. 'They asked to search me,' he says, 'and said it was under the Terrorism Act. An officer went through my stuff and confiscated some bits of paper with details of other demonstrations. I was pretty amazed...these are supposed to be extraordinary powers, not used all the time.'

Mark Thomas was at the arms fair. 'You have this huge police presence, and the use of stop-and-search is endemic. So do I have reason to stop you and search you? Yes, we've established a stop-and-search zone. You can be stopped and searched for no reason other than we want to.'

Kevin challenged the use of the act, but lost at the House of Lords. The case showed that the police *do not need a good reason* to stop and search under section 44. This means that they are well within their rights effectively to give you a half-hour prison sentence just because they don't like the colour of your hair. Or skin.[96]

When new laws come in, the police need to be trained to deal with them, so they can go out and know precisely what they're doing. The thing is that the Government has been paying out shiny new laws like a broken fruit machine for quite some time. And the police are struggling to keep up.

SOCPA was seemingly tossed out of the House of Commons, and then left to its own devices. As with the Iraq war, it just doesn't seem there was ever a clear plan for what to do afterwards.

It's quite a simple equation.

Lots more law + not enough training × increased police powers = Uh oh.

The British police protects what it thinks is the establishment, and it is insufficiently trained.

WALTER WOLFGANG[97]

All these stories have involved the police. The experiences vary vastly, as do the police officers themselves.

The 'over-enthusiastic'

The policemen who arrested Milan and Maya mostly think that SOCPA is a great idea (PC Paul McInally – you know who you are!). Various police have argued that peace protestors are actually being arrested for their own safety. Just in case they clash with those well-known 'pro-war' marches and the police weren't there to keep them apart.

The 'brutal and hostile'

> When they got to me I didn't hear what the police officer was saying – he knew perfectly well I couldn't hear what he was saying because of the terrific row that we were making as demonstrators with all sorts of equipment, you know, hailers and so on, and I was picked out straight away and was arrested in a pretty brutal fashion, and I eventually had my hands handcuffed from behind and then dragged along the ground with my shorts coming down which I was wearing...and I was treated in a most hostile manner.
>
> *JOHN CATT, 82*[98]

The dogged

> Two police officers detached themselves from the police and just followed me. I was followed through a fruit market, into a housing estate, into a newsagents, into a greengrocers, I just had the police with me all day.
>
> *RICHARD*[99]

The friendly, pleasant, and totally in agreement

> I asked them for twenty minutes to think about it...to be fair, they gave me at least 10 minutes. And then finally they took me very calmly into the van, and it was all very friendly and pleasant at the police station. I said [to the arresting officer] 'I bet you guys hate SOCPA as much as

*we do,' and he went, 'Yes.' And they just confirmed my
identity, and said they'd send me a summons.*

BECCA[100]

The Godsends

*A few years ago David Blaine came to do his 'Twat in a
box' stunt by Tower Bridge. I live just down the road
and I thought it was one of the most insulting things I
had ever seen. So I bought the biggest loudhailer I
could find and went down to tell him what I thought of
him. I started off my rant on how rubbish his magic was,
how he was clearly cheating, how he was insulting the
millions of people all over the world who are dying
from hunger. What I didn't expect was the reaction
from the crowd. Clearly there are a lot of David Blaine
fans in Essex and they had obviously been bussed in
for the day. They turned nasty straight away. I had a
couple of mates who were holding them back, but
there were about fifty Blaine-ites and I was about to get
lynched. But the police were there in seconds and
surrounded me. The sergeant told the crowd that they
would protect my right to freedom of speech, and then
turned around and said, 'Carry on, son.' So I did. Then
the crowd went really mental, but the police held their
ground. After about twenty minutes or so, the sergeant
turned to me and said, 'I think you're starting to repeat
yourself now, and I've got some real work to do.' The
police drove me away from the area for my own
safety. If those coppers hadn't been there I would have
been toast.*

CHRIS ATKINS – WRITER/DIRECTOR, TAKING LIBERTIES

We are not yet living in a police state. But the state of the police
leaves a lot to be desired. The increasing propensity of the police
to monitor protestors often ends up backfiring – what they

record is often evidence of the good behaviour of the protagonists, not their misbehaviour. But the mindset has firmly established
itself – these people need to be kept an eye on.

FIT FOR PURPOSE – WATCHING THE PROTESTORS

If you go on any protest these days, legal or not, you are likely to
experience a blue-jacketed police officer shoving a video camera
in your face. Welcome to the Forward Intelligence Team (FIT).
Half way between surveillance and intimidation, these officers are
not shy when it comes to letting you know they're watching you.

> *It's designed to make you feel twice about going on a
> demonstration again. It has what the police describe as a
> 'chilling effect'.*
>
> **MARK THOMAS**[101]

FIT was set up some thirteen years ago as a tool to deal with
football hooliganism, as well as far-right demonstrations from
groups such as Combat 18 who often attached themselves to
hooligan culture. The concept was simple: the team would use
overt surveillance to make it plain to the subjects of their scrutiny
that they were being watched. In time, it became used more
generally in policing regular demonstrations, the kind that would
attract the same individuals over and over. Islington police
commander Barry Norman helped to establish it. He saw it as a
'Dixon of Dock Green' thing – 'where community policing meets
public demonstrations'. It's a nice idea, in theory.[102] He explains,

> *We took the view that a few of us [should go] out and
> [use] our intelligence to work out who the movers and
> shakers were, and we spoke to people and we got to
> know people… If you speak to them, and you act
> decently and you're a human being, you know, most
> intelligent people, and for that matter, most unintelligent
> people find it quite difficult not to talk back. And once*

> *you start to develop a rapport, then you start to, you*
> *know, diminish people's anonymity... One of the key*
> *causes of disorder in a public order situation is people's*
> *anonymity. People think that, well, no one knows who I*
> *am. And if I misbehave, then I'm never going to have to*
> *answer for my actions.*[103]

Richard, a highly articulate and intelligent activist (if you want to amuse an anarchist, ask them who their leader is), has been trailed by FIT. The team have a list of 'regulars' who they feel need to be conspicuously watched, and Richard has found himself with a mini-entourage on several occasions:

> *They're talking about you between themselves,*
> *obviously it's there to isolate you from the crowds; if you*
> *walk away from the demonstration and go through an*
> *ordinary crowd of people, you do get, 'Who is this guy*
> *that has to have two policemen following him*
> *everywhere?' It is intended to be intimidating. Now I've*
> *only had this for a day, but there are activists who have*
> *had this day in day out. That I can imagine would be*
> *very wearing; it's designed to break down your morale.*
> *It's designed to make you dispirited, ineffective, to make*
> *you feel isolated... and ultimately powerless.*

Barry Norman insists FIT is no more intrusive than a CCTV camera.

> *'[It's] not intimidation. The intention is... to develop a*
> *relationship with you. We recognise that you are a key*
> *individual in this event, and frankly, communication is*
> *what's going to make this event pass off... without too*
> *many problems. On the other hand, we also know that if*
> *we take away your anonymity, you might feel less*
> *inclined to... orchestrate some disorder.*

Richard sees it differently.

> *The police can be very effective at shutting down an*
> *individual's civil liberties... following them around,*

observation, surveillance. What they can't shut down is an idea.[104]

When it comes to free speech, it's still primarily activists who are feeling the pinch. With surveillance, however, it's the rest of us that are under the greatest pressure and facing the most severe restrictions. But for the most part, we don't even know it. Protestors being slunk after by FIT know without a doubt they're being watched; the public in general, who'd be horrified by such a direct yet fleeting intrusion into their privacy, don't realise that in fact they are being monitored and examined on a far greater scale, with consequences which could endure for a lifetime. As Richard says,

> As the technology becomes available it is used to keep tabs on the individual. If the technology was there for the Government to be able to say what everyone in the country was doing at every single moment, they would be using it.

Chapter 3

Somebody's watching me – surveillance, privacy and identity

When liberty is taken away by force it can be restored by force. When it is relinquished voluntarily by default it can never be recovered.

DOROTHY THOMPSON[1]

Jerry Fishenden is national technology officer for Microsoft in the UK. He has tried to explain to the Government the unintended consequences of the database and surveillance systems now available.

I think if we, as a society, don't have a clear vision of where we want to be in five, ten, twenty, fifty years time the technology will have an incredible ability to drive us in the wrong direction.

JERRY FISHENDEN, NATIONAL TECHNOLOGY OFFICER, MICROSOFT UK[2]

If watching and recording other people were an Olympic sport, Britain would have a guaranteed gold medal (note to 2012 Olympic committee – this might be worth looking into). It is estimated that 20 percent of the world's surveillance cameras are here, despite the fact that we have only 0.2 percent of the world's land mass. The Government seems to have been told that all evils in the world will be solved by putting stuff in a really big computer. While this provides a good way for people to get their voyeuristic fix between episodes of Big Brother, we really need to consider whether the massive accumulation of data is providing value for the money that we pour into it. Technology and policy move on so fast that by the time this book comes out half of the things we describe will be obsolete or in their next incarnation, so please forgive us for not being able to keep up.

> *To what extent should the expectation of liberty be*
> *eroded by legitimate intrusions in the interests of*
> *security of the wider public?*
>
> **NO 10 POLICY WORKING GROUP ON SECURITY, CRIME AND JUSTICE,**
> **TECHNOLOGICAL ADVANCES**[3]

> *They who would give up essential liberty to purchase a*
> *little temporary security deserve neither liberty nor safety.*
>
> **BENJAMIN FRANKLIN**[4]

Good old security. The single most important thing in life, we now come to recognise. Over the last few years it's raced to the top of the rights chart, leapfrogging over the previous popular tunes of freedom of speech and the presumption of innocence. With the threat of terrorism looming large, New Labour has drummed it into the public that security is the be-all and end-all. A recent survey suggested 70 percent of us are very willing to give up liberty for security.[5] This wilfully distorted view, with its built-in protection of public fear, has diluted the importance of our liberty. The most serious threat to our liberty in the future is also one of the softest on its feet – the unstoppable spread of surveillance, the plan for a national identity card scheme backed up by a giant computerised register, and with it the gathering by the state of an extraordinary amount of information about our lives.

SURVEILLANCE – YOU ARE WHAT YOU WATCH

If you go down to Middlesbrough town centre tonight, you'd better behave yourself. Step out of line at all, and you might hear the voice of authority. It's unlikely you'll be able to tell where it's coming from at first – you'll just be surprised and disorientated. Then you'll look up.

'Please dismount your bicycle. This is a pedestrian area. Thank you.'

'The person in the denim jacket. Please get out of the road.'

Some people might be somewhat shocked hearing a camera speak to us and tell us to shape up. Middlesbrough is the first town in the UK, the renowned world centre of CCTV surveillance, to install £50,000 worth of cameras with extra scolding capability. Councillor Barry Coppinger is pleased with the project.

'The response has been very interesting,' he told a local paper. 'A lot of people are quite surprised when they hear the voice for the first time. I think it gets to their guilty conscience. It is like a public humiliation in a way…it means the person won't do it again.' He isn't worried about the implications for privacy. 'We've had CCTV here for a number of years, and we've never had any complaints about it infringing people's freedom. People above all want to feel safe. That's what we're here to do.'[6]

We're used to the reality of CCTV cameras capturing our image many times a day, wherever we go, and it doesn't especially bother us. It's estimated there are around 4.2 million of them in Britain, one for every 14 people.[7] It's such a normal part of life now that car manufacturers are using it in their advertisements, portraying it as a bit of a sexy opportunity to show off ('You are caught on camera over three hundred times a day – give them something to watch').[8] We figure that a lot of the time CCTV helps to catch criminals, and the rest of the time the operators kick back and use the cameras to check out the pert bits of girls. We aren't usually aware of being watched, which is mostly why we don't see it as a problem. But if you think that surveillance has reached saturation, a multi-billion pound industry will tell you otherwise.

Here are a handful of proposed and current developments in the wonderful world of watching.

Facial recognition software for CCTV cameras

The best place to get a demonstration of this is the hit TV series *24*. Blair is clearly a fan, as this incredibly expensive techno trickery is being rolled out across Britain. Basically the software matches the facial images from the street to those on file. This is one of the areas where surveillance and databases come together in perfect harmony.[9] The only slight hitch at the moment is that the software is massively unreliable and could lead to the wrong people being hauled off the streets, but let's not get bogged down in boring technicalities; the Government can see that the theory is there, and sometimes it works. How many can we have?

Open access CCTV

As the number of security cameras shoots up, operators are always in short supply. Some cunning companies have realised that there is a cheap way round this dilemma – let *anyone* watch. Not only do they not have to fork out for costly operators, but the people watching actually pay for the service. Genius. For example, Shoreditch TV gives you unlimited access to any of the security cameras in the area through the internet or cable TV. Local stalkers can save themselves all the tedious lurking that usually goes with the job, and thieves know exactly where the cameras are and when any offices/homes are empty. All from the comfort of their own homes. As we said before – genius.[10]

CCTV cameras in toilets[11]

Anyone who requires an explanation on the cons of this proposal needs help.

Behavioural recognition software for CCTV cameras

This is a huge growth area in the IT industry. The software is programmed to spot behaviour and movement that's out of the ordinary.[12] Running, standing still or walking strangely will all set off an alarm.[13] We've always thought that jogging is unhealthy, so we're very pleased to see that in future it will be treated as downright suspicious.

CCTV cameras with sound

Those of you who've been paying attention are probably thinking that we've already mentioned the scheme in Middlesbrough, but remember, sound is a two-way process. Not only will cameras be allowed to talk to you, directional microphones will be able to pick up your conversation over a hundred yards.[14] Once again these will pick up anything out of the ordinary. No laughing outside in future please.

X-ray CCTV cameras
That can actually see through clothing. Really. A leaked Home Office report recently announced that the Government wants to see these in lamp posts. To stop terrorists, of course. Admittedly the leak was to the *Sun*, but it sounds suitably terrifying, so we decided to include it.[15]

Remote cameras on every policeman
These are cameras attached to the side of policemen's helmets.[16] This effectively turns every policeman into a member of FIT. They literally bolt a camera onto the side of their heads. Alternatively you could just view policemen as walking CCTV cameras. The plus-side of this is that they will probably soon be up on YouTube, which will give you something to watch when you are bored at work.

Mobile phone GPS tracking software
This handy tool is already available, and lets anyone track your position simply by knowing your phone number.[17] It might be a good idea to leave your mobile at home when you phone in sick but are actually heading to the beach for the day.

Microchips implanted in mental patients
These aren't much help with treatment, but it'll be nice to know where they are.[18] It's always cheering when you read about a new policy from your Government featuring technology originally used to keep track of household pets.

Numberplate recognition
Works the same as facial recognition, and is there to track you for when you get in your car and the cameras might not be able to see your face.[19]

GPS road tax boxes

Ostensibly there to make sure we all pay road duty correctly, they will also keep track of every vehicle in the country.[20] Germany has already tried this scheme without success[21] but, when it comes to technology, our plucky Government is never put off by previous failures.

> We need to lift our sights a little. I don't think, in the debate so far, that we have even begun to explore the benefits that we will see in, say, ten years' time.
>
> TONY BLAIR[22]

This is just a taste of what is to come in the world of surveillance. It is increasing for its own sake, mainly to enrich the people who tell us it's vitally necessary. Between 1998 and 2003 New Labour spent £170 million pounds on CCTV.[23] They then had the ingenious idea of funding a study to find out whether CCTV actually prevented crime. The study found that cameras had little effect, except in car parks, and the scheme to fund CCTV systems was stopped.[24] £170 million for a crime-reducing initiative that their own study says fails to reduce crime – quite cost-effective for government.

Fortunately, no one seems to have been put off by the little matter of scientific research and analysis, so cameras have continued to give birth to new cameras on a daily basis. The huge demand for operators means *anyone* can get a job watching CCTV monitors (sitting and judging people while drinking a cup of tea is what the English do best, after all). There are no qualifications, checks or training necessary, as they are so desperate for operators. Is anyone watching the CCTV operatives? It turns out (and this is going to shock you) that some of them have not just been watching for criminals. On 31 January 2006, two CCTV operatives in Liverpool were jailed for spying on a naked woman in her own home. The judge said, 'You only have to read the impact statements of the lady to realise the harrowing effect this had on her'.[25] Another operator was jailed for calling a phone box if a girl he fancied walked by. If she made the mistake of picking up the phone he would then subject her to a dirty call.[26] Yup, it seems that, like the internet, CCTV is mostly used for porn.

What will the future be like when every human action is filmed and recorded? In the nineteenth century, criminal law reformer  Jeremy Bentham designed the panopticon, which he believed would be the perfect prison. He took the idea of surveillance as a means of control to its logical conclusion. The concept of the design is to allow an observer sitting on the inside ring to watch the prisoners, without the prisoners knowing if they are being observed or not. This would convey a 'sentiment of an invisible omniscience' onto the people inside. In his own words, Bentham described the panopticon as 'a new mode of obtaining power of mind over mind, in a quantity hitherto without example'.

If the prison population believe they are being watched all of the time, then they will behave and conform. The design never took off, and no perfect panopticons were ever built. But if Bentham was alive today and could see the mass of surveillance available, he would no doubt congratulate us for testing his dream across an entire country.

But surveillance is just one section of the shiny new world that technology has delivered to us. As we become more and more reliant on computers to do everything from flushing the loo for us (handles really were a lot of hard work) to making new friends (who needs to actually meet people these days?) we have come to realise that nothing exists until it has been put down on a database. And there, as with everything that's built by men, size really does matter.

THE DATABASE STATE WE'RE IN

Over the past fifteen years, databases have gone from being something that IT men bore you about at parties to a controlling factor in every single area of your life. There are now databases to store information about everything, and there are quite a lot of databases that just store information about other databases. We have databases for the nation's health records, DNA, children's school reports, and criminal records. They are not naturally evil things, and we'd like to make it clear that putting information in one easy-to-find and easy-to-understand location is not always a bad thing. Statistics can be incredibly useful (you may notice that we've used a few in this book) and most areas of science and medicine can only progress by having accurate data to hand.

And it is only information, after all, being organised more effectively by the technology that's now available to us. Information is an overwhelming positive in our lives. We all have greater access to information than we've ever had before, a world of knowledge available to us through hundreds of TV channels and an unfathomable galaxy of millions of web pages.

Our own personal information is often just something we need to utilise to buy things or go places. We guard our PINs pretty closely and try and come up with unguessable passwords, but other than that we're usually quite unconcerned about the companies we give our data to.

As for the information itself, it's easy come, easy go. You hand out your name and address, phone number and mother's maiden name many times a year. You bung them in boxes on websites, scribble them on forms, and recite them automatically to call centres while thinking about what to have for lunch. Why make a fuss about putting them in one more place? It might even be useful – no more faffing about toting your passport to the bank or trying to remember where your birth certificate is. It's what we do without thinking in order to get what we want. It doesn't feel like a big deal at all.

Yet our information is more valuable than we can fully grasp. It can be bought and sold and swapped, lost or misappropriated, attributed to someone else. We do know that this can happen when our identity is stolen, but we rarely consider the implications of allowing the Government to keep our identity for itself. It may not mean loss of identity, but what it does mean is an enormous loss of control and privacy – things we largely take for granted.

*Why should they have this information?
Why should they know?... What do they
want with it? Why don't they just butt out
of it?*

BORIS JOHNSON MP[27]

The latest supercomputer wheeled out by
New Labour and the IT industry to transform
our lives is, of course, the National Identity
Register (NIR) – the database that sits behind
ID cards. In 2005 the Identity Bill became law,
and ID cards and the NIR are now becoming a reality.[28] The sheer
size of the operation is such that it will be a few years before the
cards are in our wallets and purses; like an unstoppable steam-
roller, it is only a matter of time. But before we jump feet first
into the controversy on ID cards and the gigantic computer
behind them, let's remind ourselves of the some of our favourite
databases from the last decade.

DNA database

DNA is a scientific blueprint of who we are, unique to each
individual and found in every cell of our bodies. We scatter it
everywhere we go, leaving traces of ourselves behind which
someone else can later pick up. Cunning scientist types saw how
useful this could be in detecting crime, and began to collect DNA
from crime scenes and match it to perpetrators. In 1995 a
database was set up to store the DNA of known offenders for
checking against crime-scene samples. However, over the past
three years New Labour has changed the scope of this database
massively. First, they changed the 2003 Criminal Justice Act to
enable the police to take 'non-intimate samples of DNA without
consent' of anyone who had been arrested.[29] Then the Serious
Organised Crime and Police Act made every offence arrestable.
This has meant the DNA of millions of people who have never
been charged with anything have been added to the database
(this presumably includes several of Blair's closest advisors by

now). The database currently holds 3.6 million samples; at over 5 percent of the population, this is the most comprehensive DNA database in the world, beating the second most comprehensive, Austria's, by a whopping 4 percent. Great to see we're on top of our game here as well. While DNA has proved extremely useful in the detection of crime, the massive increase in samples on the database has not actually improved the detection rate using DNA (the chances of detecting crime using DNA have remained constant at about 0.36 percent since 2003).[30] The benefits to crime detection are often misstated by police and government, who tend to report the entire number of DNA matches at crime scenes, including matches to the victim and innocent passers-by as well as criminal detections, giving a far larger number than is relevant. Once the police have taken someone's DNA, the samples are kept permanently, rather than being destroyed once identification profiles have been obtained. The pressure group Genewatch recently discovered that these samples have been used for genetic research, and that one of the private companies contracted by the police has been keeping its own mini-database.[31] There is very little regulation of this database, despite the massive importance of the information it contains.

Children

In 2005 New Labour decided to create a children's database for the purpose of protecting kids from abuse and neglect. This will build an audit trail of every child's life history, including any interaction they have with authority. Truancy records, diet, medical history and behavioural problems will all sit on a file. There are obvious concerns that this information can be compromised to harm either you or your children, and that rather than increasing the chances of catching abuse early, the lack of security in the system will mean that people are less likely to seek help.

Plans are already afoot to use this abundance of personal information to look for patterns in existing behaviour and predict the future. This is called data mining, and is currently the Government's favourite way to find everything from terrorism to fraud. New Labour wants to use the information it will automatically gather about your children to 'predict' whether they are going to get into trouble, and intervene early. When it was launched, the Government said, 'The main focus is on spotting the babies and children who may become a menace or cost to society in later life, for example having babies in their teens, underachieving at school or being delinquent.'[32] This risks setting up expectations about children among the government institutions they interact with, creating a self-fulfilling prophecy.

It is also worth noting that no other countries drain information from their citizens quite like New Labour does. Germany, which has had real totalitarian control in recent memory, is incredibly careful about what the state knows about children. It is actually illegal for a secondary school teacher to look at a child's primary-school records, as each child is supposed to start their new school with a clean slate.

Whitehall central valuation computer

It has been suggested that the valuation office agency is planning to store details on every single home in the country, to make sure that your council-tax assessments are correct. Bold new methods have been announced to keep track of every single home improvement you make.[33] These include:

- aerial photographs to make sure you haven't got a sneaky extension on the potting shed;
- thermal imaging so that they can see through walls;
- the ability of officers to enter your home at any time to see if you've been naughtily fitting a new boiler or putting up some new tiles.

Government plans for more data sharing would allow the council-tax inspectors to raid other state databases and build detailed records of anything that makes your home more valuable. This means that if someone kindly knocks a building down and you get a better view, you'll also be handed a bigger bill.

NHS database

> If I live in Bradford but fall ill in Birmingham I want the
> doctor treating me to have access to the information he
> needs to treat me.

TONY BLAIR 1998[34]

This was the beginning of Connecting for Health, the gargantuan NHS database. Blair had the wonderful plan to make a 'paperless' NHS by computerising all patient records so that they would be accessible to anyone at the touch of a button. But were Bradford's finest falling ill in Birmingham and Brummie doctors letting them die as they didn't have access to their records? No. Were IT companies who stood to make billions out of this database telling Mr Blair it would be the best thing since sliced bread? Yes.

Nine years later it's not going too well. It was initially projected to cost £1.6 billion – latest estimates are around the £20 billion mark. Apart from allergies (which are easily identifiable by wrist bands), there are very few things that doctors really need to know before they carry out emergency procedures. Any doctor would say that the £20,000,000,000 could have been much better spent on new hospitals, medical research, more doctors, nurses, equipment – all the boring things that make people well again. Accenture, one of the companies that advised New Labour to build this database, has now pulled out; it's still not ready and is already experiencing massive problems. These problems are best explained by Helen Wilkinson, an NHS manager who's had a taste of what's to come when our medical records go digital.

Having read an article about the new National Care Records, the centralised NHS database she calls 'a huge white elephant', Helen began to think about opting out. So she requested a copy of her medical records under the Data Protection Act, and discovered when she read through it that she was an alcoholic. Well, the first step is to admit you have a problem.

'It's basically a data-entry error,' she explains. A slip of an administrator's finger, then, led to two years of a serious error on

Helen's records. If she hadn't read the records, it might have taken much longer for her to find out. An investigation was started, but it took the intervention of her MP to get the offending article removed. It's enough to drive a person to drink.

It took so long to sort out Helen's records because no one knew exactly where the information had gone. It had left an invisible trail from one system to another.

'Whenever you attend a hospital appointment, your name, data of birth, postcode, NHS number, GP details, consultant details, clinic you've attended, procedure you've had done, etc, are all sent to this private company, Mackerson, in Warwick, without patient consent. And Mackerson, then send it out to your primary care trust, your local shared agency, which does the admin, strategic health authority, Department of Health, and Dr Foster. Potentially hundreds of people can access it. It's going out all over the place and just sitting on people's PCs.'[35]

The Government weren't a lot of help. They assured Helen that the mistake had been removed,[36] but she discovered it hadn't. It took an enormous effort to clean up her records, even though she works for the NHS. 'The average person in the street wouldn't know where to start,' she says, 'or have any idea of where this information had gone.' The National Care Records system, which will incorporate the current system, troubles Helen rather a lot. 'People should be worried, because potentially millions of NHS employees will have access to your records.'

Helen predicts that this system will lead to more patients withholding information from their doctors, endangering their health. Again, it's an issue of loss of trust, something that databases almost inevitably bring about. She also thinks it will lead to people opting out of the NHS altogether. She's succeeded in doing this herself, and has set up the Big Opt Out, a campaign to help others to protect their patient confidentiality. She discovered, however, that it's not easy, making this kind of exposure of your private records essentially compulsory if you want to use the NHS. They don't want to let you go without a fight.

*For me personally, I'm the only patient that I know
they've agreed to this for – they've agreed that Section
10 of the Data Protection Act applies to me, so the
Department of Health and the NHS cannot hold or store
or process any of my personal clinical details. But when
I cut my eye recently, I was told unless I go back on
these databases, I can't have my eye treated. So they are
basically denying me care because Section 10 of the
Data Protection Act applies to me.*

Helen predicts that in future we'll have 'probably one massive database. My guess is it will be the ID database with an offshoot for your criminal record; another offshoot for education; another for social services; another for health. If you read the Government's 'Transforming IT', a document issued by the Cabinet Office, that's the line it's actually taking to have joined-up government with all these databases linked. You might not have anything to hide at the moment, and you might be perfectly fit and well, but at some stage in the future you may have cancer, you may have a mental-health problem, you may be abused by a partner – all kinds of things. And you need to protect yourself for the future, to protect your privacy so that you can go and see a doctor in complete confidence, as you should be able to do.'[37]

The last part of Helen's story shows that a key danger of the database state is not with the computers, but with the people who operate them. She says, 'A receptionist that I employed had worked at University College London Hospitals, and she admitted that in her lunch hour she used the system to look up her friends, see what they've been in with, find someone's mobile phone number. So it's already happening… at the moment it can only happen within that hospital, but once the whole system's connected up, it will give everyone much more access to a whole range of personal details.'

Having built databases to manage and control every area of our life, New Labour ran out of ideas about what to do next. After a long hard brainstorming session they decided that the only way forward was to join them all up.

> *This is about sharing data in a sensible way so the customer gets a better service.*
>
> TONY BLAIR[38]

The next stage in this efficiency drive is the creation of ID cards linked to a network of databases – called the National Identity Register.

DATA, SCHMATA

Phil Booth is the national co-ordinator of No2ID, a non-partisan campaign against ID Cards. We've interviewed him on three occasions, and every time he's been on crutches – although he assures us this is nothing to do with the Home Office.

A society in which you're told who you are, how to move, how to work, where you can live, what you can do, is not a society I want to live in. It's a controlled, controlling nightmare, it's not life. I'm not saying that the ID card scheme will be that straight away. But they're putting in place something that moves towards the nightmare.

PHIL BOOTH, NO2ID[39]

When the plans for ID cards come to fruition, you'll be obliged to add another card to your untidy wallet. It might feel a bit like your driving licence, but it will be a little more comprehensive.

The first ID cards will be issued to British citizens in 2009. You'll be told to go to a special pre-planned interview at the Identity and Passport office, where you'll face a grilling to make sure you are who they think you are.

You'll use the card every time you interact with the state, in the form of your GP, your kids' school or the local library. What you do on each occasion will be added to the register. It's an all-inclusive record of the things about you that change, and the things about you that always stay the same. It retains everything about your past and your present, and will suggest a lot about your future.

The NIR will be accessible to a huge range of government officials. But it's more than just good organisation; the problem (or at least the initial problem) is that your NIR number will make it easier for civil servants – or anyone else – to find out what you've done in your life. Even if you have an unblemished record and don't care who knows your vital statistics, the banal act of consenting to being included on this database cluster adds up to something overwhelming. It means you have relinquished control of your personal details for ever, and the state then decides who to share them with or sell them to. Gordon Brown has already indicated that he wants to subsidise the NIR by charging corporations to check the identity of their customers.[40]

NOTHING WRONG HERE

You can't give up your freedoms to be more free. That doesn't make sense. With freedom comes responsibility, and the responsibility isn't just what the Government seems to mean. The responsibility that

What is the NIR?

The card is only a small part of the whole: all the information on there will be kept on the National Identity Register (NIR). The information will sit on three existing Government databases. The Department for Work and Pensions database will hold biographical information; biometric data, such as fingerprints or eye scans, will be held on the Home Office system; and the Identity and Passport Service system will hold the remaining information. In all, the Identity Cards Act 2006 provides for 49 items of data pertaining only to you to be stored on the register, and all of this will have to be handed over when you go for your compulsory ID session.

A few of the items are as follows:

- full name;
- other names by which person is or has been known;
- date of birth;
- place of birth;
- gender;
- address of principal place of residence in the UK;
- the address of every other place in the UK or elsewhere where person has a place of residence;
- identifying information;
- a photograph of head and shoulders;
- signature;
- fingerprints;
- other biometric information – this includes iris scans and DNA;
- personal reference numbers;
- National Identity Registration number;
- the number of any ID card issued;
- allocated national insurance number;
- UK passport number;
- any driver number given by a driving licence.

Politicians change their minds

'Instead of wasting hundreds of millions of pounds on compulsory ID cards as the Tory Right demand, let that money provide thousands of extra police officers on the beat in our local communities.'

TONY BLAIR, LABOUR PARTY CONFERENCE, 3 OCTOBER 1995

'ID cards... are an important, indeed essential, way of tackling illegal migration and crime in the early twenty-first century.'

TONY BLAIR, PRIME MINISTER'S QUESTIONS, 18 JANUARY 2006

Labour's plastic poll tax has no place in modern Britain... It's an ugly monument to the waste, chaos and vanity of intrusive, over-mighty government... I promise you this... in office, we will pull it down.

DAVID CAMERON

???

DAVID CAMERON 2012

comes with freedom is the responsibility to fight for freedom.

RACHEL NORTH[41]

Your identity as it manifests itself in your collected data may not be your soul, but it does, in a very real way, represent your self. To surrender it willingly and comprehensively is to give up something you will never get back. New Labour may not be cause for too much alarm to this end – their mania for data-gathering is at least based in some misguided urge to protect us – but there's no guarantee that future governments, inheriting a toybox like the NIR, won't use it to more malign and oppressive ends.

If you've got nothing to hide, why would you want to be treated as someone who has? Or as someone who might? A pre-crim, as it were. In some US states, women of reproductive age are now being told to consider themselves 'pre-pregnant' and to quit smoking and take folic acid for the health of the zygote they may find themselves incubating at any time. Do we want to be considered pre-offensive by our Government? Data mining is already used to predict our behaviour and control us accordingly – in fact, the police have started a database to compile information on, and track, the people they consider to be probable future criminals.[42] Such a line of thinking leads to wholesale suspicion of more or less everyone, almost a reversal of 'innocent until proven guilty'.

The logic persists that if you've done nothing wrong, you've nothing to worry about. But what you've done so far in your life has been governed according to the laws as they are today. A future government might not share your views on right and wrong; and don't presume that the next government, or the one after that, will hand you back your privacy and hold a mass bonfire of ID cards in Hyde Park, laying on fireworks and baked potatoes.

But maybe we're getting a little carried away. After all, lots of other countries have ID cards; don't they?

THE ID CARD – A BRIEF HISTORY (TO BE PRODUCED ON DEMAND)

> *As an online discussion grows longer, the probability of a comparison involving Nazis or Hitler approaches one.*
>
> **GOODWIN'S LAW**[46]

It's true. It seems like a good trick, something condemnatory that has the power to shock, and yet it's so commonplace as a lazy reference that using it usually means you've lost the argument in one go, and have to slink off to watch *Battlestar Galactica* in disgrace. However, sometimes you have to dig up Hitler, because Hitler is unfortunately relevant.

This is one of those times.

Hitler pioneered the use of ID cards as a means of repression, so he qualifies for inclusion here. We wouldn't be letting him in if he didn't.

In July 1938, the Nazis had introduced the 'J-stamp' for Jewish citizens.[47] It appeared on their identity cards and passports. Four months later, Jewish homes and stores were raided all across Germany on what became known as Kristallnacht; thousands of Jews were beaten to death, 30,000 were removed to concentration camps, and 1000 synagogues were ransacked or burned down. The Jews were easily singled out due to the strictly enforced identity-card system.

Meanwhile in Blighty, a national scheme mandating ID cards was introduced to help identify aliens during the war. Everyone had to carry the card at all times and produce it on demand to the police or the army. Churchill's move was made with immense reluctance; he deeply regretted the trespass made on 'our dearly valued traditional liberties',[48] and promised to scrap the cards once the war was over.

> *I had an identity card. But it only had three purposes and the Germans were at our gate in 1940, for Pete's sake. They were bombing the hell out of London night after night. Sixty thousand Londoners were killed. And what we put up with in a world war where we were in desperate risk…[it's] quite a different state of affairs to what we are confronting now.*
>
> **LORD PHILLIPS, FORMER LIBERAL DEMOCRAT PEER**[49]

It was always Churchill's fervent intention to scrap the ID cards in peacetime, but before he could, he lost the election. The Labour Government who took over opted to retain ID cards to keep everyone extra-safe. For extra-extra-safeness, they expanded the scheme, requiring more and more information to be kept on the cards. The police began to abuse the privilege of being able to stop people and demand to see their cards.

In the end, a solitary working-class bloke from Leeds put the first nail in the ID-card coffin by refusing to show his card when stopped for speeding in 1950. Clarence Henry Willcock told the officer, 'I am a Liberal, and I am against this sort of thing'. He fought his case and lost in the High Court, but in summing up Lord Chief Justice Goddard declared that 'to demand a national registration identity card from all and sundry is wholly unreasonable. This act was passed for security purposes, and not for the purposes for which it is now sought to be used. To use acts of parliament, passed for particular purposes during war, in times when the war is past, tends to turn law-abiding subjects into lawbreakers.'[50]

Willcock's fight made him a national hero, and summed up the mood of the country. People hated the cards, and wanted rid of them. It wouldn't be long before their wish was granted. In 1952, the National Registration Act was repealed and ID cards were abolished.

While they were merely unpopular in Britain, ID-card schemes have been used to deadly effect elsewhere in the world. When the Belgians ruled Rwanda they separated the entire population into Hutu and Tutsi, using physical attributes as a means of classification. Rwandans were forced to carry ID cards by the colonial Belgian Government, and retained the cards after independence. When the 1994 genocide began, a Tutsi card would get you killed at any roadblock. A million people died in a hundred days, their identification having been made simple and undeniable by the cards they carried.[51]

There is no need to look back in history to see how useful ID cards can be to those looking to massacre part of their population. Since 'sectarian fighting' began in Iraq, showing an ID card with a Sunni name at a Shia checkpoint (or vice versa) can be a death warrant.[52]

As for the massive database itself, that concept comes courtesy of the secret police in Soviet East Germany (the Stasi). The millions of files they kept ensured that they could keep track of everyone in the country.[53] People knew that they were being watched and judged, so they stayed as quiet as possible and were careful not to attract attention.

> *The reason the East Germans did it is because once you have information on a person, their medical problems, their travel arrangements, their divorces, you have much, much better control over them and therefore the society. Everything that we're doing now is what the Stasi did, but didn't have the technology to pull off.*
>
> **HENRY PORTER**[54]

The Berlin Wall came down before the Stasi could computerise their system. If they had, it would have borne a familial resemblance to New Labour's proposed NIR.

WHY ID?

We all like things to be organised, and you can't blame the Government for wanting to keep stuff tidy. However, you don't undertake a massive task like cataloguing the lives of fifty million people just for the sake of a clear desk. The Government have explained at length their reasons for the ID card scheme, and they all have two things in common:

1) they sound completely reasonable at a cursory glance;
2) they crumble under close examination.

It'll help stop terrorism

> I am convinced, as are our security services, that a
> secure Identity System will help us counter terrorism.
>
> **TONY BLAIR**[55]

> We spent a long time trying to find something interesting to write about Charles Clarke, but have failed miserably. All suggestions welcome; please email.

Not *everyone* was as convinced as Tony likes to think, though. Asked by BBC Radio 4's *Today* programme if ID cards could have prevented the London bombings, Charles Clarke said, 'I doubt it would have made a difference.'[56]

We'd all like to stop terrorism, which is why Blair's number one justification for ID cards gains support from some quarters. Many members of the public will do whatever they can to this end, and are more than willing to accept ID cards if they'll help. It seems like a patriotic duty – just as it would in wartime. The trouble is that in terms of usefulness, signs on underground trains imploring 'Be considerate – don't blow yourself up' might do just as well.

> We know the bombers were very careful to carry ID.
> Mohamed Siddique Khan actually gave his ID to three of
> the other bombers to carry and made sure it was found
> at the scene – it was found at all three train blasts. We
> also know the bombers took great care to show their

*faces to CCTV. So I don't think having a national
identification database would have stopped the
bombers, and I don't think the bombers would have felt
remotely put off by the fact that their details were
known; I think they would have welcomed it.*

RACHEL NORTH[57]

Threatening someone determined to give up his life for a political cause with a biometric card containing all the vital details of his identity is a bit like threatening him with handcuffs made of cheese. Especially if he really likes cheese. It would be wonderful if all it took to defeat terrorism was a plastic card, just as it would be wonderful if terrorists could be deterred by the bureaucratic process of filling in a SOCPA form. But complex problems require complex solutions. It's insulting to our intelligence to suggest that ID cards could act as some sort of panacea for peace. And the Government doesn't seem to have a lot of respect for our brainpower if it expects us to believe ID cards will do any more to combat terrorism than a sturdy broom.

Next.

It'll help control immigration

*In our view, identity cards, with the new technology that
is available, are necessary in the fight against illegal
immigration.*

TONY BLAIR, PRIME MINISTER'S QUESTIONS, 9 FEBRUARY 2005[58]

ID cards are nothing if not a bold, decisive move. The massive scope and huge budget of the scheme send a clear message: we, your government, are Doing Something. Most people acknowledge that our immigration services leave a lot to be desired, and that something needs to be done to improve them for the good of the country. So it's natural to want to segue the 'doing something' of ID cards with the 'something must be done' of immigration. New Labour has done just that, reassuring some and bewildering others.

Again, a sweeping move like this may cause more problems than it will solve, and since it's unlikely to solve any, it only needs to cause one problem to be an instant liability. But it's more than that. Asylum seekers are already monitored and biometric information is taken from them for identification purposes, so putting everyone else on a database is not going to add anything. People-traffickers operate outside the law, so they won't be brought onto the radar by a scheme in which they won't participate. Since Europeans have the right to travel anywhere in Europe, the only way to stop people coming in on forged passports from somewhere else in the EU is to share our details with every other country in Europe. This means that it is not just the security of *our* databases that we have to worry about. Essentially, the immigrant issue is being used as leverage – many will agree with ID cards to control immigration – even though it has never been explained how the cards will help.

There are potential dangers to using identity cards to obtain services. If healthcare is only given to those with ID cards, illegal immigrants will not go to a hospital if they are sick. There can be risks for the rest of the population in large groups of people not seeking treatment for contagious diseases.

> There is potentially a huge public-health problem with restricting access to the NHS for diseases and things like TB. You will create a little pool in the population where all of these contagious diseases will just start to get out of control. So there's a sensible case from a public-health perspective of allowing basic emergency healthcare to anybody who happens to live in our country. I mean that's a basic humane position.
>
> **PHIL BOOTH**[59]

IT'LL HELP STOP ID THEFT

> Why are ID cards so important now? Because we know, from all the available evidence, that identity fraud is on the increase.
>
> **TONY BLAIR, PRIME MINISTER'S QUESTIONS, 18 JANUARY 2006**[60]

Identity theft is a very modern malaise. It can cause serious trouble for its victims, sometimes leaving them feeling psychologically violated to an incapacitating degree. Anyone who's ever had their credit card cloned and found phantom purchases on their bill for things they'd never buy themselves knows the thoroughly unsettling sensation of a stranger wearing your face as a mask.

In 2005 there were 66,000 victims of ID fraud in the UK, and the tally is inevitably going to rise.[61] There's ample opportunity for fraudsters to obtain information. The electoral roll is available online, replete with dates of birth and home addresses. If you apply for planning permission for work on your house, the full plans will be available online, complete with your signature. And people still fish through bins for bank statements and signed documents. Once your information has been stolen, it can be difficult to secure it again. You can end up broke, or even married to an illegal immigrant without knowing it – fake marriages using stolen identities are on the increase, earning £5000 a pop for the arrangers. It can eat up months of your life and screw up your credit record.

We are told that ID cards will reduce the threat of ID theft, but again no one has explained quite how this will happen. The logic as far as we can make out is along the lines of:
1) ID theft bad
2) ergo, ID cards good
3) er, that's it really.
If anything, the NIR could actually increase ID Fraud.

> If you go down a route of storing everything in a single place it produces what is known as the 'honey pot' effect – it becomes more attractive the more you put in it. Imagine if there's a single system that contains all of my personal information, where I live, my address and date of birth, and potentially my fingerprints and scans of my eye. To criminals that's an incredibly attractive thing. People begin to try and break into these systems, and we know that no computer system is 100 percent secure.
>
> **JERRY FISHENDEN**[62]

Of course New Labour insist that even though the NIR would make more information more readily available, it would in fact protect us from identity theft or misappropriation, not make us more vulnerable to it. Because … well … it just *would*. Trust us. We do this sort of thing *all* the time …

Fraudsters are already adept at identity theft, but at present we can recover if we are victims of it. We exist in the system as sets of numbers and information which can be changed to protect us once again. When we exist in the system as biometric data – fingerprints and scans of our eyes – it's a different matter. Once those are stolen by hackers, that's it. There isn't any provision for new fingerprints or irises to replace the ones that are now being used and shared between fraudsters. The Government can't offer to provide you with a new DNA structure. You're stuffed. You can't get a loan or a mortgage ever again, and your life will no longer be your own. Because your essential identity is no longer 100 percent yours. An increasing number of companies and institutions are using our biometric information to confirm that we are who we say we are. This makes the information more and more valuable to thieves, as well as vulnerable to theft.

So instead of having a more secure society where it's easier to identify the criminal elements and deal with them

> *more effectively you end up with a future environment*
> *where it's much harder to actually incriminate criminals*
> *because their defence will be, 'Well our fingerprints are*
> *all over the place because they've been stored in at least*
> *20 or 30 different systems.'*

JERRY FISHENDEN[67]

It'll stop benefit fraud

> *When we look at the levels of benefit fraud and the*
> *problems that arise from asylum and immigration, I think*
> *that, in principle, yes, they are a good idea.*

TONY BLAIR, PRIME MINISTER'S QUESTIONS, 15 OCTOBER 2003[68]

Again, benefit fraud is a serious problem. The National Audit Office said in July 2006 that Britain is no worse off in terms of benefit fraud than most other developed countries, which is something.[69]

Let's say you are a small-time benefit fraudster, though, and you're going to fake a benefit claim. You lie and say you live on your own when your partner's moved in. You lie and say you're not working when you've got a part-time job in a restaurant and do a few bar shifts. Or, like 47-year-old Paul Appleby, you continue to claim disability up to a total of £22,300 when you're out of your wheelchair and running marathons. (Apparently he forgot to cancel it, but he went to prison in any case. Benefit fraudsters get quite short shrift when they're caught.)[70] But you'll probably make sure you put down your correct name and address carefully. Otherwise, you won't get your cheque, which, after all, is your motivation for the whole fandango. So benefit fraud generally involves lying about everything but your actual identity.

> *As far as benefit fraud is concerned, that just doesn't*
> *run, because almost all benefit fraud is because of*
> *people misrepresenting their circumstances rather than*
> *their identity.*

ROSS ANDERSON[71]

91

Even if ID cards *could* stop benefit fraud, would it be economically worth it?

> I think it was something like…two and a half billion
> pounds a year of benefit fraud. But when you actually
> look at it the amount of benefit fraud that could be
> tackled even by ID cards…it's less than a half of a
> fraction of a percent. It's like fifty million from two billion.
>
> **PHIL BOOTH, NO2ID**[72]

Back to the drawing board on that one, then.

It'll help stop crime in general

It seems from this impressive package of justification that ID cards can do everything short of helping you drop that stubborn last stone. Government and public are in unanimous agreement that crime causes a lot of grief and needs to be cracked down upon. Criminals don't want to be identified – ID cards will make it harder for them to hide. Good, no?

Seasoned criminals will be the first to embrace ID cards, which legitimise them in the eyes of the police. Successful criminals are the ones who can appropriate the appearance of innocents – so where does that leave innocents? With the appearance of criminals. This exposes a glaring contradiction among the reasons for ID cards. If they are meant to stop crime, then surely we will have to carry them at all times and can be expected to produce them on demand for the police – as is in other countries. Which is exactly what we have been assured they won't be used for.

Ross Anderson is a professor in Security Engineering at Cambridge University. What Ross doesn't know about digital information and databases you could write on the back of a ENC28J60 microchip.

> I do not like the idea that it's the citizen who
> has to show his papers to the policeman; I
> prefer the British system, where the police
> are asked to show their warrant card to the
> citizen. We must never forget that we're the
> bosses, and they're our servants.
>
> **ROSS ANDERSON**[73]

People, generally, just want to be left alone. Wanting peace and privacy doesn't make anyone a criminal, nor does being grumpy if said peace and privacy is intruded upon, however briefly. The relationship between citizen and state is always a fragile one, and once trust is lost it can be impossible to restore on either side. ID cards are the perfect tool for the scraping away of trust. At present, it appears the state is losing trust in its citizens, and its efforts to combat terrorism/identity theft/paedophilia (delete according to most outraged tabloid headline) serve only to tell us we're not trusted. We can't help but be suspicious of the Government; but it's our place to question them. We don't expect them constantly to question us when we're minding our own business.

Well... everyone else is getting them

It is true that other countries have had ID cards, or are getting them. But we've seen from the dark history of ID cards that this isn't necessarily a good thing. The other strand to this argument is that we have to have ID cards because of international obligations.

> We will need to have biometric passports because of the United States and the European Union moving towards biometric visa requirements.
>
> **TONY BLAIR, 17 MAY 2005**[74]

> Nothing is dictated to us by Europe. All countries have to agree a policy from Europe.
>
> **GEOFF HOON**[75]

Well, make your minds up!

> They say, 'Well, because of international obligations, we need a biometric passport'. And the people then say, 'Well, that sounds fine, it's an international obligation'. Then the Government switches and says, 'Oh by the way, our biometric passport involves taking all fingerprints, your iris scans, your face scan, and putting

it into a national database'. Not one other country around the world is actually doing the same thing as Britain. It's not an international obligation if no one else is doing it.

GUS HUSSEIN, LSE ECONOMIST[76]

When the ID cards bill went through parliament, all that was required by both the EU and the US[77] was that all passports contain a chip with your photo on it. Nothing else. The EU is now moving towards biometric passports which include your photo on a chip and two fingerprints. However, only two fingerprints are required, rather than all ten, and no other biometric data is necessary.[78]

The UK was one of the countries that pushed for biometric data to be added to passports.

That is why we argue that internationally consistent and coherent biometric data should be an automatic part of our visas, passports and identity cards where we have them – and would even suggest driving licences as well.

CHARLES CLARKE, EUROPEAN PARLIAMENT, 7 SEPTEMBER 2005[79]

So, it is somewhat disingenuous to imply that they are merely following someone else's orders.

Let's have a look at what the rest of Europe actually have.

France: voluntary ID cards. Used to open bank accounts, in other financial transactions, and to travel. Police may ask for confirmation of ID, but not demand card. No biometric data. However, there have been complaints that minorities are far more likely to be stopped than the rest of the population.[80] The Paris riots were sparked by the death of two youths who were supposedly running from an identity check.[81]

Germany: compulsory ID cards. PIN and other personal details. No biometric data.

Italy: compulsory ID cards. Bank accounts, financial transactions, travel. Basic personal info. No biometric data.

US: Are you sitting down? Bush resisted calls for ID cards after 9/11. Photo driving licences are usually used. Social security number used for employment purposes (and very susceptible to identify theft, incidentally).[82]

> When they say 'Oh, the rest of Europe has ID cards, we're one of two countries in the EU that doesn't have ID cards', the rest of Europe's actually laughing at the UK because they know full well what's being proposed in this country is actually unconstitutional in most of their countries. The ID card here is that invasive.
>
> **GUS HUSSEIN**[83]

IF YOU'VE GOT NOTHING TO HIDE ...

> When absolute rules like the prohibition on torture are compromised by our political rulers, how much harder to defend more subtle and qualified rights like the presumption of privacy from the chilling slogan politics of 'nothing to hide, nothing to fear'.
>
> **SHAMI CHAKRABARTI, LIBERTY**[84]

> People say, 'If you've got nothing to hide, you've got nothing to fear.' I always say, well how much do you earn then?
>
> **RICHARD FURLONG, BARRISTER**[85]

Zingy phrases tend to lose something in repetition. But there's something about 'if you've got nothing to hide, you've got nothing to fear' that endures. Why explain why, when 'why ever not?' will do?

Does anyone have nothing they want to keep private? Is every law-abiding resident of Britain content to walk around in the figurative nude before the eyes of the state? Certainly not, this is *Britain*. We all have things that we do not wish to become common knowledge. There are things we don't tell our closest friends, and could not imagine being tossed around between civil servants and from one agency to another. There are aspects of our data that are highly sensitive under any circumstances, and would cause horror if rudely released to strangers. Several politicians should know this from personal experience.

Personal data on its own, immutable as it seems, is as malleable as statistics – it can be manipulated to justify almost anything. With your data held on a database, you wouldn't know who was looking at it, what conclusions they were drawing, and how it is altering your life. What everyone has to fear, to start with, is false judgement.

Many people have already had uncomfortable experiences with the misuse of their information. Discovering they've been placed on a tenant blacklist after a disagreement with a landlord, they found that they'd have to pay to see the full details and that they'd remain on the list for two years. Finding that the bank had somehow changed their name to that of a bordello madam in a cheesy Western, new credit cards and all. Being left waiting for child-support payments or benefits or wages with no assurance of when they'd arrive, and no promise of compensation. The question should be, why would we want to submit ourselves to more of this, in glorious New Labour technicolour?

I'm not very good with the technology; I'm not very good with any aspect of it!

TONY BLAIR ON PARKINSON

We may find ourselves with more sympathy for the celebrities we enjoy bitching about if the ID cards scheme and back-up databases come to fruition. We'll understand a little more about how they feel, when nothing about them is guaranteed to remain secret. We're so comfortable in our knowledge that our information belongs to us, and that we only release it to the people we want to release it to, that we forget how fragile that assurance is. As long as we can close our curtains and stay away from reality TV auditions, we find it hard to conceive of our privacy being lost. So if we have much to lose in the impending NIR, who will benefit?

The Government has a – how to put it tactfully – rather destructive relationship with databases. It believes in their power and thinks they are a force for good. Unfortunately, they are susceptible to being hacked, prone to IT problems and, actually, fundamentally iffy in the first place. The greedy accumulation of data serves the purposes of the Government (and those who build the databases) more than it serves the needs of the people.

LABOUR AND THE IT INDUSTRY – LOVE MEANS NEVER HAVING TO SAY YOU'RE SORRY

New Labour's over-enthusiasm for law-making is almost matched by its mania for enormous

Data morsel (to hide)	Implication (to fear)
AIDS test	promiscuity, irresponsibility
name change by deed poll	undiscovered criminal activity
CCJ	generic dodginess
anti-depressants	incapability, drug dependency
arrest for unauthorised demonstration	extreme views, rotten dress sense

Criminal records mix-up
2700 people were wrongly labelled as criminals by the Criminal Records Bureau. The mislabelling caused several people to lose their jobs, and when the mistake came to light the Home Office made 'no apology for erring on the side of caution'.[68]

Tax-credit overpayment
In 2006 it emerged that the Government had overpaid tax credits by over £2 billion for the second year in a row. This has meant that families have had to find the money for repayments which they had claimed in good faith and then spent.[69]

The Child Support Agency
Set up by the Conservatives in
1993, it was almost
immediately in trouble. When
Labour took over, they decided
that they could fix it, and gave
EDS £539 million to set up a
new computer system.⁴ By
2006 the system still wasn't
working and a Public Accounts
Committee report estimated
that it would end up costing
over £1 billion. In July 2006 it
was announced that the agency
was to be scrapped.⁴⁰

Libra
This is a project set up to install
and link a computer system
across magistrates courts. It
was originally estimated to cost
£146 million, and in June 2006
it was still not fully operational
and was estimated to cost £487
million to complete.⁴⁴

Rural Payments Agency
The Department for
Environment, Food and Rural
Affairs installed a new
computer system to deal with
changes to Europe's common
agricultural policy payments,
only to find in January 2006
that it had cost £37.4 million,
double the original estimate,
and still did not work.
Payments to farmers were
massively delayed, causing
financial hardship to many.⁴⁵

Pathway
This was a project to develop
smartcards for benefits
payments which cost £698
million before it was
scrapped.⁴⁶

computerised filing systems. Millions are poured into these set-ups, and the money tends to circulate in a particularly small pool of companies. The Government is fond of using and reusing the same contractors, seemingly regardless of their performance.

There is now a database for almost every aspect of our lives, and the more ambitious their scope, the greater the cock-ups. Blair has utilised the technology even when it's not strictly necessary, like a man with a shiny new drill using it to core apples and open doors. (Or take all the doors off their hinges, in fact – make things a bit more open-plan around here. What have you got to hide that necessitates a bathroom door?) These databases have floundered in a tangle of incompetence and incomplete planning. They've been undone by the most mundane of mishaps – problems with administration, difficulties with IT. Budgets and efficiency targets tend to go out of the window. But practice makes perfect. You've got to break eggs to make an omelette. And all that.

Since coming to power in 1997 New Labour has spent upwards of £70 billion on management consultants and new IT systems. Let's just say that figure again out loud: £70 billion.⁹¹ No one knows exactly how much the proposed ID cards and the accompanying NIR will cost to set up and maintain. In 2004 The Home Office asked one of the Government's favourite consulting firms, PA Consulting, to come up with a figure. £30 million pounds of taxpayers' money later, the consultants came back with £5.8 billion – spread over ten years.[97] The workings of these calculations are a closely guarded secret. So a couple of other independent experts took it upon themselves to produce a report on the viability of the scheme as sketched by the Government. However, they found their help really wasn't appreciated at all.

THE SIMON DAVIES REPORT – MESSENGER, MEET BULLET

Simon Davies is a visiting fellow at the London School of Economics, although with typical jovial self-deprecation he claims he doesn't even remember where he's visiting from. He's also the director of human-rights group Privacy International (CPI). When the LSE asked him what he would bring to the department he replied, with uncanny foresight, 'Trouble'. His American colleague Gus Hussein also works for PI. They are both co-mentors on the LSE's Identity Project, which they set up out of concern about the lack of debate on the Government's plan for ID cards. They are what you could consider ID nerds; brave men sacrificing what could have been a full and varied social life for the sake of keeping errant statistics in line. Having been trying to engage the Government on its burgeoning ID cards policy since its inception in 2002, they'd met with a bit of a blank.

> When we suddenly wanted to participate, feed our input into the process, the response from the Government was 'Go to hell'. It was, 'We know how to do things in this country and we're going to do it the way that we've been talking about doing all along – we don't need to listen to the people'. That was quite shocking.
>
> **GUS HUSSEIN**[98]

So in 2005 they decided to assemble a group of academics to produce a detailed report, cold-calling reputable professors. As a civil-liberties campaigner, Simon would have concentrated on that angle if the project had been his alone, but he was keen to bring in impartial individuals to the joint effort. 'We'd say, "Look, will you take part in this, just as an oversight responsibility?" And we didn't look to their ideological background, we didn't look to where they stood on ID cards – we were concerned about their reputation and their skills.'

The project ended up with 16 professors ready to go. They didn't have any funding so they were doing it for nothing. The project soon revealed itself to be an enormous undertaking, with 60 researchers in all contributing and reviewing. The work accumulated at an incredible, stressful rate. But word got around, and soon experts were phoning in asking if they could help. Most asked for their names to be withheld. This was controversial stuff, and they couldn't afford to be openly associated with it, even while they were keen to be involved.

After six months, Simon and Gus had a four-hundred-page report, a labour of love. Its conclusions were startling, and showed up how many flaws there were in the Government's plans.

'The policy was going to be costly, unworkable, insecure, unpopular, and essentially a poisoned chalice for any government,' says Simon. The report was measured, however, and pointed out that the idea of ID cards was not necessarily a disastrous one in and of itself. 'We were careful to say that the report does not reject ID Cards, on the principle that they can work very well in other countries,' says Gus. 'It depends on how the card is designed. Essentially we were tearing apart the foundations of the design as done by this Government, because this Government didn't want to just build an identity card, they wanted to build a significant infrastructure for central government.'

The Government saw the report, which Simon and Gus sent to them in the interests of fairness ('we wanted to be squeaky-clean, even though we knew they weren't going to be fair'). The report didn't only show the glaring flaws, it exposed that the

Government had fabricated figures and manipulated facts to gain support.

'We thought nobody would take any notice,' says Simon. 'We thought we'd give it our best shot, but...reaching the general public through an academic report was something we never dreamed would actually work. All we wanted was to inform the debate.'

'The Monday when the report came out,' explains Gus, 'we had a meeting at parliament where Simon had a debate with the minister in charge. Much of the debate focused on the costs. And it was the Parliamentary Labour Party [who] basically attended the meeting. There was a stitch-up – they sent all their Blairites to the media, and basically they attacked Simon time and again on the cost. We left the meeting that night just feeling exhausted and kind of dejected. Here was six months of work, and all it culminated in was a fake debate in parliament with the minister. And it wasn't until the next morning when I woke up to the radio and I heard the Home Secretary Charles Clarke lambasting us, calling us technically incompetent and saying the figures were a fabrication.'

Something of a campaign began to discredit, destabilise and shush the authors of the report. This ruckus inadvertently managed to stir media and public interest.

'When the Home Secretary attacked us and the LSE as an institution, then all of a sudden people wanted to read the report. The LSE report was always named whenever the Government's proposals were named. So whenever the Government says, "Oh it's only going to cost 5.8 billion," immediately the next paragraph, in every article, was all about the LSE costings. Our report said, "OK, at best it'll cost 10.2 billion – at worst it could cost 19 billion."'

This was no good for the Government, and it was only going to get worse. The *Observer* got hold of the £19 billion figure, divided it by the population, and came up with the nice, round, damning figure of £300 per person for an ID card. This was quickly disseminated throughout the media, splashed in the tabloids. Bad, bad, bad. This was only an interpretation of the project's figures by the papers, but the project was still going to get it in the neck.[99]

'That was where the ship started to sink,' says Simon. The permanent secretary of the Home Office called Sir Howard Davies, the director of the LSE, and demanded that he stop the report's publication. The LSE receives £11 million a year from the Government, which it seemed they might lose over this. However it quickly became apparent that the bullying tactic wasn't going to work. 'The council of the LSE ordered the director to write a letter to the media saying how the Government tried to bully the LSE away from releasing the report,' says Gus.

So the Government's tack was changed, and Simon was singled out as the sole crackpot author of the collaborative report, painting him as a civil liberties nut with an agenda.

> I have been very dismayed at the degree to which noble Lords have referred to a particular report as the 'LSE report'. It was actually written by a Mr Simon Davies, who works for Privacy International, which is an international organisation that is violently opposed to identity card bills... Perhaps we should start calling it the 'Davies report'.
>
> **BARONESS CORSTON**

> My noble friend is absolutely right – it is the Davies report... I do not want to cast any aspersions on the London School of Economics... Henceforth I will refer to it only as the 'Davies report'. So we have that clarity.
>
> **BARONESS SCOTLAND OF ASTHAL, HOUSE OF LORDS DEBATE, 16 NOVEMBER 2005**[100]

'Oh, that was an incredibly astute tactic,' he acknowledges. 'You look for the one person in the team who has a very strong civil liberties connection. And you focus all your guns on that person, and in doing so argue that the entire report is... biased beyond belief and beyond any level of credibility. You make it appear as if the institution has been used, manipulated.'

> *As for the calculations made by the LSE, I think that I am*
> *right that, although the report was put out under the*
> *LSE's name, it was actually written by the leading*
> *campaigner against ID cards on the grounds of civil*
> *liberties. So I do not think that it is an entirely objective*
> *assessment.*

TONY BLAIR, PRIME MINISTER'S QUESTIONS, 18 JANUARY 2006[101]

'And the great irony,' says Gus, 'is that the first report has 18 chapters, and two of the chapters focus on cost issues, and only half a chapter focuses on human-rights implications. The rest of the report doesn't even mention the word privacy, it hardly mentions civil liberties, but they basically tried to paint it as one man's vendetta against the Government.'

'At one point, three different ministers of the Blair Government attacked us over three days, on three separate occasions,' Simon adds. You know, one in the media, one at a conference, one in a press briefing. That's how intense it was getting.'

The campaign against Simon intensified. Dirt was dug.

'Corporations were called, people who were known to be drinking friends of mine, or had [input] on this project. They were called into Whitehall to spill the dirt. It was the same story from the two or three people I heard – I was brought in, given a cup of tea, some pleasantries were exchanged, and they said, "Well, we'll cut to the chase here, what dirt have you got on Simon Davies?" To this day I don't know what they were looking for – was I involved in an arms to Iraq scandal? Did I have a dodgy credit rating? I don't know, I would have thought that all my files would have been thoroughly interrogated for them to go to that measure – obviously they couldn't find anything, so then they went to the human-intelligence gathering.'

(If only they'd had some sort of large database to refer to … say, something containing a great deal of information about every individual. So they could see a whole lifelong audit trail on Simon at a moment's notice. That would have made matters so much easier. Ho hum.)

It continued. The Government sought to sever Simon's connections with academia and business. Companies he associated with, businesses for whom he worked as a freelance consultant, were warned off. His livelihood was being cut off, bit by bit.

'I had to go round friends begging for money just to pay rent. It got that bad. I think the Government had decided that I was expendable as a human being, that they would take a look at every element of my life, see what was vulnerable, and then put pressure on to see if they could crack me. The big message of course, that was conveyed by the opposition tabloid press, is that this is part of an ongoing tactic by government to personalise. Go for the player, not the ball.'

The chief irony was that Simon had mentored the report, not written it. 'I don't have the mental capacity to write! I've got a short attention span. Mentoring is great because you make phone calls, and take people for drinks and that sort of thing. You inspire people, maybe help the direction, that's about as far as you go.' Regardless, Simon was the one singled out as a target, and his persecution soon reached crisis point. 'I think the worst moment was when a company which had promised me some work was directly approached by the Home Office and told to back off. I was already in default two months on the rent. I had to leave and move in effectively to a squat. I also had to give up my dog, Buster, which was quite traumatic. The dog was a pain sometimes, all inner-city dogs are, but I gave him to a German Shepherd rescue organisation and move into this squat. It really got to the point where I was getting desperate and wondering, you know, where do I go to from here – is this going to be my life from here on in?'

Eventually, he'd had enough. 'I was pretty devastated ... feeling pretty down. At which point I sent a letter to Tony Blair saying "You better call off the dogs, or I'm calling in the lawyers." The *Financial Times* got hold of the story, ran a piece that I'd sent this letter, and suddenly everything evaporated.'

Things went very quiet. It became clear that the project, for all the battering it had taken, had won quite a victory.

'It became evident that the Government was in trouble, and in fact everything we had been saying was exactly true. There's no question that the report was vindicated in full.'

Simon's now able to analyse the situation from a distance. It was clear enough that the Government was characteristically averse to any debate or challenge, but was there more to it than that? 'We often asked ourselves why *this* fight... and I think it was because the Government knew that it was on the ropes on so many policies. That if it let this one go it would create a domino effect which would destabilise the Government even further. This wasn't about the ID card, it wasn't even about us. It was about the authority of the Government in parliament, and... in law. And that's what was being challenged in the Government's view, although that wasn't what we set out to do. They saw that if they let this one go they could never survive in parliament on another controversial vote. So they had to win this at all costs.'

Simon's got his life back now, although sadly not his dog. He's working again. 'I feel more resilient and able to cope with pressure now. I don't think there's anything that can be thrown at me now personally that under the circumstances could be this bad. Touch wood.'

As for the future of ID cards, 'It's going to be a society in the future where your choices are so limited,' says Simon, with a degree of gloom. 'Where the path is set out and those days where you can just do what you wanted, the freedom of the open road, the freedom of choice, is going to be practically zero.'

Gus is a little more optimistic. 'Personally I hate the Big Brother analogy – do we have no better analogy of modern day than a book written in the 1940s? But it's a very powerful book... and this Government took it as a recipe for how they want to manage all their systems. In *1984* the protagonists lost – it's actually quite a depressing ending, where he gave his individuality and it's all over. What's nice is that we haven't yet given up our individuality, the struggle's still going on. So will it turn into Big Brother? Will it turn into Orwell's society? It hasn't yet, and that says a lot about human resolve. Every time the Government has tried something as bodacious and ridiculous as this, they have been mocked. They have been brought down, and that gives me a little bit of hope.'

So, to summarise.

- ID cards won't stop terrorism or crime or benefit fraud.
- Neither will a big database.
- Even if the database wasn't delayed, and didn't run into problems and get all snarled up and cost us all a lot of money.
- But if it did work it would be susceptible to being hacked by criminals.
- But if it wasn't hacked and it worked perfectly the Government could still exploit it for revenue.
- Which would mean our data would be bought and sold without our knowledge or agreement.
- Millions have already been wasted and it's not popular with parliament or much of the public.
- Though other countries in Europe have ID cards, none of them have the scope of ours.
- There are inherent flaws in the technology.
- We don't know what the consequences could be, and neither do the Government.
- It's neither feasible nor desirable.
- It may mean that privacy, in effect, becomes a thing of the past.

> *Unless people begin to understand it and really under-*
> *stand its implications, we will walk straight into this*
> *enormous mechanism, this enormous apparatus for*
> *control.*
>
> **HENRY PORTER**[102]

THE DEVIL'S IN THE PERSONAL DETAILS

> *This represents a fundamental shift in the relationship*
> *between us as individuals and the Government. In the*
> *past they have had to justify each interference with our*

privacy and our liberty. And now we will have to justify
our existence, our identity to them.

SHAMI CHAKRABARTI, LIBERTY[103]

The ingenious thing about surveillance is that it changes people's behaviour by inducing them to keep themselves in line. Many people don't see the ID card proposals as anything but benign, and they don't think of the scheme as an imposition; in fact, it would probably be quite handy. It takes a lot more furrow-browed thought to figure out that there is a mind-boggling down-side. If you willingly surrender information, then you've got little comeback – quite literally, you only have yourself to blame. It sends a powerful signal that the populace is glad to submit to the whim of its government, and accept more or less any terms and conditions it might fancy imposing in the future.

> *There are millions of people out there who care*
> *passionately about liberty, but the broad mass of the*
> *electorate basically want security, and they value*
> *security far higher than liberty. And if the Government*
> *tells them that in the name of security, this and this*
> *compromise must be made, they're on for it. That's why*
> *you're not seeing public protests. That's why people are*
> *more or less in support of ID cards.*
>
> **BORIS JOHNSON MP[104]**

Bottom line, it's just easier to get on with life and have your details exposed than to resist. Anyone travelling on London's public transport automatically now uses an Oyster pre-pay card, just because it's easier and cheaper. We naturally go the quickest and easiest route, without always thinking first if might be the safest. The sad truth is that most of the population will never make the conscious decision to hand over their privacy, it'll just happen out of convenience. History has shown that in times of division, defining people by the information on an identity card leaves the vulnerable minorities open to discrimination. At a time when we need to be looking at what unites us, should we really be creating a system so open to abuse?

Clare Short has been an MP for Birmingham Ladywood since 1983. She was International Development Secretary from 1997 until 2003, when she quit the Government over the Iraq War.

I think it's just Blair's exasperation that people do things that he can't control, and if he makes us all have a piece of plastic he thinks then he'll be able to get at us all.

CLARE SHORT[105]

The good news is that we have plenty of inspiration when it comes to resisting the big data-gobbling governmental monster. Many people are taking it upon themselves to push back against the rude demands for personal information. In October 2006, solicitor and parent Janine Fletcher discovered that 70 schools in Cumbria had taken children's fingerprints without parental consent. The schools informed parents by letter after the fact. The deliciously named campaign group Leave Them Kids Alone mobilised, and a legal challenge was prepared. A test case is coming up. We can expect more of such iffy shenanigans, but it seems we can also expect more challenges to them, from ordinary people who aren't having it.[106]

And so we come to the end of our romp through ID cards and surveillance. You may be reading this and thinking 'Fools, they didn't mention…' In the interest of brevity and coherence we have had to leave out some of our favourite arguments. If you have time and the inclination please do your own research into the following (feel free to think of your own):

- £1000 fines for forgetting to update your information on the NIR;
- the ease with which the chips in existing passports have been hacked;
- the revolving door between the Government and their favourite management-consultancy firms.

If you have any thoughts about anything we have said, or just want to shout at us for the glaring incompetence of our technical knowledge we would obviously love to hear from you. Please write to us at info@number-10.gov.uk.

Chapter 4
Detention without trial

21 NOVEMBER 2006, 9.30a.m.

We stand at the doorway of Mouloud Sihali's room. If he steps out into the corridor, or if we put a step over the threshold, he will be sent to prison. Mouloud is 30 years old, tall, good looking and under house arrest. He wears a tag around his ankle and is clearly agitated. He points to a box in the corner 'This is my tagging equipment which tells that machine over there that I am in my tiny room'. He can't leave his room until 10a.m., at which point he has to report to the police station. For the rest of the day (until his 6.30p.m. curfew) he can only wander the streets inside the random area designated by the judge. 'They gave me a map, which is about a mile and half square, of this area round my room. That's where I'm stuck. The judge just drew it, picked up the pen and drew it randomly, that is it.' Mouloud is not dangerous, hasn't hurt anyone; hasn't even plotted hurting anyone. Mouloud is not a terrorist. But, before he got to the courts to prove his innocence, he spent two years and seven months in a high-security prison, being treated as one. Today, even though a jury has pronounced him innocent, he is imprisoned in the room he calls his home. He is one of a growing number of people who New Labour has placed under house arrest.[1]

*Either someone is a terrorist, in which case he should be
in detention, or he is not, in which case he should be
able to move freely ... It must be accepted that the power
is offensive to the basic principle of the rule of law,
which is that deprivation of liberty should be through
the courts and not through politicians.*

TONY BLAIR, 10 MARCH 1993[2]

Since Blair came to power things have changed. New Labour
now has the power to place you under indefinite house arrest
without charge. This bypasses your oldest liberty – habeas corpus.

*Habeas corpus allows you to say 'you cannot hold me
here without allowing me to appear in front of a court or
charging me', and that is really an essential right. It is
not possessed by any dictatorship, or any people living
in a dictatorship in the world. But it is possessed by
Western democracies, and we must guard that as an
absolutely essential sign – as a canary down the mine. If
habeas corpus disappears and the canary dies – then we
know that our society is at great risk.*

HENRY PORTER[3]

PRODUCE THE BODY

*Does Magna Carta mean nothing to you? Did she die in
vain?*

TONY HANCOCK, HANCOCK'S HALF HOUR[4]

The year 1215. An almighty row had been going on for some
time between King John, the Pope and a gang of barons. To settle
it the Barons made the King an offer he couldn't refuse. They
rowed him out to a very small island in the middle of the Thames
at Runnymede, and said that if he wanted to row back again he
needed to sign a contract called Magna Carta, or 'Great Charter
of Freedoms'. It was essentially a contract between him (the
state) and the people that mattered in the country (i.e. those with

land and money), represented by the barons. Not surprisingly, most of the clauses were about land rights, taxation and how many soldiers the King could borrow in wartime. But buried in clause 39 was the foundation of the rule of law:[5]

> 39) No free man shall be seized or imprisoned...except by the lawful judgement of his equals or by the law of the land.[6]

The King couldn't lock someone up just because he didn't like them. For anyone to be detained against their will, the state had swiftly to produce the person in court and state what crime they were supposed to have committed, known as the charge. This was called habeas corpus, or 'produce the body': *all detention is unlawful unless it has been approved by a court.*

The principle of habeas corpus was central to the abolition of slavery. In 1772 a captain of a slave-trader ship decided to bring one of the slaves back to England. The Quakers got wind of this and issued a writ of habeas corpus. The slave, James Sommersett, was duly brought before Lord Chief Justice Mansfield. The judge pointed out that as slavery wasn't recognised in English law, it couldn't be used as a reason for detention. He ordered that the slave be released and added: 'the state of slavery is so odious, that nothing can be suffered to support it'. Some years later, Britain banned slavery altogether.[7]

In 1940, faced with the impending Blitz and the threat of German invasion, Churchill brought in regulation 18b. This gave the Government the power to detain anyone that it thought was a threat to national security without charge or trial. Churchill hated the very idea of this, and said that to detain a man without 'the judgement of his peers is in the highest degree odious, and the foundation of all totalitarian government, whether Nazi or Communist'.[8]

Over a thousand suspected fascists were locked up, though none was ever shown to be a genuine threat. In 1943, before the war was over, Churchill repealed this emergency measure and the detainees were freed.[9]

Since the war, the only other time that Britain has experimented with detention without trial was in a disastrous attempt to defeat the IRA.

Kenneth Clarke was Home Secretary between 1992 and 1993, and even though he is a Tory is fondly known as the last liberal Home Secretary. He formed an unlikely alliance with some Labour MPs, including Clare Short, to attack the Government's 90-day proposals.

The IRA restarted its campaign in the late Sixties: it was a pretty feeble organisation – I mean there was a lot of old men grumbling that there were still one or two people in Manchester gaol: and it was not really a big, important organisation. I think we put the IRA on the map and turned it into a modern political organisation by internment.

KENNETH CLARKE[10]

As a response to the threat, the British Government introduced an 'anti-terror law' called internment, which enabled them to imprison indefinitely without charge anyone they thought might be an IRA terrorist. Hundreds of Catholics were immediately locked up without any evidence and with no prospect of a trial.[11]

Michael Mansfield QC was the barrister for the Birmingham Six, the Guildford Four, the Stephen Lawrence family and Mouloud in the Ricin Trial. He is part of Legal Action Against the War, which has petitioned the International Criminal Court to ask for charges against Tony Blair, Geoff Hoon and Jack Straw over the Iraq war.

It didn't work, it divided communities, it bred people who perhaps were not necessarily going to do something controversial or even illegal as far as the state were concerned, and pushed them. It was the recruiting sergeant.

MICHAEL MANSFIELD QC[12]

Britain then lived with thirty years of terrorist attacks that resulted in the deaths of over three thousand people, until the Good Friday Agreement in 1998 formally ended the troubles. It was the New Labour Government that signed the Northern Ireland Peace Accord, which recognised that terrorism could only be defeated by engaging with communities, rather than oppressing them.[13]

Since then, the average number of deaths per year from terrorist attacks in Britain has plummeted. Even taking into account the 7 July bombings, we are statistically far safer from terrorism now than we have been for forty years.[14] But during this period of comparative safety, New Labour has tried to abolish habeas corpus in two ways:

1) The attack on the World Trade Center in 2001 was used to give the Home Secretary the power to detain you indefinitely without charge or trial.[15]

2) The 7 July bomb attacks on the London Underground and bus network were used to try to give the police the power to hold you for three months without charge.[16]

LOCK 'EM UP!

In October 2001, just weeks after 9/11, the Bush Administration passed the Patriot Act. This gave the Attorney General (the well respected libertarian and free thinker John Ashcroft) the power to detain anyone he didn't like – without trial.[17] Not wanting to be accused of aping the Americans, Blair and Blunkett waited a whole month before they passed their version, The 2001 Anti-Terrorism, Crime and Security Act.[18]

This is on record as one of the fastest laws passed in British history[19] – most MPs who voted for it didn't get time to read it first. Those that managed to catch a glimpse did ask if these authoritarian measures were really necessary, but were given soothing assurances.

Parliament was told when the legislation came in, 'Don't worry, we will always have

2001 Anti-Terrorism, Crime and Security Act
This gave the Home Secretary the power to detain indefinitely any foreign nationals without charge. As long as he:
a) believes that the person's presence in the UK is a risk to national security, and
(b) suspects that the person is a terrorist.
No evidence was required, and no one could challenge their detention.[20]

Gareth Peirce was
the solicitor for the
Birmingham Six and
the Guildford Four
and several of the
Belmarsh detainees.
She was given an
OBE in 1999, but
later returned it.

*investigated whether we could properly
prosecute someone in a criminal trial,
openly, with due process before we go to
this last resort state.' It was a lie and
parliament was completely misled.*

GARETH PEIRCE[21]

In December 2001, nine refugees were publicly arrested and locked up in Belmarsh high-security prison without charge. Blunkett completely reneged on his promise to parliament that they would attempt a normal prosecution first, and went straight for the money shot. Besides, he had to show the tabloids that he was doing something, and locking up dodgy-looking blokes with beards definitely counted as 'something'. Charges and trials need evidence and other boring things, so why bother with having to prove someone guilty when you can just assume they are?[22]

WAR ON TERROR

QUIT BRITAIN OR ROT IN JAIL

It played so well with the tabloids that he kept on doing it. Every time he needed a headline...SLAM, let's bang another one up. To be fair to Blunkett, he did say he had secret intelligence that they were all terrorists. And of course it would be shameful to accuse New Labour of exaggerating intelligence for political ends.

*Ian Loader is
Professor of
Criminology at
Oxford University.
His favourite quote
is 'security in a free
society is about
hearing a knock the
door at six o'clock
in the morning and
being confident that
it's the milkman'.*

*David Blunkett used to be fond of saying,
'If you knew what I knew you'd behave like
me'. And as a citizen of a democracy, what
are you supposed to do when the Home
Secretary says that? Because it's the nature
of democratic life that you don't give Home
Secretaries that kind of power.*

IAN LOADER[23]

None of the Belmarsh detainees (as they became known) were British citizens, and most were political refugees who had been granted asylum many years previously. Blunkett proceeded to try to deport these men back where they came from. Inconveniently, they were all from countries like Algeria and Egypt that have horrendous human-rights records. They had fled to Britain for safety. Even though there was not enough evidence against them to warrant a charge, New Labour wanted to deport them back for political expediency.[24] Blunkett and Blair were prevented from doing so by their very own Human Rights Act. This forbids anyone to be sent to countries that torture in any circumstances. So, from December 2001 to December 2004 the Belmarsh detainees stayed put.[25]

> *Why are these people locked up at all? Either they've committed a crime, which can be tried, or they haven't. And if they have committed a crime, put them on trial. Let's have due process. So, once again, the Government is undermining the rule of law.*
>
> **MICHAEL MANSFIELD QC**[26]

Now it is completely sensible to ask the question were any of these men really planning horrific terror attacks? We still don't know. But in Britain, like most civilised countries, we have a system in place for how to deal with people who the authorities believe are planning to commit murder: the police gain evidence, arrest them, charge them with conspiracy to murder, and they stand trial. If they are found guilty, then the maximum penalty is life in prison. Since 9/11, many genuine terrorists have been charged and convicted of conspiracy to murder. One example is Dhiren Barot, who was sentenced to 40 years in November 2006 for plotting to carry out terrorist atrocities.[27]

But until you have been found guilty in a court, you are innocent in the eyes of the law. This is called the presumption of innocence, and here to explain this complicated concept is a Mr David Blunkett:

He [Blair] has been tried and found guilty by some
sections of the media…I'm biased. I plead guilty to
believing the prime minister is innocent unless proven
otherwise. That's my presumption. But it's also the law.
In this country people ARE presumed innocent until
found guilty.

DAVID BLUNKETT, IN THE SUN, 2006[28]

OK, he's talking about his friend Tony Blair being quizzed by police over the alleged loans-for-peerages scandal. *Then* you're innocent until proven guilty. But back in 2001, when Blunkett was Home Secretary he clearly believed the opposite, and ordered the Belmarsh detainees to stay in solitary confinement indefinitely.

THE BRITISH GUANTANAMO BAY

The men themselves were detained for three and half
years without trial, without knowing the evidence
against them, and were driven into severe mental illness
and clinical depression through that experience.

GARETH PEIRCE[29]

They never knew what they were suspected of, and were never shown the evidence against them. Several attempted suicide. In fairness Blunkett did say that they could stop this treatment whenever they wanted, simply by getting on the next plane back to their home countries. True they could face persecution, torture or death as soon as they landed, but on the up-side Blunkett did offer to pay for the plane tickets.[30]

There was a slight problem with this new terror law: it was illegal. The European Convention on Human Rights states that everyone – from Prime Ministers to suspected terrorists – has to be given a proper charge and a fair trial before they can be imprisoned.

The reasoning for this is simple: if politicians have the power to detain without charge, they can use it for political purposes. Blunkett's behaviour is a good example of why politicians shouldn't be allowed to lock up anyone they feel like, as there is no doubt he persecuted the Belmarsh detainees to show that he was 'tough on terror'. New Labour's own Human Rights Act gave British courts the power to strike down laws that compromised our basic human rights.

Three years after the suspects had first been interned, the case reached the House of Lords, where the 2001 Anti-Terrorism, Crime and Security Act would be tested.[31]

Blunkett wasn't Home Secretary at this point. He had just 'resigned to save his party embarrassment' for the first time. Charles Clarke had just been made Home Secretary and, by happy chance, the judgement came out on his first day on the job. It didn't go well.

On 16 December 2004, eight out of nine Law Lords ruled that the 2001 law was an affront to justice and had to be scrapped. They threw out the Government's argument that human rights did not apply because terrorism was a threat to the life of the nation. The summing up could not have been more damning:[32]

> The real threat to the life of the nation comes not from terrorism but from laws such as these.
>
> **LORD HOFFMAN, LAW LORD**[33]

> Indefinite imprisonment without charge or trial is anathema in any country which observes the rule of law. It deprives the detained person of the protection a criminal trial is intended to afford.
>
> **LORD NICHOLLS, LAW LORD**[34]

The Law Lords' ruling
The law itself was illegal and had to go. The reasoning was twofold:
1) It contravened the most fundamental human right of liberty – to be free from arbitrary detention and to be presumed innocent until proven guilty.
2) It was discriminatory, as only foreign nationals could be detained without charge, making it in effect a racist law.'

The Government had anticipated this when they drafted the law back in 2001, and tried to claim a 'derogation' from the Human Rights Act. Countries can derogate from the European Convention on Human Rights if they are in a time of dire national emergency, for example another world war. With a completely straight face Blair and Blunkett said that they thought we were facing a threat equivalent to World War II, and claimed derogation so they could bypass the rule of law. This is the equivalent of New Labour saying that it wanted to bypass the rule of law as it had a note from its mum.'

The Belmarsh detainees had been under lock and key for over three years. If they had really been dangerous terrorists, surely by now the authorities had enough evidence to charge them?

> *There is an arbitrary bunch of a dozen men, and none of them interviewed by the police. That's the giveaway. If there had been a serious interest in investigating and obtaining admissible evidence to bring people to trial, where they would have rights, then that would have been done. Five years on, it hasn't happened and the men have never been spoken to by investigating police, never.*
>
> GARETH PEIRCE[37]

If you had a dozen dangerous terror suspects under lock and key, mightn't you want to ask them a question or two? This perfectly illustrates the problem with being able to detain people without charge: the police don't have to bother with boring things like interviewing people and gathering evidence. You just lock up people who you think are guilty, and go home for tea.

The Government had two options:

1) Charge the men properly. Fat chance – you need evidence for that.
2) Let the men go. This would be a humiliating climbdown and would prove that the men had been detained for political reasons.

Having been told that the 2001 anti-terror law was racist, an affront to justice and more of a threat to the British way of life than al-Qaeda, New Labour decided to go the third way: they brought in another anti-terror law that was more draconian than the first.

TAKING A LEAD FROM APARTHEID

Instead of giving themselves the power to imprison indefinitely, they took a leaf out of South Africa's book. New Labour quickly passed the 2005 Prevention of Terrorism Act, in which Charles

Clarke gave himself the power to put anyone he wanted under house arrest. And to get round the problem that the last law was racist, this new law became applicable to everyone, including British citizens. Probably not what the Law Lords had in mind when they tore up the 2001 act, but that's what you get for letting lawyers run the country. New Labour managed to ram the 2005 act through parliament in even less time than they did in 2001. When MPs went to vote they discovered that big chunks of the bill hadn't even been written. 'Don't worry!' came the response. 'We'll fill in the gaps later!'[38]

> *So the Government had to rethink its policy rather quickly. And so what it decided to do was to bring in control orders. In other words, a form of imprisonment, outside a prison, in which people would be locked up in a house or a flat.*

MICHAEL MANSFIELD QC[39]

South African justice
The idea of house arrest to suppress political dissent was pioneered in South Africa during Apartheid. Anyone who seemed to be a political threat was imprisoned in their own home. In certain cases they could jail terror suspects indefinitely without trial. The well known terrorist Nelson Mandela was locked up for 27 years before he was released and then made President of South Africa.[*]

After the Lords ruling, in early 2005, the Belmarsh detainees were finally released, but were all put under control orders (very New Labour name – much fluffier than 'house arrest'). They had strict curfews, couldn't go further than a mile from their house, were forbidden to use the phone and internet, and couldn't have visits from anyone who hadn't been vetted by the Home Office. And like the detention in Belmarsh, it's indefinite. The psychological effects of this situation are devastating. One of the men (who's in a wheelchair) is too scared even to go out into his garden in case he has contact with his neighbour. Gareth Peirce has first-hand experience of how these arbitrary powers ruin lives:[40]

> *It's a recipe for complete social isolation ... To be placed in a position where you and your family can have no visitor to your house who has not been approved by the*

119

> Home Office, subject to intense scrutiny, and to not be
> allowed to contact and meet with people outside your
> home who have not been agreed by the Home Office.
>
> The men know and the wives know, from other cases,
> that simply to lend support to a prisoner's family has
> been construed as support for international terrorism. So
> the whole family unit is in a state of abnormality, unable
> to live a normal life. It isn't just the men, but it's their
> wives, who are suffering severe depression. The children
> are living abnormal lives.
>
> Control orders are very bad for single men. They're
> isolated in a very different way, but for a family, one has
> to think in terms that it's the family under a control order,
> not just the subject of it.[42]

In early 2007, the pressure on some of the men under control orders got too much, and they chose to return to their home countries. It is a damning indictment of British justice that people are actually opting for the possibility of torture rather than remaining in Britain.

HOUSE ARREST IN REAL LIFE – MOULOUD SIHALI AND THE CURIOUS CASE OF THE LACK OF RICIN IN WOOD GREEN

In early 2003 the British Government was looking for any connection between terrorism and weapons of mass destruction. An hysterical news story appeared that answered all their prayers: poison plot in a flat in Wood Green!

One of the men charged with terrorist offences was Mouloud Sihali. He was eventually found completely innocent, but on his release was put under house arrest.[43]

We were introduced to Mouloud by Jennifer Russell and Desiree Howells, two retired headmistresses from East London. They were members of a group called Justice and Peace, which works with asylum seekers. As an act of Christian charity they spent time writing letters to people in detention centres offering them hope. They've seen the affects of house arrest first hand, and they can't believe the situation that has been forced upon this young man.

In 1997, as Blair was beginning his new life as Prime Minister, 21-year-old Mouloud had left Algeria to escape compulsory national service and to avoid serving in a civil war which had claimed 70,000 civilian lives by the following year.[44]

'I'm sorry I don't want to do military service. I don't want to kill someone or get killed in the process,' Mouloud tells us.

'He's not political,' says Jennifer. 'I had to explain to him what a pacifist was.'[45]

When he arrived in Britain, Mouloud knew no one. He walked around London until he met some other Algerians, who eventually helped him to find somewhere to stay. He hoped to get a job, earn some money and make a life for himself. He shared a room with another Algerian, an asylum seeker he'd met called David Khalef. Other refugees and asylum seekers with nowhere to go would sometimes come back to the flat, including a man called Mohammed Meguerba. In the summer of 2002, Mouloud managed to get his own room, and as Meguerba was becoming an unwelcome guest in Khalef's overcrowded bedroom, Mouloud said he could stay at his place until he found somewhere else. But the weeks progressed and Meguerba wasn't leaving... and, as they weren't the best of friends, Mouloud started to get irritated. Eventually, after an argument, Mouloud kicked Meguerba out of his flat and he left, leaving behind some bags.[46]

On 17 September 2002, Meguerba was arrested in Tottenham, and when he was asked for his ID told the police it was at

Mouloud's flat. Two days later Mouloud was arrested and taken to Belmarsh Prison. Meanwhile Meguerba suffered an epileptic fit and was released on bail. He fled the country and went back to Algeria, where he was immediately arrested, imprisoned and tortured. Meguerba told the Algerian police the names of all the people he had met while he was in the Europe, including Mouloud. The Algerian police passed this 'intelligence' on to their British counterparts, who were under intense political pressure to prove a link between terrorism and weapons of mass destruction. In January 2003, 'terror raids' took place up and down the country; anyone unfortunate enough to have met Meguerba was arrested and branded a terrorist. One of the suspects, Kamel Bourgass, who was completely unknown to Mouloud, stabbed a policeman to death as they tried to arrest him. Mouloud had been in Belmarsh for three months at this time, and was unaware of the chain of events that had been set in motion.[47]

5 January 2003. A flat in North London is raided. Twenty-two castor seeds, some apple pips and a coffee grinder are discovered.[48]

6 January 2003. Press release from Scotland Yard states categorically that Ricin has been found in Wood Green.[49] The press print this verbatim:

POISON GANG ON THE LOOSE
– huge hunt for terrorists armed with deadly Ricin

DAILY MAIL, *8 JANUARY 2003*[50]

7 January 2003. Tests are carried out at government facility Porton Down. These would prove that there was no Ricin.[51] Tony Blair publicly announces the exact opposite: 'The arrests which were made show this danger is present and real and with us now. Its potential is huge.'[52]

5 February 2003. Colin Powell goes even further. On the eve of war he tells the UN that he has found a link between 'the Ricin

Plot', al-Qaeda and Iraq: 'The Ricin that is bouncing around Europe now originated in Iraq – not in the part of Iraq that is under Saddam Hussein's control, but his security forces know all about it'.[53]

6 February 2003. On *Newsnight*, Blair backs him up to justify the impending Iraq invasion: 'What Colin Powell was talking about yesterday is correct…it would not be correct to say there is no evidence linking al-Qaeda and Iraq.'[54]

30 March 2003. Head of US forces in Iraq announces, 'And it's from this site where people were trained and poisons were developed that migrated into Europe. We think that's probably where the Ricin found in London came from.'[55]

Meanwhile Mouloud, and the other alleged plotters, sat in Belmarsh Prison awaiting trial, and would remain there for over two and a half years.

13 September 2004. 'The Ricin Trial' finally starts. Des and Jennifer, the two Catholic ladies from East London, didn't miss a single day.[56]

> Jennifer: We were going because they were strangers in
> this country, so they'd know somebody is caring for
> them.
> Des: Yes, to show that we cared as human beings, that
> they're not alone. And then of course when you heard
> the evidence and so on, you just couldn't believe it.[57]

During the trial, Blunkett went on national television and declared the men guilty.

> Al-Qaeda is seen to be, and will be demonstrated
> through the courts over months to come, to be actually
> on our doorstep and threatening our lives.

THE POLITICS SHOW, *14 NOVEMBER 2004*[58]

According to newspaper sources after the trial, he was criticised by the judge, Mr Justice Penry-Davey, for being 'in breach of the presumption of innocence'.[59] Presumably inside the courtroom the cracks in the prosecution case were starting to appear. Because of the extraordinary events that followed the trial, four members of the jury agreed to talk to us under the promise of anonymity. While they have kept their deliberations secret, they are scathing about the prosecution's case:

> *There was no mention of an al-Qaeda connection throughout the trial, and yet all the papers were full of this, that this was an al-Qaeda plot.*

> *We kept on expecting the meaty evidence to appear that explained the links between these people. But in the end the link seemed to be that they all used the Finsbury Park Mosque as a place of social activity or worship. The prosecution said, 'Here is a terrorist mosque, therefore they must all be terrorists and plotting together'. And I kept on expecting that the prosecution would eventually supply some actual evidence for this – and it never appeared, it never turned up.*

> *There was an awful lot of mudslinging, and they hoped that some of it would stick.*

> *They were trying to prey on people's prejudices. They were trying to use the fact they weren't British, they were Muslim.*

> *We were there in the Old Bailey for seven and a half months, and we kept on waiting for the prosecution to come up with some weighty evidence, and the day the prosecution closed their case I remember sitting there with my jaw open and thinking, wow – I can't believe it – what are these guys doing here?*

> *I thought Mouloud's testimony in the dock was extremely powerful, and I felt that he conducted himself extremely well in the face of a very experienced prosecutor who was constantly trying to trip him up. I admired that a lot. I thought it was very dignified. I thought it was very brave.*[60]

8 April 2005. The jury finds Mouloud and the other supposed plotters innocent.

Kamel Bourgass was found guilty of 'conspiring to cause a public nuisance'. The same man had also been found guilty of the separate crime of murdering a police officer, but this had nothing to do with terrorism, Ricin or WMDs. Mouloud had never met Bourgass, but because Meguerba had, they were linked to the same 'conspiracy' that turned out not to exist. Mouloud and seven other men were cleared of any wrongdoing, and set free.[61]

The media were caught off guard. After months of briefings from the Government and the police, the press had continued to believe that the men were guilty.

Buried at the bottom of each article, almost as an after-thought, was a brief mention that there was no poison, no plot, and that eight of the nine men who had been branded terrorists were completely innocent.

Mouloud was released, and Jennifer and Des's charity, Justice and Peace, provided his surety. After years in prison the men didn't want to be cooped up, so they cooked meals at Des's house and ate them outside in sunshine. As Mouloud had entered the country illegally, he was supposed to serve three months in prison. But as he had just served 30 months before being found innocent, they waived the sentence. He had to report to the police station twice a week, but apart from that he was a free man again. The only day he didn't do this was on 7 July 2005, when the attacks on the Underground prevented him from travelling.[62]

Two months later Mouloud's life was shattered for the second time. At 5.30 a.m. on 15 September, over thirty police, some armed and wearing riot gear, broke down Mouloud's door.[63]

'By the time I reached for the light they were there. They pushed me to the floor and then jumped on my back. I couldn't breathe, there were about eight of them, on my back, pulling me, strangling me.' Mouloud had signed at the police station the day before, so why the need to send thirty armed police in a dawn raid? The raid was carried out with the maximum publicity, part of the Government's response to tabloid headlines that were demanding action. They stamped on his leg, leaving him with a permanent limp, and locked him in Long Lartin, another maximum-security prison.[64]

This time the Government had detained him under the vague accusation that he was 'considered a threat to national security'. There was no evidence, apart from being involved in 'the Ricin Trial'. The fact that he was found completely innocent of all charges was deemed irrelevant.[65]

> Mouloud: The Home Office said, 'The jury got it wrong.
> They are wrong, we are right. This man is a threat and we
> believe he is involved in "the Ricin Plot" and that is it.'[66]

After four months he was released again, under very strict bail conditions identical to control orders, i.e. house arrest.

- He has been put in a one-room bedsit in an arbitrary area of London.

- He has no access to the internet.
- He has an eight-hour curfew.
- He has a one square mile area in which he can walk (this area initially did not include a mosque).
- He is not allowed to work, and has to live in central London on £40 a week.
- He has to report to the police station twice a day.
- He has to wear an electronic tag.

There is in fact very little that Mouloud can do, and he spends his days wandering the streets.[67]

> Mouloud: It is worse than prison because you can see your freedom outside the window but you can't go out there and enjoy yourself. My life has been destroyed practically, you know, I don't have a life and this is the reasons why they're doing this is just to push people to the limit to sign their own will, to sign their own return, you know, to make them go back to their country without fighting the courts; this is part of their psychological torture.[68]

He has the open invitation to return to Algeria. As he fled national service the best he can hope for is a jail sentence, but as he has been branded a terrorist, it is likely he will suffer worse.[69]

> Mouloud: There is no limit, absolutely no limit, you know, it's indefinite. I'm growing up and I feel that my life is being destroyed and I will never have these years back. I'll go to sleep; I'll just put my head down every night, just think, 'Maybe I'm dreaming, maybe this is just a nightmare and I'm going to wake up now and wake up in a different world, thinking that this is a nightmare but no, it's a reality. I'm living it on a daily basis, that's how it feels.[70]

Many people are afraid of spending time with Mouloud for fear of being associated with him and being branded a 'threat to national security' themselves. He is supported not only by

127

Jennifer and Des, but several of the jurors who found him innocent also now visit him regularly.

> I think what we owe Mouloud at the end of this is...the
> choice to do what he wants with his life. Because like it
> or not Britain has taken away his choices and he's...got
> no future that he can see. There's no light at the end of the
> tunnel. And I think we have to give him back his choices.
>
> **JUROR**[71]

> I've never known jurors speak out in this sense, because,
> quite rightly, they're saying, 'Well, wait a minute...Why
> have we spent all this time poring over this evidence
> you wanted us to examine in order to decide whether
> they were guilty. Now we decided they weren't, and
> you're deciding they are!' I think it's a shocking example
> of a government saying 'We don't accept this verdict'.
>
> **MICHAEL MANSFIELD QC**[72]

> The Government started using these innocent men as
> excuses to bring in new laws, they started talking about
> 90-day detention after the end of the trial.
>
> **JUROR**

NINETY-DAY DETENTION – BYPASSING OUR OLDEST PROTECTION

Habeas corpus means that not only do you have to be charged to
be detained, but that it has to happen swiftly. After an arrest there
needs to be a small amount of time during which the police
question the suspect, make enquiries and decide whether or not to
charge them. In Britain – until New Labour came along – this
period of 'pre-charge detention' has been 36 hours. In exceptional
circumstances the police could make a request to extend this to a
few days. Having this protection is pointless if they can hold you
for months before they have to charge you or let you go.[73]

After the 7/7 bombings, New Labour made a concerted effort to extend the pre-charge detention period to three months – effectively giving the police the power to hand out 90-day prison sentences.[74]

Copying Apartheid again

Being detained for 90 days before charge was also very popular in South Africa during Apartheid. Initially the police could only hold a suspect for a few days before charge, but because of the supposed terrorist threat, the Government systematically increased it. Pre-charge detention went up slice by slice to 90 days and eventually, in 1965, to 180 days. The police obtained a near perfect conviction rate, as they simply tortured anyone who didn't confess until they did. As long as they started work on the suspects as soon as they were arrested they would always crack within a couple of weeks. The brutality was easy to cover up, as the police would hold the suspects for enough time for the wounds to heal, before anyone could see them.[75]

If it seems a bit far-fetched that the British police would beat confessions out of terrorist suspects, ever heard of the Birmingham Six and the Guildford Four? In both cases innocent Irish men were arrested immediately after an IRA terrorist atrocity for little more than having Irish accents. They had confessions beaten out of them by police who were under intense political pressure to deliver results. They were convicted on these confessions and were imprisoned for many years before the miscarriages of justice were overturned. It was recognised that the police had too much power, and the laws were changed.[76]

> But the real problem here goes back to the days of the
> 1970s, before the Police and Criminal Evidence Act,
> which regulates interrogations in this country. The longer
> you hold somebody, the greater the risk that, at the end of
> the day, they may confess to something that they haven't
> done. They may give you false information. It's a bit like
> the proceeds of torture. The risk is that very unreliable

> information comes out of long periods of detention, not
> knowing whether you're going to be charged.
>
> **MICHAEL MANSFIELD QC**[77]

Blair is so obsessed with how history will view him that he has no time for studying it. In 2005, New Labour made an all-out assault in the House of Commons to give the police three months to question people before they had to be charged.[78]

> *Stunning. You know, after what had happened with*
> *Northern Ireland (wrongful convictions with full jury*
> *trials), to suggest that you can hold someone for*
> *questioning for 90 days! I still can't believe they*
> *seriously did it.*
>
> **CLARE SHORT**[79]

This offensive on our civil liberties was well timed, coming months after a terrorist attack when the public would be pliant and fearful. But the moves towards 90-day detention started well before 7/7. The first mutterings of a sweeping increase in police powers came immediately after the Ricin trial.

The quest for 90 days

8 April 2005. Mouloud and the others accused in 'the Ricin Plot' are found innocent. There was blatantly no Ricin and no plot. The Government and police, however, are either guilty of habitual lying or chronic incompetence.[80]

17 April 2005. Sir Ian Blair goes on *Breakfast with Frost* and uses the Ricin case to push for tougher laws:

> *There's real clarity now that al-Qaeda affiliates are*
> *targeting Britain.*[81]

Actually the Ricin trial proved nothing of the sort – there was no al-Qaeda link.

One of Tony Blair's proudest legacies is the politicisation of the police. The campaign to increase state power over the individual has come not only from New Labour, but also from senior members of the police force, whose careers are steered by political patronage. Theoretically the police are supposed to remain completely impartial when it comes to politics.

> *You won't find too many police officers that want to be*
> *political. We always want to be 'apolitical'.*

BARRY NORMAN, BOROUGH COMMANDER OF ISLINGTON[82]

While Barry keeps his head down, other senior members of the police force – namely Met Commissioner Ian Blair and Assistant Commissioner Andy Hayman – have become heavily involved in politics. Rather than sticking to boring things like catching criminals, Sir Ian and Andy seemingly spend most of their waking hours talking to the media. Not surprisingly, they always back whatever authoritarian measure the Government are pushing that week, presumably because:

1) The more power they have the easier their job becomes.
2) It's never a bad idea to curry favour with the people who hand out promotions and honours. Is it, Sir Ian?

Still on the sofa with Frosty and a nice cup of tea, he goes on to scare us into more authoritarian measures.

> *I mean I wasn't particularly keen on ID cards until*
> *recently ... We now have the technology, I think through*
> *iris recognition, and I think that would be very helpful.*

SIR IAN BLAIR[83]

Why stop there? It's only three weeks before the general election, so don't waste the airtime! If he really wanted to keep Tony happy he should have said, 'Before the break, Frosty, I've seen secret intelligence that Noel Edmonds is brainwashing your children by secret terrorist code and I've locked him in Belmarsh. VOTE LABOUR! Now what's happening with the weather?'

This interview was the start of a campaign to use the fear over terrorist attacks to increase pre-charge detention. In May 2005 New Labour won an unprecedented third term. Two months later the 7/7 terrorist attacks put the plan for 90 days right back to the top of the agenda.

> *I think several times that our British Government,*
> *sometimes following an American lead, has done exactly*
> *what al-Qaeda would have wanted them to do in*
> *response to the terrorist attacks. When they crashed*
> *airplanes into buildings or when they blew up London*
> *underground trains, none of those people thought they*
> *were going to win a war on a battlefield. They knew*
> *perfectly well they were going to kill innocent people and*
> *simply outrage the rest of the population. But they*
> *destabilised the system, and governments help when they*
> *start passing almost indefensible and draconian laws.*
>
> **KENNETH CLARKE**[84]

Shortly after 7/7, Tony Blair announced that he was going to defend our freedom by removing it. An alliance formed between the politically opportunistic members of the police, Tony Blair and the *Sun* newspaper to grant the police 90 days pre-charge detention.

Always the Sun

The day after the bombings, the *Sun* made it clear where it stood: 'Mayor Ken Livingstone captured London's resolve when he warned terrorists they will never destroy our free society, whatever they do'.[85]

Quite right too. But it then superbly contradicted itself a few lines further on by demanding that we remove one of the foundations of a free society.

> *Britain is crawling with suspected terrorists and those*
> *who give them succour. The Government must act*
> *without delay, round up this enemy in our midst and*
> *lock them in internment camps. Our safety must not*
> *play second fiddle to their supposed 'rights'.*
>
> *'THE SUN SAYS', 8 JULY*

Throughout July, the *Sun* thunders on that the Government isn't doing enough to protect the country from annihilation – and MPs are leaving us in peril.

But Charles Clarke, who is now regarded as a libertarian (but only compared to David Blunkett and John Reid), had been doing something. The week after the attacks Clarke started a cross-party discussion on what security changes were necessary. Together with David Davies and Mark Oaten (the Conservative and Liberal Democrat home affairs representatives), Clarke made a plan that they would present to the country when parliament reconvened in the autumn. This plan did not involve any increase in pre-charge detention. Having got a cross-party agreement, they went on their yearly holidays.

But the pressure back home from the tabloids was too much for Tony Blair. Without even calling his Home Secretary, he bashed together a plan that involved measures far more draconian than anything Charles Clarke had agreed on:[86]

On 5 August Blair proudly unveiled his 12-point terror plan.[87]

> The 12-point terror plan was just before Tony flew off to the Caribbean. I mean his skill is the management of the media, so he wants to show he's really tough and really busy; so draw up lots of commitments, and then he goes on holiday but people can think tough action is being taken... And lots of it was nonsense.
>
> **CLARE SHORT**[88]

The majority of these points were either measures that were already in place or proposals that were quietly dropped. But one part of Tony's terror plan would go on to create a full-scale political war:

In 1991, one day when he was drunk, John Reid tried to force his way into the House of Commons. An attendant stepped forward to stop him and Reid threw a punch. However, the attendant was a former SAS soldier and easily wrestled John Reid to the ground. In 2006 police found a small quantity of cannabis resin in a guest room of his house. Strangely, he wasn't arrested for any of the above.

We will also examine whether the necessary procedure can be brought about to give us a way of meeting the police and security service request that detention, pre-charge of terrorist suspects, be significantly extended.[89]

Though the number of days was not mentioned, he makes it clear that to stop terrorism he wants the police to detain people for longer without charge.

The next day Tony Blair packs his bags and goes on holiday to Cliff Richard's villa in Barbados. He returns fighting fit and determined to push through 90 days.

They like floating things at a time when they hope to catch people slightly off guard. So Blair has what he calls a summer of reflection and focus groups and all that,

*and he comes back with a 'respect agenda', and tucked
away in all of this is the 90-day business.*

MICHAEL MANSFIELD QC[90]

5 October 2005. At the behest of the Government, Assistant
Met Commissioner Andy Hayman writes a report that demands
90-days' detention without trial. He uses the Ricin case as a key
part of his logic.

> The quality of the original charging decision would also have been higher,
> and it is probable that the suspect who fled the country while on bail and
> who eventually proved to have been a prime conspirator, would have stood
> trial in this country. If that had happened, the outcome of the trial process
> might have been very different.[91]

Does this mean Hayman advocates torture? The man who
'eventually proved to have been a prime conspirator' had this
confession beaten out of him in Algeria. Hayman is implying that
had they had 90 days to hold Meguerba in the UK, then the Ricin
plotters might have been found guilty. This is cobblers: the police
let Meguerba go after only three days, even though they had the
power to hold him for a total of seven.[92] Ninety days' detention
would have made no difference. He goes on to try to scare us
with technology:

> In recent cases large numbers (hundreds) of computers and hard drives were
> seized. Much of the data was encrypted. The examination and decryption of
> such vast amounts of data takes time, and needs to be analysed before
> being incorporated into an interview strategy.[93]

So they need 90 days for the boffins to do their work. Sadly the
boffins don't agree:

> I'm sorry but this is hogwash. Ensure your encryption
> software is good and you either guess the password or
> you give up. So processing a computer that's got that
> kind of material on it is something that takes a day or so.

PROFESSOR ROSS ANDERSON[94]

Hayman's arguments go from the ridiculous –

> *There is now a need to allow extra time for regular*
> *religious observance by detainees that was not a feature*
> *in the past. This too causes delay in the investigative*
> *process during pre-charge detention.*[95]

– to the sinister:

> *light on the intentions or capabilities of the terrorist*
> *network.*[96]

Finally he lays his cards on the table: if they have 90 days they will be able to make the suspect sweat until they get what they want.

> *The police justification for extending the detention period*
> *was: 'We have a problem here because most of the*
> *defendants we arrest stay silent and, of course, a lot of the*
> *period is used up with praying, so actually it's very difficult*
> *for us to have a good period of time with them, and we*
> *feel they're just on the cusp of telling us something and we*
> *have to release them. So if we have them for 90 days it'd*
> *be much easier, basically, to crack them.*
>
> **MICHAEL MANSFIELD QC**[97]

Hayman then goes on to his *coup de grâce*. Instead of using tedious things like real case studies, he goes on to advocate demolishing our oldest liberty by using a *theoretical case study* –

Theoretical Case Study
This case study has been constructed with the assistance of the Crown Prosecution Service and draws upon issues that have arisen in many real cases ...[98]

– and proceeds to concoct a series of doomsday scenarios that have the intention of scaring the pants off anyone who reads them.

The MPs are revolting

A humiliated Charles Clarke returned from holiday and was forced to sell this policy to Labour MPs, many of whom were extremely sceptical. An unlikely alliance was formed between the Conservative Party and the Left of the Labour Party, who were prepared to defy the whips.

The debate was set for 9 November 2005, and it was starting to look like Blair might lose the vote. As the date approached Blair became almost demonic in his efforts to convince whoever would listen that we'd all die tomorrow if parliament didn't hand him our liberty.[99]

> At one point the Labour whips office were asking chief constables to ring up their Labour members of parliament to try to get them on side to give the Government a majority. That's not what a chief constable is for.
>
> **KENNETH CLARKE**[100]

Never before in the history of British politics have senior police officers waded into a political debate, especially one about whether or not they should have more power. It's rather like asking Pete Doherty if he wants more drugs.

> It's up to politicians to regulate the power and control the police to make sure that they are accountable democratically and the rule of law is applied and that our rights are protected.
>
> **MARK THOMAS**[101]

> The view of the police must be taken into account, but it is also important that there be a review of the extent to which what we seek could be achieved otherwise.
>
> **TONY BLAIR, 1993, ARGUING AGAINST AN INCREASE IN POLICE POWERS**[102]

The days before the vote descended into farce. Gordon Brown was overseas playing trainee statesman, and his plane had just landed in Israel when Tony put a call through. 'Gordon…I know you hate me but this is serious…we're in the shit…If we don't give the police the power of arbitrary detention we'll both look like muppets…Yes the *Sun* says so…get back here!' The plane turned around on the runway and flew straight back to Britain. Gordon didn't even get to buy any duty free.[103]

> *People were being bullied. The Prime Minister was just playing political games and trying to say 'I'm the only tough guy!'*
>
> CLARE SHORT[104]

The Government was on the verge of losing the vote. It was time to call in the cavalry. On the day of the vote itself, the *Sun* ran a hysterical front page demanding that MPs vote for the new Law.

The implication could not be any clearer – the victims of 7/7 demand this law. But out of the seven hundred injured in the 7 July bombings the *Sun* could not have picked a more inappropriate person to plaster over its front page.

1) The man in the photo is John Tulloch, victim of the Edgware Road bomb. They did not ask for his permission.

2) He passionately disagrees with any increase in police detention, and loathes the idea that his nightmare experience should be used for this purpose.

3) He is also Professor of Sociology and Communication at Brunel University, with (and this is the best bit) a special interest in how images are manipulated by the media.[105]

JOHN TULLOCH

> *I see the flash, and it's this nasty yellow colour. Then I suspect I'm unconscious for a while, and I'm lying in the rubble and there's this terrible sense of pain, and I could feel the blood. Dark, my glasses had gone and – but there were two young American women, who I'd been listening to, sort of off-hand as we were travelling along, as you do. And I thought I need help. And so they're the only two people I could focus on. So, I rolled over in all this glass and smoke and dirt to my left, and there they were, in a terrible state as well. And then I thought, well, this is something – that its just not me. And it was that point that this adrenaline, this hard-wired evolved thing, cuts in.[106]*

John Tulloch

With the help of Craig Stainforth, a passenger on a train which was travelling in the opposite direction, John managed to make it through the forty-five minute wait for emergency services. As he sat outside the tube station, blood pouring from the bandages wound around his bleeding head, his picture was taken. He doesn't remember this happening, but the image was to become one of the iconic memories of the day, used in the media time and time again.[107]

John is an expert on the way the media uses imagery to promote a particular message. His image was used to communicate a message he didn't believe in, and he was angrier with the politicians than the bombers.

> Now I'd seen our newspapers putting narratives over images of me and this one of the Sun is such a clear one. The Sun, like a number of tabloids, takes a totally populist view about being 'for the people', but they don't manage even to ask the person they use for this particular story. For me, the 90-day legislation is an assault on civil liberties. And that's there to put pressure on the Labour Party back benches as much as anything else, to vote the other way.[108]
>
> The implication's pretty obvious, I mean they might as well have a little speech bubble to my mouth. I was totally opposed to that legislation. And it's using my image emblematically and symptomatically, i.e.: victim, look what they do, back the ninety-day law. And they're using my image without my authorisation – to do something that I think is going to make the situation worse if anything.[109]
>
> I don't think that one should be doing the terrorists' work for them and destroying the very democratic principles that we stand for. And, to be incarcerated for lengths of time without trial is symptomatic of one of those so-called War on Terror policies. It's an enormous civil liberty to take away on sometimes very flimsy evidence.[110]

TELL TONY HE'S WRONG

On 8 November Tony Blair lost his first Commons vote to extend pre-charge detention to 90 days.[111]

> *The House of Commons stood up for what is right and*
> *for the first time since '97 we had a real parliament*
> *working to protect the interests of the country.*
>
> **CLARE SHORT**[112]

Immediately after the vote was read out, an incandescent Tony Blair stood in the House of Commons and yelled, 'We are not living in a Police State!' Well, quite. He'd just tried to make this happen but was defeated. Tony wasn't happy. In an interview with the BBC afterwards, sparks were flying.[113]

> *Well, you know, people can read the evidence.*[114]

A bit disingenuous, as there wasn't any. Forty-nine of his own MPs voted against him because there was no evidence that these extra powers were needed.[115]

> *I think the police are the experts in this.*

But they are clearly always going to ask for whatever powers they can get.

> *This isn't just one or two policemen.*

No Tony, it was two policemen – Andy Hayman and Sir Ian Blair – who had consistently and publicly campaigned for 90 days.

The compromise agreed was 28 days before charge, which many believe is far too high and will become a source of injustice and wrongful convictions.

> *To me that becomes, if you're not very careful, very*
> *close to a police state in which they pick you up and*
> *then they say later on 'We'll find evidence against you'.*
> *That's what happened in Uganda with Idi Amin.*
>
> **DR JOHN SENTAMU, THE ARCHBISHOP OF YORK ,**
> **WHO LEFT IDI AMIN'S UGANDA IN THE 1970s**[116]

141

'Brown backs 90-day detention for terror suspects'

Independent, 13 November 2006

Even though Blair was defeated over 90 days, Gordon Brown and John Reid have stated that they want to force it through in the future. They have seen the gauntlet thrown down by the rebellion of late 2005, and see the issue as a challenge to assert their authority over the party.

Even though Reid has openly admitted that there has never been a case that needed 90 days, he wants to push this power through in the future.

The price of freedom is eternal vigilance.

THOMAS JEFFERSON[117]

Chapter 5
Respect

We are being drowned, and there's no two ways about that. Inundated. I sometimes talk about parliamentary effluent – all the ghastly stuff that goes through Westminster and then out on the poor unsuspecting public.

LORD PHILLIPS

One of the streams that feeds this effluent of law-making is the 'Respect Agenda'. The British 'common law tradition' means that you can do whatever you want as long as it's not illegal, as opposed to the European system (dating back to Napoleon) which prescribes things that you can do, and everything else is against the law. Almost immediately after coming to power in '97, Blair set about dismantling the British system, by forcing through ever more controlling laws that contain and moderate behaviour inside what he sees as 'acceptable norms'. The first policy of behavioural control was the Antisocial Behaviour Order (ASBO), but this was soon followed by a whole host of mutations. These went on to form the Respect Agenda. Another part of this programme is the policy of 'summary justice', which gives the power of judge and jury to police officers so that they can decide guilt on the spot. Both parts of this agenda completely undermine the notion of the common-law tradition, essentially taking the justice out of the criminal justice system.

ASBOSIS

Antisocial behaviour orders are a classic New Labour creation. For a long time Hollywood films have been created by salesmen who actually start with the poster and the marketing campaign, and then work out what the film is going to be like as an afterthought. The same process has been occurring in Westminster, where spin doctors and marketing gurus actually dictate government policy rather than the other way around. The initial headline for lawmakers has become the equivalent of the opening weekend for a movie in Hollywood. Many policies have come into being only because some bright spark in the press office thought it would play well in the tabloids.

ASBOs are the Godzilla of law-and-order policy making. Here's how it works:

1) Government PR man reads article in tabloid with headline: 'Teenagers are hanging around on my street corner'.

2) PR and Marketing men have long lunch and decide that Antisocial Behaviour is bad and there's a good headline to be had in being seen to be doing something.

3) PR and Marketing men have a brain storming session and come up with the term: Antisocial Behaviour Orders, which can be shortened to the cool and tough-sounding ASBOs.

4) Marketing and PR men pitch ASBOs to focus group. They tell focus group it will mean that it will stop teenagers hanging around on street corners. ASBOs score well.

5) New Labour announces ASBOs just before new set of crime figures come out. Tabloids are kept happy.

6) Marketing and PR men get pat on the back and disappear to the pub for rest of week.

And that's it. Oh yes, nearly forgot...

7) Some poor sod at the Home Office actually has to make this into applicable law, then realises that it completely undermines the rule of law and the presumption of innocence. Oh well, it's not for the first time.

ASBOs are a classic example of a marketing-led product. Like Ronseal's Quickdry Woodstain, it does exactly what it says on the tin. It explains exactly what the product does, as well as being able to be compressed into a handy acronym. But cheap disposable laws are like cheap disposable consumer goods. By the time you've paid your money, got it home and then realised that it doesn't live up to its hard sell, you're stuffed. Once they've got the headline and it's passed through the House of Commons, there's no money-back guarantee. We're sat with this ever-growing collection of naff overhyped law that sits in the corner gathering dust. ASBOs are the legal equivalent of the 'All-in-one nose trimmer, foot massager and ear waxer' that you bought four years ago and have never used.

GO AND STAND IN THE NAUGHTY CORNER

At the heart of ASBOs is the desire to criminalise 'Bad Behaviour'. Even though New Labour has been responsible for thousands of new criminal offences, you still have to be found guilty of one of these to go to prison. ASBOs neatly get round this little niggle, by having tailor-made restrictions for each individual person. As supermarkets can devise unique shopping lists based on what you buy, the authorities can now delve into your life to find something it doesn't like, and make a special little crime – just for you. If you are doing something that isn't against the law, but someone else doesn't like, they can go to a magistrates' court and get one of these orders that bans you acting in that way. If you break the ASBO you go to jail.[1]

As with terrorism, New Labour have tried to convince us that antisocial behaviour is an entirely new problem. The reality is that it has always been with us, but we just live in a permissive society where we don't send people to jail unless they break the law – even if they do things we don't like. Tearaways as teenagers quite often grow up into decent and law-abiding citizens. Many of us have been guilty of acts that could be termed not entirely social as a teenager, but we were tolerated and were allowed to grow out of them. Had we been imprisoned for drinking cider on street corners and occasionally being sarcastic, things might have turned out very differently. Once you start criminalising bad behaviour it can have the effect of turning badly behaving teenagers into real criminals.[2]

Under ASBO law, antisocial behaviour is defined as 'conduct which caused or was likely to cause alarm, harassment, or distress to one or more persons not of the same household as him or herself'.[3]

So at least you can't be served an ASBO by your flatmate. That would be silly. And there have never been ASBOs given for silly things. Definitely not.

For you to be served with an ASBO, the case only needs to be proved to *the balance of probabilities* – a far lower standard of evidence than is normally needed to put someone in prison. But if you break the ASBO then you can be imprisoned for up to five years, without the criminal burden of proof ever being met. Another ancient protection bites the dust.[4]

Levels of proof
The 'balance of probabilities' is the level of evidence used in civil proceedings: divorces, libel, copyright infringement etc. This is when the penalties and punishments are financial. As no one is going to get locked up, the standard is much lower. The 'beyond reasonable doubt' is for criminal cases and is a much higher test, because it potentially involves depriving someone of their liberty – i.e. putting them in prison. Beyond reasonable doubt raises the bar to being pretty damn certain that they are guilty before they do any time.[5]

The upshot is that people are now going to jail for doing things that are not illegal, and the evidence against them would not be enough to convict in a criminal court. Quite often they are used by neighbours to settle scores, with the side with more money and legal resources winning. When used against unruly teenagers on street corners (the problem they were invented to solve) the teenagers either ignore them or go to another street corner.

BADGE OF HONOUR

The argument against ASBOs might flounder if they actually worked, but the evidence is to the contrary. They are supposed to be a preventative measure, so if they are breached more often than not,

Sensible uses of ASBOs

- A 13-year-old was served an order banning him from using the word 'grass' anywhere in England and Wales.[8]

- A 16-year-old boy was banned from showing his tattoos, wearing a single golf glove, or wearing a balaclava in public anywhere in the country.[9]

- Thought to be the oldest recipient of an order, an 87-year-old has, among other things, been forbidden from being sarcastic to his neighbours. He was found guilty of breaking the terms of his order on three separate occasions.[8]

- A 57-year-old homeless alcoholic was banned from carrying or consuming alcohol in a public place and entering licensed premises. Unsurprisingly he breached the order within two weeks.[9]

- A 26-year-old West Lothian man has been made the subject of an ASBO after playing the Band Aid single 'Do they know it's Christmas' dozens of times daily, to the annoyance of neighbours. He has been banned from 'playing loud music, stamping his feet and dropping objects'.[10]

- A 38-year-old father of five recently escaped an ASBO banning him from his home following noisy rows with his new wife, but he was banned from getting into any more noisy rows with her.[11]

- A young Scottish woman received an ASBO banning her from answering the front door in her underwear. She also faces the threat of jail if she is seen in her garden or windows in just knickers and a bra.[12]

- A 50-year-old woman was served with an ASBO by magistrates in Northallerton, North Yorkshire, after she threw three sticks of rhubarb at her elderly brother.[13]

- A one-legged beggar on crutches with learning difficulties was given an ASBO preventing him from begging.[14]

- Thirteen-year-old triplets from Kent, who had all been born prematurely and suffer from severe developmental delay, were given a two-year ASBO. All three have ADHD, two have epilepsy, and one has a speech impediment.[15]

- A 15-year-old with Tourette Syndrome was ASBOed with a condition that he does not swear in public.[16]

then by definition they are not working. The Home Office released figures showing that 47 percent of ASBOs had been breached by the end of 2005, which means that they would just about get away with calling the policy a success. The National Audit Office then published the real figures, which showed that actually 55 percent of ASBOs had been breached, tipping the balance firmly into failure.[17]

A magistrate is quoted as saying that the orders were being used as a 'badge of honour...and they are going to carry that label with them for a long time'. One mother of three children issued with orders was quoted as saying, 'Some of their friends are left out now because they're not on an ASBO. I think they all want one. I know a boy that's hell-bent on getting an ASBO because he feels left out.' They are also used completely unevenly. One area in Coventry refuses to use them, but has still managed to reduce crime by 10 percent.[18]

Remember Plane Stupid? They recently had to fight off an attempt to have ASBOs served on them by the Crown Prosecution Service (CPS). The case was heard in Loughborough Magistrates Court, and the CPS accused them of being 'highly organised extremists' – again blurring the line between peaceful activists and terrorists. Plane Stupid won the day, but this is another example of a law being used in ways it was not intended to be used, in order to suppress dissent.[19]

SUPERASBOS

Once the shine had started to come off ASBOs and the public started to get the feeling that they might have been sold a dud, the Marketing man and the PR man were ordered out of the pub and told to come up with another headline-grabber. Every great movie deserves a sequel, they told each other. So they bunged the word 'super' at the front of the word ASBO to create the 'superASBO', and they were back in the bar before their champagne went flat.

Meanwhile the poor sod at the Home Office who had to enact it into law started to cry.

This latest authoritarian wheeze has two elements:

1) Serious crime prevention orders: these were announced in July 2006, and are supposed to target organised criminals the police 'know' to be guilty but do not have the evidence to prosecute. If the police believe you are a criminal, but can't prove it, then they will be able to go to a court and apply for one of these orders, again with the standard of proof being the balance of probabilities. The penalties are:
   - travel restrictions;
   - limiting phone use to a prescribed list of numbers;
   - restrictions on financial dealings, such as requiring the use only of specified credit cards and bank accounts;
   - restrictions on the amount of cash carried.[20]

   The other orders that have been given the term superASBOs are much more sinister.

2) Violent offender orders: these will feel familiar to anyone who has seen Hollywood movie *Minority Report,* and are there to prevent you carrying out crimes that have *not yet been committed*. No one is sure how the Home Office will be predicting the details of these future crimes, but Mystic Meg has been seen spending a lot of time in Whitehall recently. In January 2007 a leaked Home Office document revealed that they would use data mining of public databases to predict whether or not you are to be considered a risk. The paper lists a series of risk factors, including a person's formative years and upbringing, 'cognitive deficiencies' and 'a history of substance abuse or mental health issues'. If the data suggests that you will break the law in the future, you will be put on a restraining order (again with the civil standard of proof). The justifications for this policy will be completely self-fulfilling:
   - If someone is given a superASBO, and doesn't commit a crime, then they can say it's been a success.
   - If someone is given a superASBO, and does commit a crime, then they can proudly say that they are correctly identifying criminals.[21]

As these have yet to come into force, we still don't know the exact details of how either order will work, but in fairness the Home Office probably don't either. We'll have to wait until the night it goes before parliament.

BABY ASBOS
(WE'RE NOT MAKING THIS UP – HONESTLY)

What does Hollywood do when it has run out of ideas for sequels? It goes for the prequel. Not content with criminalising the teenage and adult population, New Labour has set about trying to bring in ASBOs for the under-10s. Soon children will be able to have an ASBO before they can walk. And what's the point in being able to walk if you're going to spend the rest of your life in prison anyway? This is a policy so daft and counterproductive that even the Government's own Children's Commissioner thinks it's a terrible idea. Professor Aynsley-Green is not a 'dewy-eyed liberalist' (in his own words), and supports normal ASBOs. But he sees this 'worrying' development as 'part of the incessant programme of policy towards punishment and control' of children. When pressed on the proposals, he said the Government was 'speaking with forked tongue'.[22]

And finally...

(It's natural to think this is utter nonsense. Please use the footnotes and look this up.)

It was only a matter of time. In his dying days in office, Blair has pushed authoritarianism to its logical conclusion.

'WE CAN CLAMP DOWN ON ANTISOCIAL CHILDREN BEFORE BIRTH,' SAYS BLAIR

GUARDIAN, 1 SEPTEMBER 2006[23]

*This one about identifying troublesome children in the
foetus – this is eugenics, the sort of thing Hitler talked
about.*

TONY BENN[24]

I know we've tried to put a ban on Nazi analogies, so we'll talk about Sweden instead.

We think of Sweden as a land filled with tall blond people. Well, it turns out that this isn't exactly an accident. In 1935, the Sterilisation Act was passed, allowing the Swedish Government to sterilise forcibly people considered socially unfit, and to purify the Swedish race. Around 63,000 people, mostly women, were sterilised during the period that the act was in force, some of them children. The people chosen for sterilisation were those of mixed race, low intelligence or with physical defects, and there is some evidence that some people that were merely sexually promiscuous or just didn't fit in were also included. The Sterilisation Act was not repealed until 1976.[25]

What Blair has set in motion is a programme whereby 'problem children' will be spotted before they are born. This will be made possible by extensive data mining of the NHS, DNA, children and identity databases to try and predict if your child is going to turn into a tearaway while it's still in the womb. If your unborn baby triggers any alarms you will be ordered to go to pre-parenting classes and your child will have an ASBO served before the umbilical cord is cut. If you argue with these measures you will face various punishments, including prison. This has the advantage for the authorities that they are actually getting two convictions for the price of one, and that they can save themselves the bother of arresting your little bundle of joy if he or she is born into custody.

SUMMARY JUSTICE

> *We're fighting twenty-first-century crime with*
> *nineteenth-century methods.*
>
> *TONY BLAIR[26]*

> Eric Metcalfe is the
> policy director at
> Justice – an all-party
> law reform and
> human-rights NGO.
> The head of Justice
> – Lord Steyn –
> called the Attorney
> General's advice on
> the legality of the
> Iraq War 'scraping
> the bottom of the
> legal barrel'.

> *Summary justice is just police discretion.*
> *It's shortcutting the courts, shortcutting the*
> *legal process and just simply saying 'We'll*
> *let frontline police officers handle this'.*
> *The nature of the rule of law is that you*
> *don't entrust police with incredible*
> *powers. Who's going to be there to protect*
> *you when the police suddenly become*
> *more arbitrary in their decision-making?*
> *When they decide to give you a fine*
> *because they don't like the look of you?*
>
> *ERIC METCALFE[27]*

At the heart of summary justice are fixed penalty notices for public order offences. This is where the policeman can decide that your behaviour is likely to cause harassment, alarm or distress to others. The policeman then becomes judge, prosecutor and jury – and you get handed the fine. It's then up to you to challenge it and get it overturned, otherwise non-payment of the fine means they can send in the bailiffs. Bottom line, guilty until proven innocent. The best way to illustrate how summary justice can be misused is by swearing. A lot.[28]

> *Take away the right to say 'fuck' and you take away the*
> *right to say 'fuck the government'.*
>
> *LENNY BRUCE[29]*

Readers of a sensitive disposition may want to skip the next bit. Lots of perfectly decent people curse like dockers rather often; lots of other perfectly decent people are genuinely shocked by it. Arguments still rage in the media, and in front rooms, as to the relative offensiveness of one rude word or another. They're just words, after all. Rude ones, but legitimate ones. Swearing, ubiquitous as it is, is generally tolerated in our free society. And it should go without saying that there's a clear and recognisable difference between swearing at someone – an act of verbal aggression, a prelude to possible violence – and swearing to them as a natural part of normal conversation. Our simple table clarifies the difference.

Fairly straightforward. Unfortunately, the police don't always recognise this crucial difference between the crude and the dangerous. In the last year several individuals have fallen foul of this inability to discern nuance. You don't know who you might be offending, and what it might cost you – 80 quid, or even your liberty. Tony, for all his tough talk on terrorism, is a sensitive flower.

EFF

In February 2006, student Kurt Walker happened upon his mate in the street and stopped for a chat. He was on his way to the youth centre in Kent where he worked as a volunteer. The conversation went something like this:

Swearing at (active)	Swearing to (passive)
'You motherfucker, I'm gonna fuck up your socks.'	'Fuck me, did you see they threw a guy out of the Labour Party conference for saying 'Nonsense'? What bastards.'
'Fucking look at me again and I'll put you in the ground you fuckbasket'	'What a lot of bollocks the Serious Crime and Police Act is – I can hardly even say the name without fucking chortling.'
'One more fucking word out of you and I'll fuck up your spanner box'	'What? John Reid can just put me under house arrest because he feels like it. Are you fucking joking?'
'That's fucking it. I'm going to fucking thump you all the way to Chichester.'	'How much did you say the National Identity Register would cost? That's fucking insane!'

> Walker: Hello mate.
>
> Mate: Alright mate. What have you been up to?
>
> Walker: Fuck all, mate.

Whereupon a passing policewoman slapped the astonished student's mild pottymouth with an £80 fine – what you might expect to get for being found drunk and disorderly, or committing £500 worth of damage. Walker told the press he was 'shocked', and said, 'In my eyes I have not committed any crime whatsoever.' Swearing, to him, was 'normal'. Dover District Council (whose anti-social behaviour unit works closely with Kent Police), however, didn't agree, aligning themselves firmly with the WPC. 'Swearing and abusive behaviour certainly is not normal behaviour,' said Councillor Julie Rook. 'I feel it should never be used in a public place.' A police spokeswoman shrugged that 'the public expect us to tackle antisocial behaviour. If Mr Walker is not happy he can have his case decided by a court.' In fact, the case was dropped a month later without anyone having to go to court, pay a fine, or receive one.[30]

If the police are now empowered to fine passing citizens for dropping the odd oath, they could at least produce some sort of tariff for their fines. So we all know exactly where we stand and what we can and can't say if we're a bit skint.

Since society's instinct to equate illegal with immoral is pretty strong, and our memories can be short, there's a danger that the criminal-isation of normal behaviour will become enshrined not just in law, but in the psyche of our society. Lots of people don't really care a row of buttons if some little oik is made to pay for saying something rude. But perhaps they should. First they came for the little oiks, and all that.

Or flogging T-shirts with 'Bollocks' on them.

Swearing price list	
'Fuck'	£80
'Fuck' (muttered under breath)	£75
'Fuck' (if minor injury to hand, inside cheek or toe is proven to be involved)	£60
'Bugger'	£50
'Arse'/'Wank'/'Scruttocks'/'Minge'	£40
'I do think Dave Cameron has some brave ideas even if he is a smarmy Tory who looks like Data from Star Trek'	£1500 + thumbscrews

NEVER MIND THE...

Toby Rhodes was furious about Blair's decision to ban foxhunting with the Hunting Act of 2004 – a move that was seen, even by many who opposed the traditional bloodthirsty gallivanting itself, to be cynical and unworkable. Since Toby produced T-shirts, hats and jumpers with his friend Tom Williams, he had a readily available outlet for his disgust with what he considered to be an unjust law. His feelings manifested themselves in what would become an immensely popular design with his customers – the slogan 'BOLLOCKS TO BLAIR'. Well, it's not 'I♥NY', but it gets the message across.

The T-shirts had been selling well for 18 months when Toby and Tom displayed the T-shirts at their stand at the Royal Norfolk Show in the summer of 2006. They had done a roaring trade at country fairs full of people livid about the ban. However, this time police officers handed out an £80 fine to both stallholders. They offered to take the display down, but the police said that the offence had already been committed. 'It's ridiculous,' said Toby. 'Totally out of proportion.'

The Norfolk police stuck to their guns, stating, 'Officers from Norfolk Constabulary issued two fixed penalty notices, each with a value of £80, at the Royal Norfolk Show in relation to two trade stands displaying T-shirts emblazoned with offensive language. The notices were issued under Section 5 of the Public Order Act as the language was deemed to cause harassment, distress or alarm at an event where a cross-section of people were present, including families and young children who may have found the displays offensive.'[31]

When pressed, the police had to admit that no one had actually complained. Only that they might do.

A twenty-something woman was stopped by police and ordered to take hers off. She pointed out that she only had a bra on under the shirt, but the police told her to take it off anyway. She refused, at which point they marched her to a waiting police car in tears.[32]

The 'Bollocks' shirts are still available. Wear one at your own risk.

SHH ...

Like students and foxhunters, 24-year-old Phil Bennett isn't outwardly the sort of bloke everyone would immediately embrace to their bosom. He likes heavy metal and is partial to a mosh. He wears disquieting T-shirts with bones and things on them. But he's a nice, personable bloke, and as a Cambridge physics graduate, very well educated. In summer 2006 he travelled two hundred and fifty miles from Preston to see renowned screamers My Ruin at the Garage in north London, but had a little more trouble getting out of Highbury and Islington station than he anticipated.[33]

A metal detector was in place, which Phil and his friend Jo were happy enough to pass through. Phil, having some understanding of the inadequacies of the instrument, remarked to his mate, 'This is a piece of shit machine, it wouldn't stop anyone'. In his opinion as a physics graduate, it's nothing more than 'security theatre. I don't think having your tube station monitored by a metal detector is going to stop anyone. I think they're more for reassuring people that they are being watched. Being seen to be doing something is not actually doing anything. So as such it's not a valid machine – it's just a piece of shit.' All of this he said later – at the time, he restricted himself to just the 'piece of shit' bit. But that was enough. Silly Phil.[34]

Within moments of his off-hand comment he was being physically pulled aside by three policemen and questioned. 'I was interrogated for about twenty minutes,' Phil says, 'about where I was from, why I was coming down to London, and where I'd been that day.' What was he being detained for? 'For causing offence. I received an £80 fixed penalty notice, saying "You have caused a disturbance, this is an antisocial behaviour, public order offence – please give us £80". I tried to pay it then, but they wouldn't let me.'

Meanwhile, Jo was 'standing outside hyperventilating and getting very agitated about police state Britain, and "1984", and fascist blah-di-blah. I was getting a bit dramatic.' When she asked if they were nearly done, the police told her to be quiet or she would be arrested herself. Phil was eventually allowed to go with her to the gig, clutching his public order offence sheet, the sheet quoting him as saying 'piece of shit machine'. Their alliance would be brief – during a particularly enthusiastic mosh, Phil lost the sheet along with his glasses. He did his best to track down a copy, but the British Transport Police didn't seem to have any record of his offence.[35]

'You can't be stopped just for criticising a piece of kit,' says Phil. 'That's not an arrestable offence. It shouldn't be anyway. You should be able to discuss the methods they're using between your friends without being pulled over and arrested. They just don't expect people to challenge them, because it's more expensive to challenge it than it is to just pay the fine and walk off. If no one challenges it then they're going to carry on doing it.'[36]

Phil says that the officers who questioned him seemed to be enjoying themselves, which is easy enough to believe – people want to enjoy their job. But if they find hauling someone aside and fining them for hurting a metal detector's feelings fun, there's something wrong. Worse, if the police feel it is now their job to keep the public intimidated, then a dangerous shift has occurred. At least in real terms they can't fine everyone who says 'fuck', 'shit' or 'bollocks', even in relation to Tony Blair. They wouldn't have any time to arrest people for standing in Parliament Square or anything.[37]

SUMMARY JUSTICE GETS EXTENDED

On 20 January 2007 the Home Office announced that as fixed penalty notices were such a success they were going to be extending them to many other crimes. Under the proposals, fines would be handed out for offences including assault, threatening behaviour, theft up to the value of £200, obstructing or assaulting a police officer, possession of cannabis and drunkenness.[38] So between super-ASBOs, baby ASBOs, foetal ASBOs, vanilla ASBOs, control orders and fixed penalty notices, it seems like they've got pretty much everything covered. Very soon there won't actually be any need for any semblance of justice or the presumption of innocence. Guilt will be either decided on the spot by police or by the Home Secretary based on suspicion alone. Evidence will become a peripheral antiquity, the legal equivalent of the royal family – it'll still be there but it won't actually serve any purpose. This is already happening in most areas of the criminal justice system as we have seen. But there is one area of justice where New Labour have successfully removed the need for evidence completely. This is when we are required to give up British citizens and send them to foreign countries that have decided they have done wrong – extradition.

Chapter 6
Extradition

It all started on the internet. Alex Stone is a blind computer science graduate from south London who had worked for a bank for ten years. In May 2003 he joined an email list for blind people, and started chatting to a woman called Alma from Kansas City. They started talking regularly on the phone as well as emailing each other. After a few months they decided they wanted to meet, so Alex made plans to fly out to Kansas City and spend a holiday with Alma that August.[1]

A few months earlier, in another part of America, David Blunkett was signing a piece of paper that would devastate Alex's life.

On 31 March 2003, the Home Secretary had flown to Washington to sign a new extradition treaty on behalf of the UK. On the surface, it appeared to be a little bit of administration and

David Blunkett and John Ashcroft signing the new extradition treaty

not very newsworthy. The consequences would ruin many ordinary people's lives.

The treaty removes the requirement on the US to provide evidence when requesting the extradition of people from the UK.[2] In effect, all the US has to do is fill in a form and then, bang, you'd be flown off to America to stand trial, whether or not there is a shred of evidence against you. We signed away our right to be protected by British law, and hardly anyone noticed.

> *The first duty of any government is the protection of its own citizens.*
>
> **GEOFF HOON, MINISTER FOR EUROPE**[3]

The problem with the treaty is that, by signing it, our Government completely reneged on its primary duty.

In 2003, as his friendship with Alma was blossoming, Alex Stone was still blissfully unaware of the world of political treaties. Alex and Alma spent a wonderful fortnight together, and Alex met Alma's son, one-year-old Zachary. In the light of his new relationship, he decided to take the redundancy offer he'd been made, and to move out to the US to be with Alma: 'It was exactly what I wanted to do; I wanted to go and live out there and be with her'.[4]

Alex sorted out his life in the UK and flew back to Kansas City in November 2003. He hadn't been there long when the trouble began. Zachary developed a cold that wouldn't get better. He was clearly unwell, so Alma's mother took him to hospital to be looked at. While he was there, the doctors decided to X-ray him, and discovered that both of his arms and both of his legs were broken.

Alma rushed to hospital to be with Zachary, and Alex stayed at home in her apartment. But over the next four or five days, Alex began to feel uncomfortable, and gradually realised that suspicion was falling on him. 'Because I was new on the scene, it was convenient for them to suspect me rather than look at their own family.'[5]

Things got worse when a friend of the family came round to the apartment to warn him. The friend said Alma's family might try to 'do something stupid'. Feeling threatened, Alex moved out of Alma's apartment into a motel. Another four days went past and, after no further contact with Alma, the police turned up. He was taken in for questioning and accused of having injured the child. The only other people who could have injured Zachary were members of Alma's family, and according to the police they were all 'very nice people'.

Alex wasn't charged, and he was taken back to his motel. He contacted a lawyer, who told him that as he hadn't been charged with anything he was free to go, and ought to get out of the US as quickly as possible. So he did; he flew home to London straight away. He'd been in the US less than a month.

Back in home he discovered that the papers and TV news reports in Missouri were full of stories saying he had been charged with injuring Zachary, and that he was now in prison. Despite the inaccuracy of the reports, the fact that he had been formally charged with the crime meant things were getting more serious. First-degree assault on a minor can carry a sentence of up to 30 years in the US.[6]

Nothing happened for a year. Then, in November 2004, Alex's neighbour at his old flat phoned to say that three policemen had been knocking at his door. Alex was advised to turn himself in. Two days later he presented himself at Charing Cross Police Station, where he was arrested and extradition proceedings began.

Over the following months, and several more court appearances, he discovered that he had absolutely no defence under the Extradition Act. Simply by charging Alex with the crime, the US had the right to extradite him. Thanks to David Blunkett's new law, the British legal system was impotent to protect him. At the end of April 2005, Alex's family drove him to Gatwick Airport, where he was handed over to the Scotland Yard extradition squad, handcuffed, shackled, and put on a private jet to the US.

He was then transferred across the country in 'holding cells', and his journey ended in the county jail in (the ironically named) Liberty, Missouri. He was locked up for 23 hours a day. He was allowed to take his laptop with him to write letters, but they didn't give him a printer, so he couldn't print them or send them back. It took several months to get him a scanner so that he could scan in and read the letters that were sent to him. He couldn't make international calls or send emails, so he had no contact with his family in London for many months. When his father came to visit him in September, there was a glass screen between them, and they had to talk using a telephone. For Alex, his dad might as well have been in London.

He was in jail for six and a half months. In November, Alex's mother helped to secure bail, but he had to remain in the US. By February, his lawyers went to the public prosecutor and, in Alex's words, 'They said, look, you've got no evidence here, have you? This is not going to stand up in court, so why don't you just drop it?' But the prosecutors were stuck because, having gone to the trouble of extraditing Alex, they needed to find him guilty of something. Alex and his lawyers negotiated a plea bargain. He passed a polygraph test, pleaded guilty to fleeing the country (despite the fact that he did it solely on the advice of a US lawyer), and flew home to the UK in the first week of March 2006. He'd been stuck in legal limbo for over 10 months.

There is another reason why the prosecutors were prepared to accept the plea bargain. Alma's brother had a child who was discovered to have similar injuries that dated from a time when Alex wasn't even in the country. The mother of that child and the grandmother were prepared to testify against a family member who was suspected of injuring both children. For Alex, it was simply a case of being in the wrong place at the wrong time.

Now Alex is living in London and looking for work with a 16-month hole in his CV. 'It is very difficult to prove you haven't done something. This has robbed me of two and a half years of my life and cost me around £50,000 – money I will not get back. I feel angry about it, but most of all I feel very sad.'[7]

Had David Blunkett not signed that extradition treaty back in 2003, Alex would almost certainly not have had to go through those years of hell. Under the old rules the US prosecutors would first have had to show that there was a case to answer in a British court before they could put him on a plane. As the evidence against Alex was shambolic, the case would have been thrown out and Alex would have been protected. By banishing evidence from extradition proceedings, Blunkett and Blair have left us all at the mercy of the US criminal justice system.

DAVID BERMINGHAM AND THE NATWEST THREE

> *Well it's outrageous! Here you've got a guy, the crime he's meant to have committed took place in this country against UK interests and yet the British authorities don't want to do anything against him. It's the Americans, who've found some tangential involvement in the Enron business, who want to extradite him. And simply on their say-so, without any evidence, he's being supermagnetically suctioned over to America.*

BORIS JOHNSON MP[8]

If the case of the NatWest Three started out as being about three fat cats who looked as if they had been caught with their fingers in the till, it finished as an international incident which brought into sharp focus not only the Government's casual attitude to the liberties of its citizens, but also its subservience to the United States of America.

The NatWest Three are David Bermingham, Giles Darby and Gary Mulgrew. Three forty-something men of very differing backgrounds who had worked at a division of NatWest Bank in early 2000, when their crime is alleged to have taken place.

Mulgrew is a tall, dark, charismatic Glaswegian who had been the boss of the NatWest structured finance group, for whom the other two worked. Darby was born in India, but was brought up in Wiltshire, and has the affable nature of a country boy made good. Bermingham is ex-army, with a stiff upper lip, and speaks in precise, clipped tones. Although the most junior of the three when they worked together as colleagues, it was Bermingham who was to become their unofficial spokesman when their story exploded.

None of the men comes across remotely as the stereotypical investment banker. There are no expensive suits, braces, Armani shoes, Rolex watches or slicked-back hair that one associates with the *Wall Street* caricature of a banker. All three are family men, and they have ten children between them.

All three worked for Greenwich NatWest in the late nineties and 2000. During that time they became involved with the energy giant Enron. Although these days Enron is now a byword for fraud, at the time it was the company to do business with. Between leaving NatWest and joining a new employer in the summer of 2000, they entered into a deal with Andy Fastow, Chief Financial Officer of Enron. This deal was to make them something in the region of seven million dollars.[9] The men have never denied receiving the money, all of which was declared in their tax returns. By the end of 2001, the cracks were starting to appear in the Enron empire.[10]

> David: On 8 November 2001, Enron made an
> announcement which shook my world to the core,
> because hidden in amongst that announcement were
> some details about the transaction in which Gary, Giles
> and I had been personally involved the previous year.

It suddenly seemed to him that Enron might not have been playing straight dice. David, Gary and Giles immediately did something typically British. They came forward straight away to tell the authorities everything they knew.

> We spent three or four hours with the Financial Services
> Authority, with their enforcement people. We had a
> taped, transcribed interview with them and they said,
> 'Look it's fantastic that you've come forward'.[11]

The Financial Services Authority (FSA) then asked them if they could share the information with their counterparts in the US (the Securities and Exchanges Commission). They all agreed, keen to make sure they were as co-operative as they could be. Ironically it was this desire to be honest that would lead to charges being brought against them in the US some months later.

In early December 2001 Enron filed for bankruptcy protection, leaving thousands in Houston out of work and without a pension.

A year previously the company had been worth $70 billion on the US stock market, and in filing for bankruptcy they were effectively saying, 'We're now worthless'. At the time this was the largest ever single bankruptcy in US corporate history. A vast amount of money had been lost by a huge number of investors, and the stink of criminality was strong. The Enron task force was set up, but as is often the case in the US, anyone who was approached by the FBI had reached for their lawyer and had 'taken the Fifth'. The task force needed a breakthrough.

> David: At the end of June 2002, I was watching the BBC breakfast news and I was on it. I was one of the first three people, along with Gary and Giles, to be criminally charged in respect of the whole Enron debacle.

David's wife – Emma – clearly remembers the day that the charges were announced: 'David came into the bathroom and said, "I've got to go to London – go and have a look at the headlines on the news," and it was about eight o'clock in the morning. So I went and saw my husband on the news, and the day went very wrong and very bizarre after that. My reaction was shock and horror and disbelief. But with three children you have to carry on, and act as if not an awful lot has gone wrong.' [12]

Charging someone in the US is very different to the process to Britain. A prosecutor can go to a grand jury, tell them that he believes that someone has committed a crime – and a charge is issued. The standard of evidence needed is cursory, and there is a saying in the US that 'a determined prosecutor could indict a ham sandwich'. The information that the NatWest Three had naively volunteered was used against them to get the charges. The Enron

What they did or didn't do

Although the alleged scheme to defraud their employer (according to the charging documents) seems to have been fiendishly complicated, the core allegation is that the men conspired with two senior executives of Enron to defraud NatWest of seven million dollars through convincing the bank to sell an asset that it owned at an undervalue, and then profiting themselves from the subsequent on-sale of that same asset. The men have always strongly denied the allegations.

task force was then able to use these charges to start working up the Enron ladder. A chain of charges and plea bargains followed, eventually leading right up to the heads of Enron, Jeff Skilling and Ken Lay.

But back in 2002, even though there were US charges against them, David, Giles and Gary at least had some legal protections. The old rules of extradition still applied – if the US wanted to demand them in court in America, it would have to show that there was a case to answer in front of a British judge. For over a year and a half this did not happen, presumably as the evidence against them was not strong enough. When the charges were first brought, what press coverage there was was confined to the business pages of the newspapers. What nobody could possibly have known at that stage was that the Home Office was well on its way to creating a perfect political storm. During the whole of 2002, officials from the Home Office were secretly negotiating the new extradition treaty with the US, which would remove the obligation for the US to provide any evidence to extradite UK citizens.

EVIDENCE SCHMEVIDENCE

After 9/11 the US started seeing itself as 'the policeman of the world', and made a series of extradition requests to Britain. One of them was for a young man called Lotfi Raissi, who was accused by the FBI of being involved in the 9/11 attacks. Without even questioning the reasoning behind this accusation, Lotfi was arrested by the British police in an extremely brutal fashion, carried naked from his house at 3 a.m. and locked in Belmarsh high-security prison.

> From that day…I was locked up in a cell facing the
> most serious allegations imaginable. In my case I feel as
> though the world perceived me as a guilty man and that
> I had to try and prove that I was innocent.[13]

He stayed in Belmarsh for five months, with the world's media declaring him guilty. Eventually he came to have an extradition hearing. As this was under the old rules, evidence still had to be presented in a British court. After five months of investigating by the FBI, CIA, MI5 and MI6, the evidence supplied to prove that Lotfi was a terrorist mastermind was:

1) he is a Muslim;

2) he has a pilot's license.

Not surprisingly, the judge threw out the case. If that had happened under the new rules then Lotfi would have probably never been seen again.

Presumably to avoid embarrassing cases like this, the US wanted to remove the inconvenient bureaucracy of evidence. In the spring of 2003 the treaty was signed, and later that year the Extradition Act 2003 went through parliament, but at the time the crucial part about letting the US haul off our citizens without proof was left out. This bit was slipped in later on while no one was looking.

> They whacked it through at the end of a parliamentary session; there was no scrutiny of it at all, hardly any debate… Whether or not it fell foul of the rules is an open question.
>
> **BORIS JOHNSON MP**[14]

Apart from giving the US complete *carte blanche* to extradite British citizens, there was one other glaring problem with the treaty: it was completely unbalanced. Under the terms of the treaty, the US no longer needs to provide evidence to support an extradition request for a UK subject. However, if the UK wishes to extradite someone from the US, it must still satisfy an American court of exactly the same evidential burden as under the previous treaty, that of 'probable cause'.[15] Since this provision is written into the US constitution, it is not something that the US could ever have given up. The treaty gave away our rights of protection to a country who would never, could never, extend the same courtesy to us. In the face of US demands, our Government simply rolled over and waved their legs in the air.

We're agreeing to extradite people to America ... without
any evidence being supplied by the Americans, when if
we want anyone to come from America to this country
to face trial (which of course never happens; it never
happened in thirty years of the IRA atrocities when they
had many IRA suspects in America), we have to supply
evidence to the Americans. So there's a grotesque
asymmetry in the arrangements.

BORIS JOHNSON MP[16]

If there was any doubt as to who was the driving force behind
it, you only have to take a cursory look at the treaty document
itself. Take a look at the second heading on the first page:

ARTICLE 2

Extraditable Offenses

1.   An offense shall be an extraditable offense if the conduct on which the offense is based
is punishable under the laws in both States by deprivation of liberty for a period of one year
or more or by a more severe penalty.

2.   An offense shall also be an extraditable offense if it consists of an attempt or a
conspiracy to commit, participation in the commission of, aiding or abetting, counseling or
procuring the commission of, or being an accessory before or after the fact to any offense
described in paragraph 1 of this Article.

3.   For the purposes of this Article, an offense shall be an extraditable offense:

----

1.   Treaty Series No. 16 (1977) Cmnd 6723

The British spelling of 'offence' is with a 'c', whereas standard
American spelling has an 's'. American spelling persists throughout the document.

As the treaty passed into law, the only significant high-profile
critic of the bill, Menzies Campbell, warned that it would not be
long before the constituents of the MPs on the select committee
would feel the force of the new provisions. One of the MPs on

the select committee was David Lepper, the Labour MP for Brighton and Hove.[17] Gary Mulgrew is one of his constituents.

Though the NatWest Three were charged in June 2002, the US did not seek extradition of the three men until February 2004, one month after the new Extradition Act came into effect. They were arrested in April and bailed to appear before a magistrate for an extradition hearing in September 2004. A valid charging document, specifying the offence, was all that was needed.

The Three weren't going to keep quiet, and the case started to gain notoriety. A website was set up appropriately titled friendsextradited.org. While city bankers do not often gain public sympathy, there was something about the case that rattled people's sense of fair play. Why were we sending people to Texas to stand trial for a crime that supposedly took place in Britain, against a British bank, by British citizens?

> *This is not about whether they are guilty or innocent –*
> *they may well have a case to answer. It's the treatment*
> *of a British citizen in another jurisdiction that really does*
> *worry me.*
>
> **SIR DIGBY JONES**[18]

The NatWest Three's message was easily understood: 'Try us by all means, but try us here'. The subtext was equally clear: 'If it can happen to us, it could happen to anyone'.

And it wasn't just bankers who were facing this problem. Since the Extradition Act came into force dozens of extradition requests have been filed that had nothing to do with international terrorism. One of the few cases where there was a terrorism link was that of Babar Ahmad, a case that also seemed to be riddled with injustice. But as the NatWest Three were first to be requested, everyone else was waiting to see the outcome of their case. If they lost, then everyone else would be likely to follow them in chains to the US.

Predictably they lost the first round. In October 2004, Magistrate Nicholas Evans ticked the relevant box and ordered their case to be sent to the Home Secretary. In May 2005 Charles Clarke ruled

Babar Ahmad is a computing expert from south London. He was originally arrested by the UK police in December 2003 but released after six days without charge. He was then rearrested on 5 August 2004 on an extradition warrant from the US. Babar has been held in prison since that time, fighting the extradition request. He is charged with using US-based websites to recruit fighters and raise funds for terrorism in Afghanistan and Chechnya. Though Babar was based in the UK, since the website was based in Connecticut and Nevada, the US has claimed jurisdiction. The case has incensed many people who feel that terror suspects are being deported to America when the British police do not have enough evidence to support a case which would stand up in a British court. There are fears that he will be transferred to Guantanamo rather than receive an open and fair trial. Babar also made allegations of physical abuse by the British police and many of his supporters feel that he is being transferred to America as a way of keeping him quiet. 'My son is not a terrorist – he is a junior IT support officer' – Ashtaq Ahmad

against the men. They appealed. Their case was referred to the High Court, with their appeal due to be heard in November of 2005.[19]

The Serious Fraud Office hadn't even opened a file on them, and ironically this would have actually helped their situation. The NatWest Three were so convinced of their innocence, and so determined that if there were a case to answer it should be answered in the UK, that they took the SFO to court – for not taking them to court. In effect, they wanted the SFO to investigate their case – so that they could show there was no case to answer.

We know that if they investigate they will find there is no evidence. They will find that this is a fabrication and that is why they've refused to do it. It would be so monumentally embarrassing, in the very first high-profile extradition case for this Government, for it to turn out that the American charges are a tissue of lies, which is what they are.

DAVID BERMINGHAM[20]

In November 2005 the High Court heard both the appeal to the extradition and the judicial review of the SFO's lack of action back to back. And in February 2006 the Three lost both cases. By this time the NGO Liberty had also taken up their case, and Shami Chakrabarti stood with the three men on the High Court steps. It was an emotionally charged moment, as the three men knew that their options were running out:

> *This is a violation of fundamental rights: why will the US*
> *Government not allow similar traffic for its own citizens*
> *in the other direction?*

SHAMI CHAKRABARTI[21]

They immediately petitioned the House of Lords, and were stuck in a legal limbo while they waited for the Lords to decide whether to hear the case. The wait became agonising, as there was no indication as to when they would give a decision – it could be weeks or months.

What emerged over the following months was an extraordinary alliance of civil libertarians, left-wing crusties, city businessmen, journalists, MPs and oddballs. Several more cases came to light of people who were facing a similar fate. The US had requested the extradition of Gary McKinnon, an unemployed computer programmer and UFO enthusiast from Glasgow. Gary had been accused of hacking into NASA's computers. The fact that NASA had failed to set passwords for their systems and, in effect, left all the doors open, won't stop them sending Gary to prison for 70 years if he is found guilty.

As the months wore on the NatWest Three started facing up to the probability that they would soon be going to Texas to face trial. Once there, innocence was unlikely to be of much help. Ninety-eight percent of people indicted in the federal criminal

The NatWest Three with
Shami Chakrabarti

system in America choose to enter into plea bargains rather than go to trial. They do this first because the costs of trial can be astronomic, and are non-refundable even if you win; second because the Federal Sentencing Guidelines, which work on a points system to determine sentence, can expose defendants to (literally) hundreds of years in prison if found guilty, as opposed to (say) one or two years for a guilty plea.

On 21 June, the House of Lords rejected the petition to have the case heard. The Three's solicitor immediately petitioned the European Court of Human Rights for an emergency stay of execution; on 27 June they lost this as well. This was their last hope. A date was set for the flight: 13 July.

At this point, the media interest became a circus. The *Telegraph* published a full-page open letter to John Reid, the new Home Secretary, urging him to stop the extradition and change the law. It was signed by nearly forty senior business figures. The *Sun* ran a headline saying 'Free the Three'. David Blunkett wrote in his regular *Sun* column that the US was behaving very badly! Karl Watkin, an entrepreneur, organised a march of business people though central London to the Home Office in protest.

The Business Against Extradition demo that took place on 29 June 2006 was an intriguing affair. For many participants, it was their first ever political demonstration. A group of suited-and-booted City gents, civil liberties campaigners and several cameramen and film crews assembled outside the Institute of Directors on a fine summer evening after work. Clutching their panama hats, brief cases and copies of the evening papers, they set off across St James's Park towards the Home Office. One man wheeled his bike dutifully along the pavement. At the centre were Shami Chakrabarti and David Bermingham. There were no banners or placards, no slogans or shouting; as the march passed through the restricted area around Whitehall, and no SOCPA authorisation had been given, there was a danger they could be arrested. When they arrived at the Home Office, there was some negotiation with the policemen on duty as to whether they were allowed to hand in their petition. A few extra signatures were hastily added, and in it went. When it was all over, everyone wandered off to the pub for a drink, except no one could remember which pub had been agreed on or how to get there. All in all, it was a thoroughly British affair.

The demonstration was carried in all the national newspapers the next day. Over the following week, speculation reached fever pitch that the Government would finally be shamed into intervening on the men's behalf.

As the campaign intensified and the Government was put on the back foot, the fact that a PR company had been employed was one of the things the Government used to attack and try to discredit the campaign. Of course, using PR people is something they'd never do. The Government spin machine also insisted on calling the men the Enron Three, as a way of making a negative association between the men and the collapsed energy giant. This was in spite of the fact that the US had asserted from the outset that the men had stolen the money from NatWest, not Enron.

We interviewed David at his house two days before the extradition. He had been up all night on the phone to his US lawyers, preparing for his impending arrival and trying to find a way to obtain bail once they landed. His gallows humour was still strong – when asked if he thought that the Government would save the day, he looked out of his kitchen window and wondered aloud whether he had just seen a pig flying past.[22]

We drank coffee on the porch of his house, and the interview was continually interrupted by the stream of calls from journalists and well-wishers. People were still fighting to keep them in the UK, but David had become resigned to their fate.

> In my view it's entirely political. The only people who can stop it are the Government. If they want to stop it, they will, and if they don't they won't. It's a political decision, not a legal one. So let's just get over there and sort it out and get this law changed for other people.[23]

The next day – 24 hours before they were due to leave for Texas – questions were put to Tony Blair in Prime Minister's Questions by Menzies Campbell on the impending extradition. Blair read out a carefully worded reply:

> *... in the Attorney General's view the test that the US applies, that of probable cause, is roughly analogous to the one that we apply in this country...*[24]

'Roughly Analogous'? If the British want to extradite an American citizen, we have to provide evidence. When the US want to extradite a British citizen, they don't.

> *... the case for extradition was mounted originally under the old law not the new law.*

It is rare that Blair is actually caught out lying, but this is one such occasion. The new law came into force on 1 January 2004.

STATUTORY INSTRUMENTS

2003 No. 3109

EXTRADITION

The Extradition Act 2003 (Part 1 Designated Authorities) Order 2003

Made - - - - -	*1st December 2003*
Laid before Parliament	*3rd December 2003*
Coming into force - -	*1st January 2004*

The Secretary of State, in exercise of the powers conferred on him by section 2(9) and (10) of the Extradition Act 2003(a), hereby makes the following Order:

1. This Order may be cited as the Extradition Act 2003 (Part 1 Designated Authorities) Order 2003 and shall come into force on 1st January 2004.

2. The National Criminal Intelligence Service and the Crown Agent of the Crown Office are hereby designated for the purposes of Part 1 of the Extradition Act 2003.

Home Office
1st December 2003

Caroline Flint
Parliamentary Under-Secretary of State

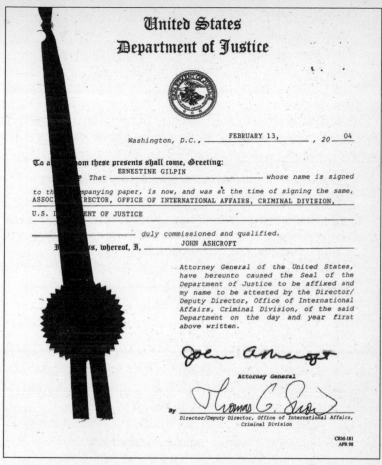

United States
Department of Justice

Washington, D.C., _____ FEBRUARY 13, _____ , 20 __ 04 __

To all to whom these presents shall come, Greeting:

_____ That __ ERNESTINE GILPIN _____ whose name is signed

to the accompanying paper, is now, and was at the time of signing the same,
ASSOCIATE DIRECTOR, OFFICE OF INTERNATIONAL AFFAIRS, CRIMINAL DIVISION,

U.S. DEPARTMENT OF JUSTICE

_____ duly commissioned and qualified.
__ JOHN ASHCROFT __

In witness, whereof, I, _____

Attorney General of the United States,
have hereunto caused the Seal of the
Department of Justice to be affixed and
my name to be attested by the Director/
Deputy Director, Office of International
Affairs, Criminal Division, of the said
Department on the day and year first
above written.

Attorney General

By _____
Director/Deputy Director, Office of International Affairs,
Criminal Division

CRM-181
APR 98

The extradition requests were made on 13 February 2004 – over
a month later.

Later that day, the Speaker of the House of Commons, Michael
Martin, took the unusual decision of allowing an emergency
debate. It was requested by the Liberal Democrat MP Nick Clegg,
and covered both the treaty and the NatWest Three's case. The
Government, in the form of Solicitor General Mike O'Brien, made
it clear that they believed the men to be guilty, and that the best
place for these British citizens was in a jail in Texas. He was
assailed from all sides – Boris was taking no prisoners:

> *If the torrent of allegations that the Solicitor General read*
> *out against the three are so compelling, why cannot he*
> *put them on trial in this country? It is not too late for him*
> *to do that. He has the power at the stroke of a pen.*

BORIS JOHNSON MP[25]

He was probably surprised to have his argument supported by the left-wing MP George Galloway, no fan of bankers:

> *All we want is a special relationship that does not*
> *resemble that between Miss Lewinsky and a former*
> *United States President: unequal, disreputable and with*
> *the junior partner always on their knees. That is not the*
> *kind of special relationship that we want, but as the*
> *Honourable Member for Henley [Boris Johnson]*
> *powerfully made clear, it is exactly the kind of special*
> *relationship that most people in Britain think that we*
> *have with the United States of America.*

GEORGE GALLOWAY MP[26]

The day ended with MPs from all sides showing their dismay at the way the Government had behaved. All other debates were cancelled, and the MPs went home in disgust. Not exactly the storming of the Bastille, but it's the best they could do.

Later that day there was another twist. Sky News broke the story that Neil Coulbeck, a former colleague of the NatWest Three, and a man targeted to have been a witness for the US Government in the case against the men, had been found dead near his home in Essex. There were reports from 'friends of the family' that he had been put under enormous pressure by the FBI, and that this may have contributed to his suicide. We may never know the truth. His inquest has yet to be held.

Behind the scenes, the pressure on the Government was starting to work. Baroness Scotland was in the US and was doing her best to show that she was actually trying to make the US ratify the treaty. She went to Washington to put pressure on Senator John Kerry, but Kerry was too busy to see her. Go Britain!

But she did start to put pressure on the Justice Department to give the men bail, and there is little doubt this was because of the embarrassment that was being felt back in the UK. That evening David Bermingham said goodbye to his children and they went to stay with their grandparents.

The following morning he left his home with his wife and drove to Croydon Police station, accompanied by some intrepid members of the British press in cars, vans and even motorcycles. The rest of the press corps were waiting for them at the police station, and as David and Emma got out of the car, they practically had to fight their way through the photographers to get to the station door. Just before he went in, David turned to the media and had one last thing to say:

'It is a very sad day, because I suspect that most of you are British and you got let down today by your own Government. Get them out.'[27]

And he went inside.

> Emma: I don't think I was there: I might have been there in body but I certainly wasn't there in mind. I came back home and I switched on the television and they were obviously rerunning what had happened in the morning, and I just thought 'Gosh,' it just didn't feel like that had been me. What I was thinking was 'this is horrible'.[28]

The extradition was carried live on all of the major television stations, one of which even had a helicopter following the police van from Croydon to Gatwick, and caught the men being loaded onto the plane, which was also full of press. On arrival some nine hours later in Houston, Texas, the men spent over an hour being processed at the US customs and immigration facility at George Bush Intercontinental Airport, put into chains and then transported by van to the Federal Court House prior to being incarcerated in the Federal Detention Centre pending a bail hearing the following day.

Unfortunately for the UK Government, one enterprising photographer managed to get a photo of the men in their hand and foot chains, and within an hour this was being beamed around all of the news wires. It was obviously too much for Blair. An urgent appeal was made to Alberto Gonzales, the US Attorney General. He sent one of his representatives to the court house, and the men were taken out of their chains and spirited away. The following day, the US Government did not oppose their bail, provided that each put up bond of $1 million, submit themselves to curfew, electronic tagging, travel only within Houston and its immediate surroundings, and an undertaking not to associate together, other than in the presence of their attorneys.

With the exception of the curfew, which has been removed, the men remain on these bail conditions today. Their trial is set for September 2007, some three years after the UK magistrate said that to try the case in the UK now would introduce unnecessary delay.

There seems little doubt that the extradition of the NatWest Three was agreed at a very early stage between the UK and US Governments. Historically, extradition has consisted very much of horse-trading, but the stakes for the Government in this case were incredibly high. They had forced through parliament on the back of the 'War Against Terror' a very contentious law which paid only lip-service to the concept of defendants' rights and due process. It would have been catastrophic for New Labour for the NatWest Three to have had their case investigated in the UK, and either for no charges to result, or for the men to have won in court. This could not be allowed to happen.

Even though the horse has well and truly bolted in his case, Bermingham continues to lobby for law change from his flat in Texas.

> Lots of other countries have built-in protections that
> oblige the extraditing country to supply prima facie
> evidence, and we've just done this super-poodle deal.
> It's an insult to poodles what we've done.
>
> **BORIS JOHNSON MP**[29]

As if to rub salt in the wounds of how pathetic the British had been in negotiating the original treaty, in 2006 the US Senate received treaties for Latvia, Estonia and Malta which all required US prosecutors to provide evidence. Not wanting to insult the good people of these fine countries, but how much more embarrassing does it get? It remains to be seen whether either Iraq or Afghanistan will negotiate extradition treaties with the US in the future, but the smart money is that if they do they will get a better deal for their people than Britain.

HOW CAN THIS AFFECT ME?

It's harder to stay out of the way of the US justice system than you might think. Because of the nature of electronic mail servers, sending an email to your friend suggesting a quick pint will probably be routed through at least one US server. By arranging an after work drink you have inadvertently entered US jurisdiction and made that meeting a potential conspiracy organised on US soil. An overzealous US prosecutor could take the email, along with a spurious allegation that you went to the pub to discuss terrorism, and get a grand jury indictment within hours. He could then request your extradition, and far from defending you against this idiotic allegation, the British Government would arrest you and put you on the next plane to the US. You could produce mountains of evidence that the nearest you came to discussing terrorism was hoping that Tottenham thrash the Arsenal next week, but a British judge would be powerless to do anything about it.

The 2003 Extradition Act has made Britain effectively the fifty-first state of the US when it comes to criminal justice.

Chapter 7

Torture

The worst thing was the sound of a woman screaming next door, which at that point I believed was my wife. An FBI agent told me, 'After 9/11, the rules changed. We have new laws, and according to them you're already convicted. The US has done with fighting wars with its hands tied behind its back.'

MOAZZAM BEGG, EX-GUANTANAMO DETAINEE¹

I know it's hard on America... destiny put you in this place in history, in this moment in time and the task is yours to do... You're not going to be alone. We'll be with you in this fight for liberty.

TONY BLAIR, TO US CONGRESS, 18 JULY 2003

As a response to the unimaginable brutality of the Second World War, both Britain and the US established a series of human-rights declarations. Central to these declarations was an absolute ban on torture, and that it could never be justified in any circumstances.

But, led once again by the US, we are blithely chopping away at the last leg we have to stand on when we condemn other nations for their use of this most inhumane of acts. The people who are suffering for it are suffering the unimaginable, and if they are released they are carefully forgotten by a Government to whom they are little more than an uncomfortable embarrassment.

Blair kindly gave Bush the British cloak of respectability and squandered the British reputation of decency and fairness. Together they sent out a message to the world: 'In the War Against Terror, torture is cool'. When Tony Blair and George Bush stood shoulder to shoulder and declared that the inmates of Guantanamo Bay were 'bad people', it gave *carte blanche* to every dictator in the world to imprison and torture dissenters without condemnation from the West. While thousands have been imprisoned illegally and tortured by the US with British support, countless more have suffered in other countries whose governments are following George Bush and Tony Blair's lead.

A BRIEF HISTORY OF TORTURE

Torture is as old as civilisation itself. Most countries have a history of it somewhere in the closet, and Britain is no exception. During the sixteenth century, as the official British religion flipped every decade, the Catholics and Protestants took it in turns to do beastly things to each other. Embarrassingly, we British seem rather proud of our history of human degradation, as today the historical sites where most of the cruelty took place are now tourist attractions. If you're ever at a loose end in the capital, check out the London Dungeon or the Tower of London, and spend money celebrating Britain's history of dishing out pain and misery for religious coercion. Do other countries rejoice in their history of barbarism in this way? We did hear that Disneyland Florida will soon open Guantanamo World, in which American Tourists put on oversize orange jumpsuits and get waterboarded by a comedy cartoon character of Dick Cheney.

International law defines torture as follows: 'Any act by which severe pain or suffering, whether physical or mental, is intentionally inflicted on a person for such purposes as obtaining from him or a third person information or a confession, punishing, or intimidating or coercing him or a third person'.[2]

We can break the reasons for torture down into three categories.

1) *Punitive torture. Severe pain or suffering intentionally inflicted on a person to punish them. Or just for the hell of it.* Criminals (and suspected criminals) are tortured under the dubious logic that if you brutalise someone enough they won't do it again, and that's only if they're lucky enough to survive. And even, say the advocates, if they die during the correction process it'll send out a message to others. The physical abuse of prisoners as a punishment was given up by most civilised countries well over a hundred years ago.

2) *Coercive torture. Severe pain or suffering intentionally inflicted on a person to make them change their minds.* These days it is political coercion that leads people into the torture cell. Anyone who voices political dissent in China, Algeria, Saudi Arabia, Chechnya, Syria, Iran (among many others)[3] is likely to be locked up by the Government and brutalised until they toe the party line. While it's easy to point the finger at these less enlightened societies, most European countries have a bloody history of coercive torture, for example Britain's religious schizophrenia of the sixteenth century.

If you lived in Spain at the turn of the fifteenth century, and were suspected of being anything less than a card-carrying Catholic, you would be at the mercy of the Spanish Inquisition. This could involve levels of pain infliction so unimaginable that even describing them would make most people sick. When the victim relented and promised to change their worshipping habits to make the pain stop, they were promptly killed, but now stood a better chance of getting into heaven.

Amnesty is a movement of ordinary people from across the world standing up for humanity and human rights, and has over a quarter of a million supporters in the UK.

3) *Extractive torture. Severe pain or suffering intentionally inflicted on a person for such purposes as obtaining information or a confession.*

People will confess to all sorts of things when they're being tortured. It doesn't take much imagination to put yourself in

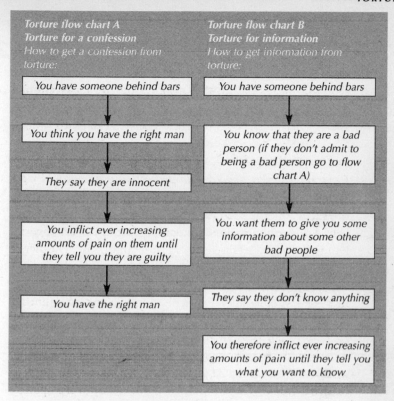

Torture flow chart A
Torture for a confession
How to get a confession from torture:

| You have someone behind bars |

↓

| You think you have the right man |

| They say they are innocent |

↓

| You inflict ever increasing amounts of pain on them until they tell you they are guilty |

↓

| You have the right man |

Torture flow chart B
Torture for information
How to get information from torture:

| You have someone behind bars |

↓

| You know that they are a bad person (if they don't admit to being a bad person go to flow chart A) |

↓

| You want them to give you some information about some other bad people |

↓

| They say they don't know anything |

↓

| You therefore inflict ever increasing amounts of pain until they tell you what you want to know |

that situation and know what your own limits would be and how you would sign up to practically anything.

KATE ALLEN, DIRECTOR, AMNESTY INTERNATIONAL UK[4]

THE END OF THE TWENTIETH CENTURY – TORTURE NEARLY DIES

It was the United States that led the world in…putting forward a new system of international law, to ensure that the horrors of the Second World War were not repeated…There were times when the US itself hasn't followed the rules, but they've

Philippe Sands is a QC and Professor of Law at University College London. In 2005 he wrote Lawless World: The Making And Breaking of Global Rules.

never before said 'We're going to shred the rules we
created because they no longer suit our interests'.

PHILIPPE SANDS QC[5]

The years following the Second World War were a high point for human rights, but the Cold War ushered in a new era of covert abuse. Both the US and Russia were guilty of instigating many atrocities over the next few decades. During the Russian occupation of Afghanistan in the 1980s civilians were systematically tortured and murdered. US soldiers committed medieval atrocities during the Vietnam War.

In 1984, Britain, the US and most other countries in the world signed the Convention against Torture. It stated very simply:

> 2.2: No exceptional circumstances whatsoever, whether a state of war or a threat of war, internal political instability or any other public emergency, may be invoked as a justification of torture.
> 3.1: No State Party shall expel, return or extradite a person to another State where there are substantial grounds for believing that he would be in danger of being subjected to torture.[6]

When Tony Blair came to power in 1997, New Labour promised a foreign policy with an 'ethical dimension'. Robin Cook, then Foreign Secretary, promised to put human rights at the top of the agenda when deciding which countries we would do business with. New Labour was going to export human rights to every corner of the globe. It seemed that we were on the way to a torture-free world. It's a pity that our 'oldest ally', with whom Britain shares a 'special relationship', would be the country that broke these fundamental protections, and led Britain down the same path.[7]

9/11 – TORTURE IS BACK ON THE MENU

The 19 hijackers who murdered just under three thousand people on 11 September 2001 also gave the Neo-conservatives an excuse to shatter the prohibition from torture.

> *A lot of the people in the Bush Administration (Mr*
> *Rumsfeld, Mr Cheney, Mr Wolfowitz) had, back in the*
> *late '90s, committed themselves to a rewriting of global*
> *rules, that they felt undermined American sovereignty,*
> *American security, American hegemonic power. So 9/11*
> *comes along and it's a wonderful opportunity to remake*
> *the rules.*

> **PHILIPPE SANDS QC**[8]

Five days after 9/11, US Vice President Dick Cheney couldn't have been clearer. The US Government needed to 'work through, sort of, the dark side'. Cheney went on, 'A lot of what needs to be done here will have to be done quietly, without any discussion, using sources and methods that are available to our intelligence agencies, if we're going to be successful. That's the world these folks operate in. And so it's going to be vital for us to use any means at our disposal, basically, to achieve our objective.'[9]

At this time that Tony Blair was an up-and-coming actor on the world stage. His one meeting with George Bush prior to 9/11 had generated the profound and historic agreement:

> Bush: 'We both use Colgate toothpaste.'

But now Blair had a chance at a starring role, and all he had to do was to agree to whatever the Bush Administration asked.

'We, therefore, here in Britain stand shoulder to shoulder with our American friends in this hour of tragedy, and we, like them, will not rest until this evil is driven from our world.'

Blair pledged allegiance to the Bush Administration, and gave full British support in the 'War Against Terror' – whatever the tactics.

> *I think Tony personally got a taste for the world stage at*
> *that point, and loved it, and loved being the only leader*
> *in the world that could pick up the phone to the*
> *President of the US.*

> **CLARE SHORT**

In return for the limelight, Blair had promised British support on 'modernising' the rules of torture.

Individuals in Washington were already concocting a scheme which would allow the US to take prisoners and remove them from all constraints of legal protection. So the idea was to find a place outside the US, so that the US constitutional protection didn't apply, in which foreigners could be held, detained and questioned with intrusive new rules of interrogation.

Step 1: Find a place to do it.

Step 2: Determine unilaterally, as President Bush did in January 2002, that the detainees are not entitled to any rights under the Geneva Conventions on the treatment of prisoners of war.

Step 3: Bring the detainees in and subject them to a legal black hole.

PHILIPPE SANDS QC[10]

Condoleezza Rice, known as Condi to her friends and anyone else that doesn't know how to spell Condoleezza, is the Secretary of State and the friendly face of the Republican Party.

Jack Straw is a Labour politician and, of course, a lawyer. In 1966 he was branded a 'troublemaker... acting with malice aforethought' by the Foreign Office, and in 1969 he was considered enough of a security risk to warrant an MI5 file. This does not seem to have stopped him running both the Home and Foreign Offices. It is believed that he was removed from his position in the Foreign Office at the request of the US for stating that it would be 'nuts' to bomb Iran.

The Bush Administration and New Labour continually argued that torture does not take place.

The United States does not permit, tolerate, or condone torture under any circumstances.

CONDOLEEZZA RICE, US SECRETARY OF STATE[11]

The British Government does not support torture in any circumstances. Full stop. We do not support the obtaining of intelligence by torture, or its use.

JACK STRAW[12]

These denials are maintained through a classic piece of double-speak. Lawyers were brought in to change what the word 'torture' actually meant.

THE DOUBLESPEAK OF TORTURE

The universally accepted definition of 'torture' is:

> *Any act by which severe pain or suffering, whether physical or mental, is intentionally inflicted on a person.*
>
> **CONVENTION AGAINST TORTURE 1984**[13]

Months after 9/11, in January 2002, a series of memos were sent to the White House that attempted to redefine as the word as:

> *Severe pain that must be equivalent in intensity to the pain accompanying serious physical injury, such as organ failure, impairment of bodily function, or even death.*[14]

When pushed to define 'severe pain', the lawyers came back with:

> *to the level of death, organ failure, or the permanent impairment of a significant body function.'*
>
> **JUSTICE DEPARTMENT MEMO TO WHITE HOUSE COUNSEL ALBERTO GONZALES**[15]

For a cruel or inhuman psychological technique to rise to the level of mental torture, the Justice Department argued, the psychological harm must last 'months or even years'.

According to the Bush Administration, as long as your heart was still beating then you hadn't been tortured. This is a familiar tactic to anyone who has read *Through The Looking Glass* by Lewis Carroll.

Being lawyers, Tony Blair and Jack Straw have always accepted the assurances that the US doesn't use torture based on this absurd new meaning.

THE US TAKES OFF THE GLOVES– BRITAIN HOLDS THEM

The Bush Administration embarked on a bloodthirsty campaign of revenge against… well, anyone who was unfortunate enough to get in their way. This involved all three forms of torture: punitive, coercive and extractive, and manifested itself in two ways. First the US set up a series of torture camps around the world where they could do what they wanted with impunity. The three best known were Bagram airbase in Afghanistan, Abu Ghraib in Iraq and Guantanamo Bay in Cuba. Second, the CIA, through its programme of 'Extraordinary Rendition', flew suspects around the globe to secret locations in countries that practise torture, known as black sites.

US TORTURE CAMPS

The best person to tell us what it's like in a US torture camp is someone who's been to two of them, Moazzam Begg.

I received a knock on the door, twelve o' clock at night on 31 January 2002. And I opened the door to face several un-uniformed… officers perhaps, who pointed a gun at me, pointed tasers, electric stun guns, pushed me into the front room of where I was living, put a hood over my head. Just before the head was covered, I saw them walking towards my room, where the children had been sleeping, and I told them not to go in. After that they pushed me down to the ground, shackled my hands behind my back, shackled my legs and physically carried me off into the back of the vehicle.[16]

188

He was kidnapped from his home in Islamabad, Pakistan, illegally imprisoned, tortured, taken to Bagram airbase and eventually to Guantanamo Bay. Three years later, on 25 January 2005, he landed back in the UK at RAF Northholt and was released without charge.

Moazzam was born and brought up in Birmingham, where his family had settled after leaving India and Pakistan. He opened an Islamic bookshop back in Birmingham, where he ran discussion groups, raised funds for Islamic charities and made translations from Arabic.

As practising Muslims, Moazzam and his wife Zaynab wanted to experience living in an Islamic society. With all the work he had already done for humanitarian causes, it was a logical, if brave, decision to move to Afghanistan with their children to work in schools and help dig wells in the drought-stricken parts of the north-west. Unfortunately for them, they chose to go in the summer of 2001. It wasn't until several days after 9/11 that they discovered exactly what had happened in New York and Washington. During October, as the likelihood of the US bombing Afghanistan increased, they decided to leave and go to Islamabad, where they thought they would be safer. Three months after arriving, on the last day of January, Moazzam was kidnapped.

He believes he was targeted for abduction because he had evacuated to Pakistan from Afghanistan and wasn't known locally. The Americans were offering a bounty of $5000 per head for suspects, and it's easy to see why someone might have pointed the finger at him: 'In places like Pakistan, where poverty is rife, it's easy. If you're offering somebody $5000, then they're set for the next decade or so.'

He was held in a house in Islamabad for a couple of weeks. His guards were Pakistanis, but those who had seized him were Americans. When the Americans were out of earshot, he was able to speak to the guards in Urdu. It was clear that they were acting under American orders, and felt uncomfortable about doing so. He was interrogated four times, mostly about what he was doing in Afghanistan and his links to Muslim organisations.

'On the first occasion, the British intelligence were present.' He asked them to contact the British consulate and get him a lawyer. They refused. It was clear that he wasn't giving them the information they wanted. 'I was questioned twice by American intelligence, and then I was shipped off to Kandahar.'

Kandahar was the US military holding base for detainees who had been captured in the 'War Against Terror' in Afghanistan. 'I was held there for about six weeks, and I think that was probably some of the worst treatment. Particularly the processing part, where we were stripped naked using knives to cut off our clothes... I was spat at, sworn at, kicked, punched, dragged around naked, photographed. There were dogs barking at us. And then I watched the same humiliating process taking place with the other detainees. And the ridiculous questions that I was asked initially, when I was brought in, were standard. I heard them actually being asked of the other detainees. "When was the last time you saw Osama Bin Laden?" "When was the last time you saw Mullah Omar?" These were the questions they were asking everybody.'

Unlike in Islamabad, in Kandahar it was clear who was holding him. 'It seemed rather bizarre, actually, these people in FBI caps, with their casual clothing, questioning me. I was shivering because it was in the middle of the winter; I was naked and shackled and they were asking me about when was the last time I saw Osama Bin Laden. When he realised, this particular interrogator, that I was from England, he started talking to me about Shakespeare.'

Early on in Kandahar, it became clear that the prisoners were in legal limbo. The constant fudging by the US about their status, and their eventual designation as 'enemy combatants', began there. This phrase is meaningless in international law.

> *You're either a warrior, subject to the rules of war and armed conflict, or you are a criminal subject to the rules of criminal justice. There's no middle ground, and there's no legal black hole.*
>
> **PHILIPPE SANDS QC**[17]

At no point was he charged with an offence, or presented with evidence against him, so he could not be considered a criminal. The other alternative, to call them prisoners of war, was clearly considered and then rejected. 'We were held and that's all that mattered. We were initially given enemy prisoner-of-war cards, but they were taken away soon after, because that meant that we would have prisoner-of-war rights.'

After processing, the prisoners were held in pens in a large barn, brightly illuminated day and night. They were not allowed to move or talk to people. He was interrogated several times by the Americans, and also by an MI5 agent. Moazzam was unable to tell them any more than they already knew. The MI5 agent told him that the Americans were in charge and that MI5 were there as guests.

Moazzam was held there for six weeks, until he was moved to Bagram. On arrival, there was the same humiliating processing procedure, involving full body cavity searches and being photographed naked. Again the prisoners were shackled and put in cells behind concertina wire, sometimes six to a cell. Halved oil drums were used as toilets, and only emptied every few days. Water was rationed to two small bottles a day for drinking, and cold water for washing once a week.

The interrogations continued, and the Americans used their now-infamous 'enhanced questioning techniques' on Moazzam. These included 'being hogtied, having my hands tied behind my back, having a hood placed over my head, being kicked and punched and sworn at, spat at.'

They started to question Moazzam about files they had found on his laptop, which they had seized from his house in Islamabad. 'On that laptop, in my temporary internet files, were stored all sorts of pictures from the websites that I visit. My home page is the BBC World Service and so it happened that, amongst the pictures they printed off my hard disk to show me, were pictures of the Pope, a BBC reporter, a camel spider, a man on the beach, and so on. They picked up on the picture of the Pope. "Why have you got a picture of the Pope on your hard disk? Are you planning something against him?" This was the ludicrous way in which they tried to trump up some sort of plot that I may have been involved in.'

If the questioning was laughable, the threats certainly weren't. 'They threatened to break my fingers and to have me sent to Egypt or Syria for further torture; to be raped, to be electrocuted.'

The degrading treatment, beatings and fruitless interrogations were not the worst of Bagram for Moazzam. 'During my time there, I saw some of the worst ever atrocities and abuses that I've seen in incarceration, which culminated in the deaths of two detainees, which I witnessed.' One was a young Afghan who had tried to escape; two American guards jumped on him and beat him to death. Later Moazzam found out that he had been due to be released in a few weeks.

The turnover at Bagram was high; there were new arrivals every week, and planeloads of people being taken on to Guantanamo Bay. The name was well known among the detainees, and in January 2003, a year after his capture, Moazzam learned that he too was destined for Cuba: 'I was actually almost looking forward to it because I was told that this will be the beginning of an end.'

Hooded and shackled, fitted with earmuffs, goggles, facemasks and nappies, the detainees were loaded up onto the plane for the two-day flight to Cuba, during which he passed out. His next memory is of being processed at Camp Echo, or Eskimo as it was called then, and being issued with the trademark orange jumpsuit. He was then taken to a new cell, even smaller than the dog kennel he had got used to in Bagram. And he was alone. 'I was held in solitary confinement, in a tiny little cell measuring 8 feet by 6 feet, for approximately twenty months.'

The day after Moazzam arrived in Guantanamo Bay, FBI interrogators brought a typed confession that they wanted him to sign. They were asking him to confess to being a member of al-Qaeda, and to knowing several of its key figures. Moazzam was allowed to make some corrections and changes, but eventually agreed to sign.

Moazzam's story is similar to that of many of the detainees at Bagram and Guantanamo: Muslim men brought by US intelligence with British support, 'rendered' around the world and finally deposited in the legal black hole that is Guantanamo Bay. To compare the Guantanamo military tribunals to a kangaroo court would be an insult to kangaroos.

> *So the tribunals that were originally proposed in November 2001 were completely inconsistent with the system of rules the US had set in place since the Second World War. Individuals would not have access to the evidence on the basis of which they were being criminally prosecuted, and secondly the President would effectively be judge and jury in these proceedings, as well as prosecutor, because ultimately the President would decide who sat on these tribunals.*
>
> **PHILIPPE SANDS QC**[18]

> *I am the decider!*
>
> **GEORGE W. BUSH**[19]

George W. Bush as judge, jury and prosecutor? Go for the kangaroo any day of the week.

The great irony is that some of the people imprisoned in Guantanamo Bay will have committed serious crimes, and could be a threat to Britain and America. But as none of the detainees has been charged or brought before a court there is no way of determining who is innocent and who is guilty. The US has declared them all guilty and proved it through confessions extracted under torture.

BLAIR STANDS BY HIS MAN

> *The only thing necessary for the triumph of evil is for good men to do nothing.*
>
> **EDMUND BURKE**

Throughout Moazzam's ordeal, Blair continued to give the Bush Administration Britain's support on Guantanamo Bay, while every other civilised country in the world condemned it.[20] In the summer of 2003, news of the treatment of prisoners in Guantanamo came to light. As Bush was also facing some tough questions on Iraq, Blair jumped on the next plane to Washington.

17 JULY 2003 PRESS CONFERENCE

President Bush starts off by making it clear that when it comes to the 'War Against Terror', Britain is firmly alongside the US. 'From the outset, the Prime Minister and I have understood that we are allies in this war – a war requiring great effort and patience and fortitude. The British and American peoples will hold firm once again, and we will prevail.'[21] Look everyone, the Brits are with us! They wouldn't do anything nasty, would they?

Tony Blair then dutifully lavished praise on Bush: 'I would like to pay tribute to your leadership in these difficult times. Because ever since September 11, the task of leadership has been an arduous one, and I believe that you have fulfilled it with tremendous conviction, determination and courage.' Blair is then restrained from kneeling down in front of Bush.

Bush is then asked about whether or not the people at Guantanamo will be getting justice, and replies, 'No, the only thing I know for certain is that these are bad people, and we look forward to working closely with the Blair Government to deal with the issue'. This phrase completely subverts the rule of law. Not one person in Guantanamo Bay had been charged at this point, but the President has decided they are all guilty. And Bush specifically uses Blair to ram this point home.

Blair then jumps in to back him up: 'But I think, again, it's important just to realise the context in which all this arises ... and the context was a situation in which the al-Qaeda and the Taliban were operating together in Afghanistan against American and British forces.'

Bush then thanks Blair for his crucial public support: 'Good job. Thank you. Appreciate your country.'

By allowing Bush to continue with torture, Blair is himself committing a crime.

> *There's footage of President Bush speaking about the*
> *importance of getting the right information out of*
> *individuals he characterised as criminals at*
> *Guantanamo, and in many of those shots Mr Blair is*
> *standing right beside him, silent. In international law*
> *that's not good enough. Once credible information*
> *emerges, in relation to abuse or standards of treatment*
> *falling below international standards, it is necessary for*
> *the Government to act to satisfy itself that abuse is not*
> *taking place.*
>
> *PHILIPPE SANDS[22]*

While Blair was sanitising the image of Guantanamo Bay, Moazzam Begg and other British citizens were still being held there.

One day, Moazzam was shackled, taken out of his cell and spent seven hours lying on the floor of a room. Eventually, one of the Foreign Office men turned up. The good news was that he was now eligible for a military commission. 'They said that if I pleaded guilty to a crime, which hadn't been defined at this point, then I would have access to the law. I would have access to a court. It's bizarre. They said until you actually agree to plead guilty, you won't be given access to a lawyer.'[23]

> *I didn't believe that America would do something like*
> *this. I was afraid that I'd be sent to Egypt and Egypt*
> *would do it. Or perhaps, you know, they might send me*
> *to Syria. And often the Americans would say well, you*
> *know, you're treated here a lot better than you are if you*
> *would've been taken in custody by a Third World*
> *country. But that's such a dangerous path to follow*
> *because what they're saying is that they're on a par with*
> *some of these Third World countries by using these*
> *methods.*

Meanwhile human-rights lawyers Gareth Peirce and Clive Stafford Smith, along with relentless campaigning by Moazzam's father and Zaynab, had raised the profile of the British detainees

Clive Stafford Smith is a lawyer who has spent twenty-five years fighting against the death penalty in the US. More recently Clive was the first British lawyer to be admitted to Guantanamo to represent several of the inmates.

in Guantanamo. Law lords including Lord Steyn added weight to the campaign.

Finally, Moazzam was visited by Clive Stafford Smith, who advised him that the best way to make things happen was to embarrass the Americans. He took detailed notes and produced a thirty-page document on all the degrading treatment, humiliation and torture that Moazzam had been through. He also told him that he would soon be going home. It was the good news he hardly dared believe in.

The embarrassment finally worked, and Bush agreed to let the British citizens go home. On 25 January 2005, Moazzam landed back in England. After thinking of nothing but release for three years, it was a strangely underwhelming experience. 'I wasn't as elated as I had imagined because I wasn't stepping off the plane and going straight home or into the open arms of my family. It was into Paddington Green police station, where I was given some peripheral questioning. I met Gareth Peirce. She was the first friendly face that I saw in all these years. And eventually, when I was released, I met my father, my brother, my wife, my children for the first time in all these years. It wasn't this emotional explosion or volcano of emotion when I met them. It was a sort of very dignified, simple affair. Hugs and embraces. They had more tears in their eyes than I did. I think I'd just become a little distant after all that solitude.'

After a period of adjustment, Moazzam got on with his life. He was never charged with any offence, either as a criminal or as a prisoner of war, much less as an 'enemy combatant', so he used this phrase as the title of the book that he has written about his experiences. Even though the detention and abuse was at the hands of the Americans, he feels that the British intelligence services, in their complicity, were equally to blame. 'I always maintained the myth in my mind that the Brits will never stoop as low as the Americans. The Brits are always there coming in to save the day. It's hard for me to accept because I feel – despite all of what's taken place – I am British. I began to question that. It seemed to me that, for every little thing that the Americans felt they were justified in doing, the Brits were there, behind them, patting them on the back.' While Moazzam believes the British are as guilty as the Americans in the practice of torture, the two countries differ in one respect. The US doesn't allow the torture of its own citizens. It seems British citizens enjoy no such favours.

As more news of what was going on inside Guantanamo leaked out, the world unanimously condemned what was going on.

Guantanamo Bay is a byword for abuse.

KATE ALLEN[24]

A Gulag of our times.

AMNESTY INTERNATIONAL[25]

a shocking affront to the principles of democracy

LORD FALCONER[26]

in breach of every fundamental legal principle and directly at odds with the very values the War on Terror purports to defend

EARLY DAY MOTIONS, HOUSE OF COMMONS[27]

unacceptable in terms of human rights

MARGARET BECKETT[28]

America's idea of what is torture is not the same as ours and does not appear to coincide with that of most civilised nations.

MR JUSTICE COLLINS[29]

It is time, in my view, it should close.

LORD GOLDSMITH, ATTORNEY GENERAL[30]

an international disgrace

GASPAR LLAMAZARES, SPANISH POLITICIAN[31]

> *Waterboarding is a torture technique which simulates the sensation of drowning. This is sometimes in the form of dunking a person headfirst in water. Another way of waterboarding is to strap a person to a board, wrap their face with cloth or cellophane and then pour water into their mouth. The person believes they are being killed so it is a form of mock suicide which is illegal under international law.*

Well, almost unanimously.

I don't think the United States is being unreasonable.

TONY BLAIR[32]

Tony Blair has loyally either defended it or avoided talking about it – even after the Bush Administration actually admitted that torture is taking place:

US radio host: 'Would you agree that waterboarding is a no-brainer?'

Dick Cheney (US Vice President): 'It's a no-brainer for me'.[33]

After massive domestic and international pressure to get Guantanamo shut down, in 2006 Blair shifted his language slightly, and daringly called it an 'anomaly'. After extensive research, this is the only time that this word has been used to describe a torture camp. The dictionary definition of anomaly is:

Deviation (better or not) compared to what is expected.

So while it is different to normality, it isn't necessarily a bad thing. Whenever Blair is questioned about Guantanamo he repeats this word over and over again and refuses point-blank to condemn it.

Thanks to his family's protests and campaigning, Moazzam was returned home to them, and all the British citizens were eventually released. But several long-term British residents are still in Guantanamo Bay, and are unlikely to be released any time soon. The British Government, which at one stage gave these people political asylum and protection, has now abandoned them.

OMAR DEGHAYES

Omar's story starts back in Libya. His father, Amer, was a leading Libyan trade unionist and lawyer. He was asked by the Gaddafi Government to spy on people he knew who had been politically active in the past. He refused to co-operate, knowing that he could be killed for it. He was given a period of time to think about it. He still refused, and was picked up by the Libyan secret police. After three days, his family was told he had committed suicide in prison. Amnesty International investigated his death and produced a report with evidence showing he had been tortured and murdered.

After his death, Amer's wife Zohra and her sons Abu bakr, Omar and Taher, and daughter Amani were terrified. People who had been friends of the family were frightened to associate with them. As soon as they could they fled the country and settled in Sussex, near Brighton. They had friends in the area, and it seemed a natural choice. They were granted refugee status in 1987 and settled into life in Britain. The brothers were close as they grew up, Abu bakr said: 'We went to mosque together and talked about religion. Omar was very argumentative and would always go to books and bring me back quotations that proved his side was right.'[34] Omar studied law at the University of Wolverhampton, and his ambition was to become a human-rights lawyer. He sat his exams, but because he didn't pass them all first time he decided to take a bit of time off to go travelling before returning to study.

The rest of the Deghayes family applied for and were granted British citizenship, though Omar hadn't completed his application before he went travelling. He was called for an interview at the Home Office, but he missed it because he had already left the UK. Because he has been in American prisons for nearly five years now, he has not been able to renew his refugee status in the UK either. Missing that interview with the Home Office might still cost him his life.

On his travels, Omar visited Malaysia, India, Pakistan and finally Afghanistan. While there he fell in love, got married and had a baby. Towards the end of 2001, when Suleiman was just a few months old, the US-led bombing of Afghanistan began, and Omar and his wife fled to Lahore in Pakistan to safety. They planned to return to the UK as soon as possible.

This part of Omar's story is remarkably like Moazzam Begg's. He was arrested in Pakistan, after a tip-off by local bounty hunters, and taken to the detention centre at Bagram in Afghanistan.

Like Moazzam, Omar has said that the abuse and torture he suffered there was the worst of all the places he has been held. He likened it to footage he had seen of Nazi concentration camps. He was locked in a box with very little air for prolonged periods, and guards had forced petrol and benzene up the anuses of prisoners, causing horrible burns.

In September 2002 he was transferred to Guantanamo Bay. Here, Omar believes he has been singled out for particularly brutal treatment because of his legal training. Because he is aware of his rights under the Geneva Conventions, he has been vocal in his criticism of the abuse he has suffered. He has been made to wear a special jumpsuit reserved for troublemakers. When he challenged the guards, he was repeatedly sprayed in the face with pepper spray, and one guard gouged at his right eyeball with his finger-nails. Omar has always had a weak right eye; when he was a child he was taken to Switzerland frequently for treatment. He is now completely blind in that eye; it has glazed over and become milky-white.

Early on, the British Government washed its hands of Omar and the other British residents still held in Guantanamo. The Government has argued that since they are not British citizens, there is nothing they can do.

They should ask for help from their own governments.

GEOFF HOON[35]

We have met Amani, Omar's sister, several times over the past year as she's been campaigning to the Government for his release, but she has been routinely turned away.

> *The Foreign Office has been quite disgraceful throughout*
> *the detention. Initially, they used to write to us in*
> *standardised letters saying, 'We should seek help from*
> *the Libyan Government because he's not British'.*
>
> **AMANI DEGHAYES**

Though he has been interrogated many times by the CIA, FBI and MI5, the most worrying development was when the CIA flew in the Libyan secret police from Tripoli to pile on the pressure. In 2004, Libyan intelligence officials interrogated and threatened Omar. Amani learned that 'these Libyan officials told him that "Your problem is not with the Americans; your problem is with us, and if you return to us we'll torture you and kill you".'

According to their obligations under the absolute ban on torture,[36] neither the US nor Britain can deport anyone to a country where they believe they will be tortured. This, at least in theory, should protect Omar from being returned to Libya. But to sidestep their obligations to protect people from torture the UK Government has signed a memorandum of understanding with Libya. This is an agreement that if certain individuals are returned to a country the Libyan Government agrees not to torture them. New Labour has signed these with several countries with long and detailed histories of human-rights abuses, including Algeria, Syria and Egypt.

> *These countries have promised the international*
> *community that they will torture nobody, and our reports*
> *year after year show that they systematically and routinely*
> *use torture. The British Government thinks that by getting*
> *the signature of those governments saying that they won't*
> *torture a particular individual. It's an absolute nonsense to*
> *think that's worth the paper that it is written on.*
>
> **KATE ALLEN**[37]

Taking Britain's lead, Sweden has also started signing up to these agreements. A recent case showed just how meaningless the assurances are:

> The Swedish Government sent back an individual to
> Egypt. They were allowed to make visits to monitor the
> assurances that they had received from the Egyptian
> Government, and they visited him in prison and he
> said, 'I've been tortured'. What happens in that
> situation? The memorandum, the assurances which
> you've received, have become worthless. The Egyptian
> Government is not going to give this individual back
> and, you know, the diplomats walk away and wring
> their hands. You can't run the risk that these
> individuals will be sent back.
>
> **ERIC METCALFE, JUSTICE**

In Amani's opinion, the memorandum is another nail in Omar's coffin. 'Worse still, the human-rights organisation in Libya, which is run by the son of Gaddafi, is going to oversee that such torture doesn't occur. It's just a complete joke.'

> I think that Tony Blair's approach to Guantanamo is
> shocking actually. People held without charge, without
> due process, apparently indefinitely, with the Prime
> Minister apparently turning a blind eye to the whole
> thing, and not taking active steps to ensure their
> minimum rights under international law are maintained.
> I think that says a lot about the man.
>
> **PHILIPPE SANDS**[38]

Suicide attempts are common at Guantanamo, and three detainees killed themselves in June 2006. The Bush Administration was devastated by this news, and offered its sincerest condolences to the families:

> There were means and methods for protestation, and
> certainly taking their own lives was not necessary. But it
> certainly is a good PR move to draw attention.
>
> **DEPUTY ASSISTANT SECRETARY OF STATE COLEEN GRAFFY**[39]

Believe it or not, Coleen Graffy's job description is to find ways to improve the image of the US in the Arab world.

Far from being shut down, Guantanamo continues to flourish. Halliburton (Dick Cheney's old company) recently won a thirty-million-dollar contract to build a brand spanking new jail.[40] Tony Blair has always craved a place in the history books, and he will now have it, as the British Prime Minister who helped the Bush Administration build torture camps.

ABU GHRAIB – TORTURE GOES PUBLIC

In April 2004 the CBS news programme *60 Minutes* ran a report that showed a series of photographs from the US-controlled military prison of Abu Ghraib. The photos showed US military personnel putting Iraqi detainees through humiliating and disgusting ordeals that clearly constituted torture by any sane definition of the word.

A handful of low-ranking US soldiers were either discharged or given small prison terms.[41]

> *There's been of course a big effort to hang out to dry people who are much lower down the food chain, but I think ultimately it will become clear that the decisions reached right to the top.*

> **PHILIPPE SANDS[42]**

And what of Tony Blair and New Labour when this scandal broke? Well Blair had actually been told about the widespread torture in Iraq months before the photos were made public, but did nothing. Ann Clwyd, the Prime Minister's Special Envoy on Human Rights in Iraq, had a meeting with Iraqi Minister Abdel Bassan Turki in September 2003, two months before the worst abuses took place. Turki made it clear that there were increasing reports of abuses in Iraqi prisons. Clwyd came back to London and raised concerns with Tony Blair personally at a meeting on 15 October 2003. Blair did nothing, and the worst acts at Abu

Ghraib took place in November and December 2003, *after* this warning.[43]

But the word was out. Faced with photographic evidence that the US was routinely torturing prisoners, a change of tactics was called for. A new plan was put into action by the US to allow its torture spree to continue, and this plan would need the help of its friend and ally: Great Britain.

EXTRAORDINARY RENDITION – BRITAIN JOINS IN THE FUN

During 2005 evidence had begun to leak out that Britain was neck deep in the Bush Administration's torture tactics.

'Ordinary Rendition' had been going on for some time. The authorities would smuggle people back to the US to face justice.

> Rendition had been going on for decades back to the nineteenth century, but that always involved in the old style of Rendition bringing people back to a courtroom to go before a judge and jury to face charges in public.
>
> **STEPHEN GREY, AUTHOR, GHOST PLANE**

Extraordinary Rendition is the exact opposite, as it involves flying people to countries other than the US that openly practise torture. The CIA uses Gulfstream jets to deposit people in secret locations in countries like Algeria, Egypt, Syria and Uzbekistan. They are handed over to the local authorities with a list of questions. The suspect is then tortured and the answers are handed back to the CIA. The benefits to the countries themselves are obvious:

> The Egyptians were only too glad to have all these dissidents sent back to them. And in return many of these countries got, sort of, diplomatic support, got money and they got good intelligence about people who were against their regime.
>
> **STEPHEN GREY**

Stephen Grey was one of the first people to break the Extraordinary Rendition story.

> I used the flight logs of CIA planes and found a way of
> tracing the CIA planes around the world and was able
> to identify the CIA's fleet and show that the stories
> they were telling (the few who were released or could
> get to see a lawyer) were exactly right. There really
> were flights into Egypt, there were flights into
> Uzbekistan, flights into Morocco that matched exactly
> what these prisoners were saying.

The logs that Stephen had were secret, and not available to the
prisoners, so they could not have made up the stories to match
the logs.

The problem for the CIA was that it's quite a long trip to the
countries that offer discreet and economical torture services.
Passing through European airspace, these CIA
flights need to refuel on the way.

During 2005, substantial evidence came to
light that CIA torture flights had not only
passed through British airspace but had used
UK airports to refuel.[44] The Bush Administration
itself admitted in late 2005 that it was using
Extraordinary Rendition, and that European
governments were involved. This put New
Labour in a tight spot: under international law,
flying people from a jurisdiction that doesn't
torture to one that does is completely illegal.
Not only that, but any government who fac-
ilitates this is as culpable as the torturers
themselves.

As soon as this evidence came to light, Blair
was challenged in the House of Commons:

> Charles Kennedy (then Liberal Democrat
> leader): To what extent... have the
> Government co-operated in the transport

Torture techniques

Syria
the German Chair,
which is designed
to stretch a
prisoner's spine, in
some cases to
breaking point

Uzbekistan
boiling prisoners
alive

Egypt
electric shock
treatment

Morocco
cutting people up
with broken
bottles

America has
rendered to all these
countries.

*of terrorist suspects to Afghanistan and elsewhere,
apparently for torture purposes?*

*Tony Blair: First, let me draw a very clear distinction
indeed between the idea of suspects being taken from
one country to another and any sense whatever that
ourselves, the United States or anyone condones the
use of torture. Torture cannot be justified in any set of
circumstances at all. The practice of Rendition as
described by Secretary of State Condoleezza Rice has
been American policy for many years… However, it
must be applied in accordance with international
conventions, and I accept entirely Secretary of State
Rice's assurance that it has been.*

Blair, clinging to the denials by the Bush Administration, using
the lawyers' new definition of what constitutes torture.

*Mr Kennedy: Given that assurance, can the Prime
Minister therefore explain why the published
evidence shows that almost four hundred flights have
passed through 18 British airports in the period of
concern? When was he as Prime Minister first made
aware of that policy, and when did he approve it?*

*Mr Blair: In respect of airports, I do not know what the
right honourable gentleman is referring to.[45]*

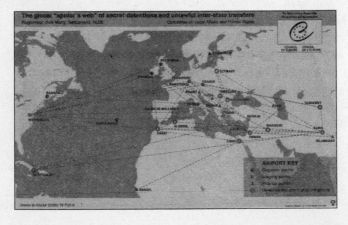

Rather than actually answer the question, Blair just pretends he doesn't know what airports are. This is political equivalent of sticking your fingers in your ears and going, 'La la la, I can't hear you!'

> *When you're the prime minister of a country, you've got a positive duty to find out what's going on and to satisfy yourself that there's no wrongdoing. It is simply not good enough to bury your head in the sand and say you don't know.*
>
> **PHILIPPE SANDS[46]**

At a press conference in Downing Street a few days later, he was even more clear-cut.

> *Question: Amnesty International, a number of politicians in the House of Commons have come up and furnished you with flight details and asked for an inquiry. Given that you are concerned that if it is illegal you would want to stop it, should you not find out whether it is illegal?*
> *Mr Blair: I have absolutely no evidence to suggest that anything illegal has been happening here at all, and I am not going to start ordering inquiries into this, that and the next thing when I have got no evidence to show whether this is right or not. And I honestly, it is like all this stuff about camps in Europe or something, I don't know, I have never heard of such a thing, I can't tell you whether such a thing exists.[47]*

Blair has in fact been given a mass of evidence from Amnesty International that points towards British complicity.

> *There is so much evidence that planes have used the UK in the process of Rendition, and we really want to see a proper public enquiry into that.*
>
> **KATE ALLEN[48]**

We had a meeting with Geoff Hoon (Minister for Europe) to discuss whether he wanted to appear in the film (he refused). We discussed the Rendition issue with him and asked him why the Government refused to investigate the mass of evidence it had been provided by Amnesty International. He said there wasn't any evidence, and called Amnesty 'crackpots'.

When Constitutional Affairs Minister Harriet Harman was asked whether the UK was complicit in torture flights, she set the record straight: 'I think if we didn't know about it we wouldn't know whether we didn't know about it'.[49] Clearly New Labour have been taking lessons in clarity from Donald Rumsfeld.

A European parliament investigation also handed over a report to the British Government which contained detailed evidence that Extraordinary Rendition had been taking place. Baroness Ludford and her team took dozens of statements from torture victims which matched exactly to the CIA flight logs that the witnesses could not have had access to.

> I think we do have to be seriously troubled by what appears to have taken place, both by the British Government and up to a dozen other European governments, there does seem to have been some systemic failure for Europe to live up to its human-rights commitments and aspirations.
>
> **BARONESS SARAH LUDFORD MEP**

Aside from the criminal charges Blair and other members of New Labour may face for the invasion of Iraq, there is another case for their refusal to investigate torture flights.

> If evidence emerges to show that the PM knew, or should have known, that this type of activity was going on, then he is open to the possibility of criminal charge for complicity in torture.
>
> **PHILIPPE SANDS**[50]

Let no one fault Blair's devotion to the Bush Administration if he's prepared to go to jail to defend them. The irony is that even though Blair may find himself in chokey in a few years, Bush will never see the inside of an International Criminal Court. Great Britain, along with practically every country in the world, is a signatory to the International Criminal Court in The Hague, which outlaws torture and complicity in torture. By not ordering a full enquiry, Blair has made himself open to prosecution. George Bush is off the hook, as the US refused to sign up to the court. Incidentally, the only other leader who refused to sign up to the International Criminal Court was Saddam Hussein.[51]

How many people have suffered as a result of this practice?

> There are official figures for the number of people
> arrested; there were more than ten thousand processed
> in Afghanistan and barely seven hundred in
> Guantanamo. So the difference is the people that have
> gone missing.
>
> **STEPHEN GREY**

The practice still continues to this day.

> It's wrong because of what it does to the victim of torture,
> to the torturer and to wider society. It's also desperately
> counter-productive; if there are people who think that
> Western democracy or democracy is hypocritical, is anti
> people of certain religions, this is the way to prove it. You
> cannot talk about democratic values, you cannot say that
> you want to spread them round the globe if the means of
> spreading them is torture.
>
> **SHAMI CHAKRABARTI**[52]

BRINGING TORTURE HOME

New Labour has signed up to the Bush Administration's belief that information extracted under torture can 'save lives'.

> *The right to be protected from torture and ill-treatment*
> *must be considered side by side with the right to be*
> *protected from the death and destruction caused by*
> *indiscriminate terrorism.*
>
> *The view of my Government is that this balance is*
> *not right for the circumstances which we now face –*
> *circumstances very different from those faced by the*
> *founding fathers of the European Convention on*
> *Human Rights.*
>
> CHARLES CLARKE, 7 SEPTEMBER 2005[53]

Yet again New Labour trying to convince us that we are in a more dangerous situation now than we were in the 1940s, when these declarations on human rights were agreed. Not only does it show how they will twist history to the point of barefaced lying, but it shows contempt for the public who elected them.

TORTURE AS EVIDENCE

For hundreds of years, evidence that is likely to have come from torture has been inadmissible in a British court. One of the first acts of the long parliament in 1640 was to abolish the Court of Star Chamber, where torture evidence had been received, and later that year the last torture warrant in our history was issued. Unsurprisingly, the British Home Secretary that tried to change this was David Blunkett, as part of the Government's attempts to deport the Belmarsh detainees back to Algeria where, ironically, they were likely to face torture themselves.

In eight of the deportations the Government wanted to use evidence that had clearly come from a torture cell. The Home Office spent public money concocting an argument that torture evidence was admissible because no British officers were in the room. They went on to argue that Britain was under no obligation even to *ask* if evidence had come from torture, and won in the Court of Appeal in 2004. Amnesty International were so appalled that Britain was openly advocating torture that it appealed the decision to the House Of Lords.

The Law Lords were equally horrified at the idea, and ruled unanimously against New Labour.[54] Lord Bingham of Cornhill, the former Lord Chief Justice who headed the panel, said English law had regarded 'torture and its fruits' with abhorrence for more than five hundred years.

> The principles of the common law, standing alone, in my opinion compel the exclusion of third-party torture evidence as unreliable, unfair, offensive to ordinary standards of humanity and decency.
>
> **LORD BINGHAM**[55]

TORTURE AS INTELLIGENCE

While the Government lost the fight to bring torture into the courtroom, it has succeeded in giving it value as intelligence.

> And so we've now got a debate about whether it is desirable or possible to use torture, and the Americans are slowly working up [that] actually torture works. They're getting the public to be anaesthetised to that idea. It's the ticking bomb argument, and I don't know of any cases where the ticking bomb has been stopped by the use of torture.
>
> **MICHAEL MANSFIELD QC**[56]

While Moazzam Begg was being interrogated in Bagram, he discovered just how dangerous torture 'intelligence' can be:

> And they said also that the senior, most high-ranking member of Al-Qaeda that they had in custody to date, at that point, had been in the very room where I'd been and, according to what the interrogator said, had been 'playing games', so they sent him to Egypt, and that he told his whole story there within hours. Now the

> *interesting thing I learnt about this was that this was the*
> *very confession that was used to say that there was a*
> *tangible link between al-Qaeda and Saddam Hussein,*
> *and they used it as a pretext to justify the war in Iraq. Of*
> *course, this confession was found to be said under*
> *torture, and useless, many years after.*

Lord Carlile is the Government's independent reviewer of government terrorism policy, and does his best to convince the public that torture is sometimes necessary.

> *If we received information that there was going to be a*
> *bomb in a football ground, the Government would be*
> *failing in its duty if it ignored this information.*
>
> **LORD CARLILE OF BERRIEW QC**

But the Government cannot point to a single instance where anything like this has actually taken place. The only times torture intelligence has been used it has led to miscarriages of justice, as in the Ricin case. It's also impossible to keep our hands clean as Lord Carlile hopes.

> *If you are part of a global system you have to exchange*
> *this information, but don't pretend you can somehow sit*
> *on your island divorced from what's going on around the*
> *world, because we are all working together on this. If*
> *the information comes from the Egyptians or the Uzbeks*
> *and it's obtained under torture, and we use it, we've*
> *asked for it.*
>
> **STEPHEN GREY**

Popular culture is as much to blame as the politicians, and never is this more obvious than in hit TV series *24*. Most episodes of *24* involve Jack Bauer doing something horrific to a baddie to get vital information. Occasionally, for a bit of variety, Jack gets tortured by the baddies, and soon Jack and the baddies will be torturing each other simultaneously in a surreal sadomasochistic torturefest. The torture in *24* is at complete odds with reality:

- No one ever dies during Jack's grizzly antics. In fact, after a few hours, the torture victim is often laughing and joking about it and patting Jack on the back.
- Jack always tortures the right person. He hardly ever accidentally ties up the wrong person and electrocutes their genitals by mistake.
- Jack always gets *extremely valuable information* from torturing the villain. He never gets told absolute rubbish that is concocted to stop the pain. He then takes this *extremely valuable information* (that he would otherwise *not have had unless he had tortured*) and goes on to save lots of American lives.
- Jack always knows when to stop. He manages to know that a particular piece of information is the truth, as opposed to the denials that preceded it and the gibberish that is about to follow.

The creator of *24*, Joel Surnow, is a big fan of torture: 'I think torture does work. It would work on me! I believe torture has been around since the beginning of time because it works. If you have ten minutes to stop a nuclear bomb, tell me what you're going to do.'

Apart from Tony Blair, there are other impressionable media-obsessed people influenced by the show. In February 2007 US Brigadier General Patrick Finnegan actually approached the producers of *24* and asked them to tone the torture down, as it was encouraging American troops in the field. 'They should do a show where torture backfires. The kids see it and say, "If torture is wrong, what about *24*?".'

Sorry to have to do this, but we need to tell one more story in this chapter. It should dispel the myth once and for all that useful information can come from torture.

SANDY MITCHELL

'I had been told: "It's already been decided you're going to be executed. It's just a case of where and when now". There was one particular day I thought they were going to execute me. The guards were there with their blindfold, the ankle chains and the handcuffs. The hood was put on me. The chains were put on me. Normally I'd be taken to a room for interrogation and beating. I was told to kneel down, and it just came to me that this is it. I'm about to be executed now. I'm going to die, and all I could think of at the time was my wife and son. Dying is just something that I've learned to live with. None of us get out of this alive. So I just prayed that God would look after my wife and Matthew. And then I got this slap in the back of the neck and my bowels failed me, and I think I passed out for a few seconds. When I came round I could hear the laughing of my interrogators. It was just their sense of humour. It was their way of softening me up for another interrogation session.'[57]

Sandy Mitchell, a British man, was arrested, imprisoned and tortured in Saudi jails, constantly under threat of execution, until he was released in August 2003. Jim Cottle, another British man, was among several other men who shared the same ordeal.

The first duty of any government is to protect its own citizens

GEOFF HOON

But while British citizens were being tortured in Saudi Arabia, our Government did everything but protect them. In order to maintain good relations with one of the most powerful countries in the Middle East and secure lucrative arms contracts for BAe Systems, New Labour went out of its way to appease the Saudi regime and left its own people to rot. This sell-out continued after the men's release, when Sandy, Jim and the other torture victims tried to bring the Saudi Arabian Government to account for the horrific treatment they had endured. Tony Blair's

Government successfully intervened in the highest court in Britain to make sure that the Saudi torturers could evade justice.

Sandy Mitchell is a straightforward kind of guy. He left his native Glasgow in 1973, but he still has a soft Scots accent that twenty-five years living and working in the Middle East hasn't eradicated. He isn't the type to make things up or exaggerate for effect. And yet his story is so unbelievably horrific that, if it weren't Sandy telling it, you wouldn't believe it. You wouldn't want to believe it.

He rose to become chief anaesthetic technician at the Security Forces Hospital in Riyadh in Saudi Arabia. He was as integrated into life in Saudi Arabia as any ex-pat could be. However, like most ex-pats, he also liked a drink. Legally, it's a dry country, but the civilian police and religious police turn a blind eye, as everyone knows what goes on. The ex-pat drinking culture consists mostly of people meeting up on a compound for a few home-brewed beers after work – nothing more dangerous. Yet this was the pretext that the Saudis used to arrest and torture Sandy before framing him for a series of bombings later discovered to have been carried out by Islamic militants.

The first car bomb went off on 17 November 2000, killing a British engineer, Christopher Rodway. Two days after the first bomb, a police sergeant friend of Sandy's told him that the Ministry of Interior were going to blame it on Westerners. It was at this time that a friend of Sandy's, Jim Cottle, decided to leave Saudi Arabia and return to Britain.

A few weeks later, two more jeeps were blown up by car bombs as they left a bar on one of the compounds. They were driven by a group of people going on to a party after the bar had closed. 'One of my friends, Ross Skevins, is a paramedic, and he stopped and gave first aid to the driver and his passenger in the first vehicle. The secret police turned up within minutes, and the emergency services turned up shortly afterwards. The fable about there being a turf war amongst ex-patriots was created by the Ministry of Interior because they wanted to divert attention away from the problem with Islamic militants targeting Westerners.' A few days later, Ross was arrested and taken to the Ministry of Interior.

Ten days later the secret police came for Sandy. It was 7 a.m. on a normal working day. 'I was on the way to the hospital where I worked. I parked the car, and as I got out I was just attacked and jumped on, hooded, put some chains on, manacled, and bundled into this vehicle.'

He was taken to a small room and waited for a few hours. Finally the hood was taken off and he saw some uniformed officers. The two men were Khaled and Ibrahim, employees of the secret police, and later the prosecutors at his trial. They were also his torturers. 'They told me, before you leave this place you're going to confess to these bombings or you'll go mad with what we're going to do to you. They weren't interested in the truth. They just wanted the confessions.'

The abuse began straight away. 'It was as if they were in a rush to break me and get me to confess as quickly as possible. All they really wanted was a quick confession, and they could sort out the details later.' It started with being beaten up – two men holding his arms and legs while the others kicked, punched, slapped and spat at him. When they got tired they gave it a rest. Soon his shirt was covered in his own blood and vomit and the phlegm of his torturers.

This softened him up before the proper torture began. A favourite method was called 'the chicken position', in which the victim is suspended from a metal bar to make the beating easier. 'You're handcuffed at the wrists and at your ankles. A metal bar is shoved behind your knees. You're hoisted up between two desks making it easy for them to beat the soles of your feet and buttocks with an axe handle. This would go on continuously, and then they would let you down and then they would go next door and do the same to Bill Sampson, my friend. And it would rotate all through the night, them doing this.'

The days weren't any easier. He was kept standing up with one arm chained to his cell door above his head for eight days. One thing that remains in his mind about this time is the extraordinary fact that the shackles that held him were made in Britain, by a company called Hiatts. He couldn't sit, sleep or move. The pain in his raised arm was almost unendurable. 'After the fifth night, what really broke me was when they said, 'OK, your wife is a Thai national. We can do anything we want to her.' I knew exactly what they meant by that. So I said, OK, I'll confess to anything you want. Just leave my wife alone.'

Confessing convincingly to a crime you didn't commit isn't easy. At first, Sandy confessed to the bombing and said he had done it alone. He was tortured and beaten and told that Bill Sampson – a Canadian – had already confessed to the bombing. So Sandy confessed to carrying out the bombing with Bill Sampson.

Through suggestion and torture, the Saudis eventually got the confession they wanted. Sandy was now ready for the video cameras. They took hours and hours of video footage, making the men repeat over and over the agreed confession until they got it exactly how they wanted it. It was edited down into one shorter tape ready for broadcast on Saudi TV, where Sandy, Bill and Ross confessed that they were ordered to carry out the explosion in November that killed Christopher Rodway.

The videotape of the confession shows just how meaningless information extracted under torture is. As Sandy says, 'I was absolutely zombified at the time. We had been continuously interrogated, beaten, abused, tortured, and hadn't slept for nine days. You get to the point where you just say anything just to stop the pain. If they'd taken me at that precise moment to the square and they executed me, I would have been grateful for it.'

While all this was happening to Sandy, the British Foreign Office were doing nothing to help. They were completely aware of what was happening to the British citizens they are charged with protecting (they had speedily brought home some of the embassy staff so that they did not share the same fate). When the US Government discovered that an American citizen, Mike Sedlak, had also been picked up, they lost no time in getting him released. Even though the US and Saudi Governments are financially joined at the hip, the US State Department hit the roof and immediately secured the release of their man. Sandy, on the other hand, was left at the mercy of Saudi justice. 'Quite simply, the Americans wouldn't take the bullshit that the Saudis were feeding to them. Unfortunately, the British Government weren't as staunch when it came to standing up to the Saudis.' The reason for the Foreign Office looking the other way goes right to the heart of the New Labour machine.

> *The British Government is absolutely entwined with BAe Systems, which is Britain's biggest arms dealer, which is the largest recipient of state subsidy.*
>
> *There is a huge amount of corporate and diplomatic worth put in the relationship with Saudi Arabia, far above the rights and interests of individual citizens like Sandy Mitchell.*
>
> **MARK THOMAS**

After the taped confessions were secured, Sandy was transferred to al-Ha'ir prison, a top security prison for political offenders. He was kept in solitary confinement which went on for 15 months.

Meanwhile Jim Cottle had returned to Britain, but a few months later he got a call from his old boss offering Jim a new six-month contract in Bahrain. Jim wasn't interested in returning to Saudi, but after a bit of persuasion he agreed to fly out to Bahrain to meet his boss. 'He said he'd meet me at the Bahraini Airport. When I landed at Bahrain, I got to the immigration desk and I was arrested by the Bahrain police and the Saudi secret police.

Sandy Mitchell's confession

After about an hour of sitting in a room and waiting, they drove me straight to the border and handed me over to the Saudi secret police.'[58] As soon as he was over the border, he was shackled and blindfolded and taken to the interrogation centre in Riyadh.

The torture began on the first night. They took Jim upstairs and asked him about the car bombs. They said they had two witnesses who would testify that he had done it. They wanted him to confess. He said no, and the familiar pattern of beatings began. It carried on for nine days and nights.

Jim held out and refused to confess. Eventually, they brought in James Lee, another captured Brit and a friend of Jim's who had already 'confessed' to the bombings and claimed Jim had helped him. He said that James was lying. 'They beat me to a pulp that night because I called James Lee a liar.' Eventually he cracked: 'Every bit of confession was beaten out of me for the next four weeks. Eventually they were helping me, telling me which way I went. I was beaten for 10 weeks, and you can't take it any more. I had, maybe, three nights when I wasn't touched in 10 whole weeks.' His confession was also videoed and broadcast on TV.

Sandy was still in solitary confinement. 'My only visitors were my interrogator; they could come, have me taken out my cell, taken upstairs and beaten. They wanted me to modify the confession because they'd obviously arrested more people and they wanted to include them into the plot.' It was one of the hardest periods of his time in prison. He tried to commit suicide twice. 'Looking back on it, it was probably a selfish thing to do because my wife and son were still in Saudi Arabia. OK, if I'd died, then they'd have no reason to go after my wife and son, but I couldn't endure the pain any more and the agony. At the same time, I knew that it was impossible for me to help Noi and Matthew.'

His trial took place in June 2001, six months after he was arrested and tortured for his confession. The trial consisted of one of the torturers, Ibrahim, who was the state prosecutor as well as being a captain in the Saudi secret police, reading out the confession in court before three judges. The judges passed a sentence of execution, and asked Sandy if he wanted to ask the court for mercy. He told them to shove it. 'If they're going to take my head, what little dignity I had left I was going to keep.' The whole trial lasted about ten minutes.

After confessing, Jim did have a trial like Sandy's, with three judges and his two torturers as state prosecutors. He was brave enough to plead not guilty. There was a quick conference in Arabic, then Jim was taken outside and beaten up again by Khaled and Ibrahim. He was led back in and pleaded guilty. He was told he was going to be beheaded. For the rest of the time he was imprisoned, they used the fear of execution as a method of psychological torture. He was kept in solitary confinement for a year.

Both Sandy and Jim were fortunate in one respect. They both had determined family members back in the UK who were not as frightened of upsetting the Saudis as the British Government seemed to be. Sandy had his sister, Margaret Dunn, and Jim had his girlfriend, Mary Martini.

Sandy's sister had found out about Sandy and Bill's televised confessions on the morning they were due to be broadcast, back in January. She was shocked, and she phoned the Foreign Office immediately to find out what was going on. The Foreign Office didn't know anything about the televised confessions; it was news to them as well. Mary had found out through a friend that Jim hadn't turned up for a meeting during his trip to Bahrain.

When they saw the televised confessions, both Margaret and Mary knew something was seriously wrong. The men looked terrible, all bloodshot eyes and battered faces. They spoke in a completely uncharacteristic way, with stilted voices and using words they wouldn't ordinarily have used. They weren't told about the trials or the death sentences that had been passed. After that, they constantly pestered the Foreign Office for news of the men, and to find out what they were doing to help them.

Mary had her first meeting with Baroness Amos from the Foreign Office on 11 September 2001. From the outset, Mary was told not to speak to the press for fear of making things worse. 'All the time they were going on to me about the press. "We prefer the softly softly approach. We don't want you to rock the boat. The last thing you need to do is upset the Saudis. If we embarrass them, that'll be it. There's nothing we can do."' For several months Mary did as she was told.

Mary was fortunate in that the embassy staff were at least visiting Jim in prison once a month during this time. However, they lied to her about his condition, saying he was being treated well, that the food was good and that he had been joking around during their visit. They failed to forward on a whole bundle of letters to the prison, because Mary hadn't attached enough postage. When she hadn't received any replies, and she asked if he was allowed to write back, they told her that if he wanted to write, he could. This was also a lie – Jim was desperate to write, but was denied pens and paper for eighteen months.

The Foreign Office also used emotional blackmail to prevent Mary talking to the press. They told her that Jim had sent a message to Mary specifically asking her not to talk to the press. She assumed he had been threatened in some way – that if she publicised his case back in the UK he would be punished or worse. Jim never said such a thing or sent any message to Mary about the press during his time in prison. In fact, Jim says, 'If I'd known about it I would have egged her on because I knew myself the only way to get to the Saudis is to embarrass them. All they ever want to do is save face.' Gradually it dawned on Mary that the Government was doing nothing.

At the start of 2002, the story was beginning to gain exposure in the press, and Margaret was also pestering Foreign Office ministers for news and action on Sandy's behalf. Eventually, she managed to get a meeting with the Foreign Secretary, Jack Straw. She was told beforehand, 'You can have ten minutes with the Foreign Secretary, because he's a very busy man'. Jack Straw spent most of the ten minutes describing his trip to India, and Margaret could not get her point across to him. He finished off by saying, 'We're doing everything we can'. The reality is that they were doing nothing at all. Sandy is in no doubt why: 'They did nothing because they just didn't want to upset the apple cart. Saudi Arabia is a trading partner. The BAe Systems contract was worth 20 billion pounds to the British Government.'

During this period, all the families asked the Foreign Office for each other's phone numbers, so they could be in touch and support each other. The Foreign Office said to each family that the other families didn't want to give out their phone numbers. Later on, once they had all got in touch, they discovered they had all been told the same lie. The victims' families were much easier for the Foreign Office to deal with if they were kept isolated from one another.

Mary was in touch with Human Rights Watch and Amnesty International. A UN inspector managed to get in to see Jim, and gave Mary an accurate report of Jim's condition.

When the next Foreign Office report came in, saying as usual that Jim was in good spirits and being treated well, Mary told them that she knew the truth. They were amazed. After agonising over the decision for a long time, this was one of the incidents that made Mary finally decide it was time to talk to the press. A combination of Mary and Margaret's public shaming of the UK Government eventually forced them into action.

Ironically, the 9/11 attacks on America did a lot to help the men's conditions. As it became clear that al-Qaeda was a global problem and not just a local Saudi one, it was easier for the Saudis to acknowledge that the car bombings had been carried out by Islamic militants targeting Westerners. Jim remembers his food in prison started getting better.

In May 2003, nine suicide bombers targeted a compound in Riyadh, killing 35 and injuring two hundred. It was no longer possible to deny that this was a sustained al-Qaeda campaign against Western targets within Saudi Arabia. A few days after the bombing, five Saudi prisoners from Guantanamo Bay were released in exchange for Sandy, Bill, Jim and the others.

Even though the Saudi prisoners were released in May, the Government still did not push for the release of the British men, and left them to sit in jail until August 2003. Someone at the Foreign Office clearly had a sick sense of humour, as just before the release they tried to get the families to pay for the men's flights. They told Margaret, 'We need Sandy to sign a declaration saying that he will pay his fare back home.' Margaret said hell will freeze over first, and on this occasion the Foreign Office backed down.

Finally Sandy and Jim were driven to the airport, where there was an RAF medical crew waiting. Sandy: 'There was a team specifically for medevacing hostages and prisoners of war, and these guys were really good. We occupied all of the business class compartment of the aircraft. When we landed we were taken to a VIP wing because the Foreign Office did not want us speaking to the media about our ordeal. I met my sister and my family, my wife and son. Matthew had grown so much – the last time I saw him in Riyadh he was a little fat bundle, and now he was quite tall. I cuddled my family and they drove me home. It was just so unreal, because for 32 months everything I saw was grey, there was no plants, no trees, no grass in the prison. Everything was grey. The next morning I woke up and looked out of the window. There was all these trees, fields and plant life and the sort of things you take for granted now, but then it was just so beautiful to me.'

Sandy's recovery was going to take a long time. 'The night after I came home, I came out of the kitchen and my sister said to me, "Could you turn the light off?" I was absolutely shocked, because I had never had any control over anything for 32 months, so the thought of turning the light switch off just totally confused me. It took me a long time to learn how to do some basic things again.'

When they landed in the UK, the men were effectively destitute. No one asked Jim if he had anywhere to live. Mary remembers meeting Jim at the airport and vomiting in the car all the way home as he told her about what he'd been through. Mary took him in, though he had trouble claiming any disability benefit because he'd lived out of the country for so long. Sandy also felt completely abandoned. 'I got some help from local MPs, but we got absolutely no help from the Government, absolutely none.'

He was offered no financial support. 'In the end I was given £92 a week for myself and my son and my wife. That £92 a week was to look after the three of us. So I had to get off my backside and say well I've got to provide some form of support to my family so, as difficult as it was, I just had to make the effort and I got some agency work. This was difficult, as technically I was a convicted criminal, a convicted terrorist and spy, and the British Government were not prepared to give us a letter saying that we were innocent.' To this day the Government has refused to provide this letter.

Eventually they decided to seek compensation from the Saudi Government. 'After we realised the Saudis were not going to put their own house in order, they were not going to redress the injustice done to us, they were not even going to give us back the possessions they stole from us, that's when we decided we were going to take legal action.' Initially the Saudis claimed that they were not tortured. 'We went to the Parker Institute. They have a number of forensic tests they can do, and they confirmed that we were tortured. The Saudi Government then changed its stance from "No we haven't been tortured" to "We want state immunity".'

State immunity is a legal defence that countries can give when being sued. Anticipating this, Sandy's legal team also took action against the individual torturers themselves: Khaled and Ibrahim.

When the case came to trial in the Court of Appeal, they won on the grounds that the prohibition from torture was so important that it took a higher precedent than state immunity. The Saudi Government were furious, and appealed the case to the House of Lords.

It is at this point that the British Government gave its final slap to Sandy and the other victims. At the behest of the Saudis, New Labour intervened in the House of Lords appeal. Lord Goldsmith did not support the British citizens who had been tortured, but backed the Saudi Government that had done the torturing. The intervention worked, and Sandy and the other victims lost, and went home penniless. A spokesman for the Department of Constitutional Affairs actually said: 'The UK Government condemns torture in all its forms and works to eradicate it wherever it occurs'. A spokesman for *Taking Liberties* said, 'Bollocks.'

The legal precedent means that no British citizen will be able to seek recompense from torture from a foreign government ever again. Sandy: 'Any one of us can be tortured now; the British Government has put commercial interests before human interest.'

One of the other victims was eventually granted an audience with Jack Straw. The first thing Straw said was, 'For a man that's been tortured you're looking remarkably well.' Sandy was deeply upset when he heard what Straw had said: 'Most people thankfully don't know what its like to be tortured. Torture is not just getting beaten up, it's not just the pain; it's the humiliation. The fact you're degraded to such a level where you'll say anything to stop the pain. You're in absolute agony. And the fact that you see the pleasure that people take while they're torturing you, that is so disturbing, just sometimes you just cannot describe something like that. The sheer evilness of it. And the fact that we have no legal redress in this country for being tortured is just incredible.'

Sandy has written about his experiences in his book *Saudi Babylon*, and now campaigns against torture whenever he can.

BUSH AND BLAIR SEND OUT A CLEAR MESSAGE

The numbers at Guantanamo Bay are currently under a thousand. The numbers of those tortured by Extraordinary Rendition are estimated at ten thousand. No one is getting hauled off the streets of London and tortured (except perhaps Mouloud Sihali), so why should we be bothered? Whether we like it or not, developing nations around the world watch Britain, and how we treat people echoes round the world.

We at Amnesty have been used in the UK to having a very good relationship with the UK Government on this issue of torture, and we have been used, over many years, to being able to congratulate the British Government on its programme of work to eliminate torture worldwide. In the last year or so we've been unable to do that. The UK Government's example here is a particularly appalling one to the rest of the world. It sends a green light to many regimes with far fewer scruples and much more appalling records in terms of human rights, and we find at Amnesty International that the UK's record on this is being quoted to us. It makes our work harder with regimes like the Chinese, the Syrians, and others that have deeply worrying human-rights records.

KATE ALLEN[59]

LOOKING TO THE FUTURE: REID BELIEVES IN TORTURE TOO

Will this support of the Bush Administration's bloodlust end when Blair moves on? Unlikely. Other ministers have independently followed in the footsteps of the White House in trying to rewrite the rules on torture. Alberto Gonzales (the lawyer who changed the meaning of torture) has since been promoted to Attorney General in the US. He has always made clear he believes the Geneva Conventions are a waste of time:

In my judgement, this new paradigm renders obsolete Geneva's strict limitations on questioning of enemy prisoners and renders quaint some of its provisions.[60]

In 2006, his counterpart in the UK John Reid took the first steps in making sweeping changes to the Geneva Conventions:

Article 3 of the Geneva Conventions sets fundamental standards of treatment in all non-international armed conflict, standards that are upheld by the laws of any civilised state. However, I believe we must ask serious questions about whether or not further developments in international law in this area are necessary.

JOHN REID[61]

Following the most insane elements of the Bush Administration in tearing up the protections of the individual is not, it seems, limited to Tony Blair alone.

Chapter 8

Why?

On the evening of 7 July 2005, Rachel North started writing a blog. Even before she had got all the glass out of her hair she began to talk about her experience and feelings online. Her blog became massively popular, and she has now quit her job in advertising to become a full-time writer. She has campaigned against the Government's reaction to the bombings and believes the first mistake is to see the attacks as an act of war:

> *It's not a war. There are no rules here. If you start acting in a world when you say you are in a war and the other side has no rules then you don't have any rules either. So you have Guantanamo, you have torture, you have Rendition, you have things that should appal and disgust and shame any democratic country that puts its name to them.*

No one, least of all Rachel, is in any doubt that we are under threat. 'They may attack us – but we are a democratic people, a civilised people; we can probably take it. What we can't take is a gradual erosion of our civil liberties, of everything that makes us worth defending in order to do something that is not a war, against people who are not soldiers.' She believes that as soon as you start calling it a war then you've already lost, 'I wasn't blown up in an act of war. People didn't die on my train in an act of war.

I'm not going to sink to the level of people who do that because they say, well, anything goes – it doesn't. There are some things that are more important than being able to have a safe journey in to work.'

Have the rules of the game really changed? 'I didn't change them. I didn't get off that train saying the rules of the game had changed. I got on that train a civilised person; I got blown up with civilised people. I do not want to throw away my decency in order to continue a war that I never called, that I never bought into, that I never believed in. This isn't a war, and don't make it into one; it dignifies it.'

But she also believes that politicians benefit from the rhetoric of battle. 'Whilst it may be politically appropriate and easy to corral people into camps of good people and bad people, that's not how it works. Al-Qaeda is not a mobilised series of crack battalions ready to leap into action at a moment's notice, it's just an idea. The only way you can defeat an idea is with another idea. The only way you can give an idea substance is by your words and your actions. If your words and your actions are talking of freedom, talking of heroism, talking of honour but they are not free, they are not heroes and they are dishonourable, then they are worthless. That is what we need to hold on to; we need to show what we are doing is worthwhile.'

Rachel also doesn't believe that the Government is eroding our liberty as part of a grand conspiracy. 'I think they probably genuinely think, in a slightly panicky way, that they are doing the right thing. It's very difficult to say to people who haven't been blown up, and probably feel very responsible for the people who have, "It's okay, calm down". I'd like to say it: don't panic! One person got on my train with a bomb, nine hundred others kept calm and looked after each other, thousands of others wanted to help us, London got back to work the following day, we haven't had another 7/7 since. It's do-able. But if we go around thinking that every day is going to be a July...that's what it's actually like in Iraq.'[1]

IRAQ

Wars seem to make prime ministers popular.

**TONY BLAIR, SUPPOSEDLY SAID TO A FRIEND
ABOUT THE FALKLANDS WAR IN 1982**[2]

The invasion of Iraq was a central plank in the 'War Against Terror', and its effects have been at the heart of the erosion of British liberty. The clampdown on dissent kicked into gear as a response to the war – New Labour simply could not handle the strength and volume of the opinion against them. Rather than debate with those who were against the war, the response was to shut down any discussion.

Since the invasion, the Government has restricted our freedoms to make us safer from terrorism, but no one is now in any doubt that the threat from terrorism has *increased* thanks to the invasions of Iraq and Afghanistan. It is impossible to tell the story of *Taking Liberties* without delving into the Iraq debacle.

Crispin Black was a soldier before he worked for the Government in military intelligence and then defence intelligence. He sat on the Government's Joint Intelligence Committee and briefed No 10 on terrorism.

I think most people accept that the Taliban had harboured Bin Laden, and that needed to be put right. I think invading Afghanistan enjoyed near unanimous support. Now, whether it could be successful or not is a different matter: you know, read Kipling.

CRISPIN BLACK[3]

The plan to invade Iraq began in America almost straight after 9/11. Tony Blair was swiftly brought onboard, and they set out to convince the rest of the world that Saddam Hussein and the 'War Against Terror' were linked through terrorism and those irrepressible WMDs.[4]

This twisting of the truth culminated in the 'dodgy dossier' of September 2002 that made the infamous and spectacularly wrong claim that Saddam could attack British interests within 45 minutes.[5] They shook every piece of intelligence they could from the security services and wheeled out the Ricin case to link Saddam with terrorism. This should hopefully not be earth-shattering news to anyone by now, but it is deeply relevant when looking at how our liberties are being taken away. The methods and language used by the Government to convince us that Saddam needed to be taken out is remarkably similar to that used when the Government talks about terrorism.

> *My judgement, as Prime Minister, is that this threat is real, growing, and of an entirely different nature to any conventional threat to our security that Britain has faced before.*
>
> **TONY BLAIR, TALKING ABOUT SADDAM HUSSEIN**[6]

> *It is perfectly obvious that this country faces a terrorist threat the like of which we have not faced before.*
>
> **TONY BLAIR, ARGUING FOR CONTROL ORDERS**[7]

> *The threat is real*
>
> *…people should have faith with the authorities.*
>
> **TONY BLAIR, TALKING ABOUT SADDAM…OR WAS IT ABOUT TERRORISM?**[8]

MAKE IT LEGAL

Throughout the assault on our civil liberties, New Labour has consistently undermined the rule of law. Never was this more obvious than during the build-up to war, when the Government twisted the legality of the invasion as well as the intelligence to support it. The Attorney General, Lord Goldsmith, is the legal advisor to the Government. His advice is supposed to be independent and free from political pressure. When the Government began discussing the invasion, Goldsmith was asked to give his legal opinion on Britain's case for war. Originally, he felt that the war would be illegal without a second UN resolution expressly authorising force.[9] Britain and the US dutifully wheeled their

travelling circus off to the UN and put on a cracking performance (Colin Powell's 'artist's impressions' of what WMDs 'might'
look like was probably a highlight[10]), but sadly they failed to
convince, and the resolution did not go through.[11] This left Britain
in something of a tricky position, and Lord Goldsmith came under
immense pressure to change his opinion.[12] Finally, ten days before
the war broke out he changed his mind, and stated unequivocally
that the war was legal.[13]

FROM BAGHDAD TO LONDON

George Bush declared the hostilities at an end on 2 May 2003 –
on board an aircraft carrier in the middle of the ocean, nowhere
near Iraq.[14] If he had actually gone to Baghdad he might have
noticed that this was a little premature.

Saddam Hussein's Iraq rarely featured on anyone's top ten
holiday destinations. But one of its few redeeming features was an
absence of Islamic extremist terrorism. Since the invasion, militant
fighters have flooded into Iraq, turning the country into a blood-
bath. New Labour are still in complete denial about this, and
senior figures in the army have become infected by New Labour's
doublespeak:

> There is a very intense sectarian conflict going on … I do
> not see that as civil war.
>
> **GENERAL SIR ROBERT FRY**[15]

The civilian death toll is at least two hundred thousand (opinions
vary wildly on this figure), and this has hugely increased global
resentment towards the US and UK.

> Just before the invasion of Iraq, me and my mate Sam
> turned up at Geoff Hoon's constituency surgery. Above the
> door there's a sign across his surgery, it says, 'Geoff Hoon,
> New Labour Constituency Surgery'. And we stuck a
> homemade banner that we'd got above the constituency
> door, and it just read 'al-Qaeda recruiting office'.
>
> **MARK THOMAS**[16]

The deterioration of Iraq

Security

Iraqi civilians killed by violence (does not include murders):

May 2003	260
August 2005	2489
December 2005	534

Total no of civilians killed May 2003–December 2005 (not including crime) — 19,500

Number of daily attacks by insurgents and militias:

August 2003	16–18
August 2004	70–90
October 2005	180–185

Internally displaced persons in Iraq:

(Since April) 2003	100,000
November 2006	650,000

Estimated strength of insurgency nationwide:

November 2003	5000
October 2006	20,000–30,000

Estimated no of foreign fighters in the insurgency:

January 2004	300–500
November 2006	800–2000

Economic and quality-of-life indicators

Doctors in Iraq:

Iraqi physicians registered before 2003 invasion	34,000
Iraqi physicians who have left since the invasion	12,000 (estimate)
Iraqi physicians murdered since the invasion	2000
Iraqi physicians kidnapped	250

People with potable water availability:

Pre-war level (2003)	12.9 million
Status as of 21/3/2006	9.7 million

Average hours of electricity per day in Baghdad:

Estimated pre-war level	16–24
May 2003	4–8
January 2007	4.4

Crude oil production:

Estimated pre-war level	2.5 million barrels/day (pre-war peak)
May 2003	0.3 million barrels/day
January 2007	1.66 million barrels/day

Public opinion:

Iraqi public's approval of attacks on US-led forces:

January 2006	47%
September 2006	61%

The images of dead Muslim civilians are still beamed around the world, and continue to act as a recruiting sergeant for the cause of Islamic terrorism.

TOUGH ON CRIME, TOUGH ON THE CAUSES OF CRIME

When four suicide bombers struck London on 7 July 2005, Blair shut down any discussion about the reasons behind the attack and whether there was a link between Iraq and terrorism:

> *I am afraid that I must tell the honourable gentleman that it is a form of terrorism aimed at our way of life, not at any particular government or policy.*
>
> **TONY BLAIR, HOUSE OF COMMONS DEBATE, 11 JULY 2005**[17]

However, a leaked report showed that he had been warned about an increased threat of terrorism even before the war began. On 10 February 2003 the Joint Intelligence Committee issued a secret report to Brown and Blair:

> *Al-Qaeda and associated groups continued to represent by far the greatest threat to Western interests, and that threat would be heightened by military action against Iraq.*
>
> **JIC REPORT**[18]

A few other people have also recognised that there might be a connection. Blair and Brown were explicitly warned about the risks to British civilians if they supported the US invasion of Iraq, and ignored them. Just over two years after they invaded Iraq, the JIC report proved chillingly accurate as four British suicide bombers attacked London.

Acknowledging that there is a link does not condone or excuse terrorism or the bombings on 7/7. But to deny there is a link can only make the problem worse. New Labour has ducked the discomfort of examining the events of 2005, as an independent enquiry has never been allowed.

*A public inquiry into the 7 July
bombings is not necessary, and could
divert resources from security... The
events of 7 July were an exceptional
case that has to be treated exceptionally.*

JOHN REID[19]

Rachel North believes otherwise: 'I don't see how any politician could say right now, "I am absolutely certain that I have learnt everything there is to know from the first suicide bombing attack in Europe to the extent that I am completely on top of my game". Seven hundred injured, 52 dead, and we were lucky, it could have been worse. We know that the threat hasn't gone away; in fact we're constantly told it's got worse. It seems to me absolutely barking mad that people are saying that we don't have the resources for a public enquiry. What could possibly be more important than learning from the first, the only real, suicide bombing attack on Western European soil? You've got a live one here; learn from it.'[20]

Politicians may be unhappy about discussing the causes of terrorism, but they have spent a fair amount of time trying to decide what a terrorist is. The definition has been amended several times over the last few years, and at the time of writing it is being reviewed again by Lord Carlile. Since it seems to become broader with each amendment, it should soon encompass toddlers throwing tantrums in the aisles of supermarkets.

Here is a list of all the people and organisations who believe that British foreign policy has increased the threat of terrorism in the UK:[21]

- Muslim leaders;
- Joint Terrorism Analysis Centre;
- Sadiq Khan;
- International Institute for Strategic Studies;
- David Cameron;
- US National Intelligence Estimate (US Intelligence Agencies);
- Foreign Policy in Focus;
- Martin Bell;
- the JIC;
- Home Affairs and Foreign Office;
- Michael Scheuer (22-year CIA veteran and former head of the CIA's bin Laden unit);
- Professor Robert Pape, University of Chicago;
- Juan Cole (Middle East expert);
- Chatham House;
- 79% of Londoners;
- two thirds of British people;
- EU Counter Terrorism Group.

And here is a list of all the people and organisations who believe that British Foreign Policy hasn't increased the threat of terrorism in the UK:
- Tony Blair.

A BRIEF HISTORY OF TERRORISM

At the moment New Labour has redefined terrorism in the following terms:

> The use or threat of certain types of action where the use or threat is designed to influence the Government, or to intimidate the public or a section of the public.
>
> **TERRORISM ACT 2000, AMENDED 2006**[22]

Under this definition, the following are all terrorists:

- Jesus Christ: tried to destabilise the Roman Government. Thought to be behind subversive pamphlet (the Bible) and known associate of the Father and Holy Ghost.
- Robin Hood: leader of proscribed terror organisation 'the Merry Men'.
- Mahatma Gandhi: used certain types of action known as 'peaceful protest', designed to influence the British Government to gain Indian independence.
- George Washington: advocated dangerous terrorist activities to form American state independent from British Empire.
- François Mitterrand (former President of France): committed terrorist atrocities in France in attempt to destabilise the Nazi Government (while member of French Resistance).
- Martin Luther King: labelled a terrorist by J. Edgar Hoover (head of the FBI), used actions like marches and protests to influence the Government to make life less shitty for black people.
- The Suffragettes: dangerous activists who attacked public institutions to promote subversive message that women should have the vote.

Under the 2006 Terrorism Act, anyone who *encourages or glorifies* a terrorist is also a terrorist. Blair is a practising Christian, so therefore by worshipping Jesus he is risking a seven-year jail sentence under his own law. John Reid once spent three nights in Geneva at the expense of Radovan Karadzic (top of The Hague's International War Crimes Tribunal list of wanted men) and said some nice things about him,[23] so Reid's definitely a terrorist. And as for Gordon Brown, he is a big fan of Gandhi, so he's on the list as well:

> *I could never compare myself to Gandhi or those other heroes of mine but I do take inspiration from the way that they dealt with the challenges they faced when I think about how I will deal with the challenges the country and the world faces, including the security challenge.*[24]

> **GORDON BROWN, JANUARY 2007**

Incidentally, Gordon appears to be telling us that Gandhi would deal with the 'War Against Terror' in the same way New Labour has. Does he honestly expect us to believe that Gandhi would jail people for peaceful protest, introduce ID cards, abolish habeas corpus and help the Americans torture innocents?

> *An eye for an eye makes the whole world blind.*

> **MAHATMA GANDHI**

If New Labour were to take a look at even a fraction of history they would see that it is impossible to paint terrorism in these black-and-white terms. Yesterday's terrorists frequently become tomorrow's politicians.

TERRORIST TWISTER

Twenty-five years ago, two groups of terrorists flourished on opposite sides of the world: the IRA and the Mujahedin. The IRA (Irish Republican Army) was the military wing of Sinn Fein, who wanted the British out of Northern Ireland. Now the IRA were *bad* terrorists. They bombed innocent civilians and were prepared to die for their cause. The British Government tried to stop the problem by passing draconian laws, which actually made the problem worse and increased the terrorist violence.

Several thousand miles away, another 'war' for independence was being fought. The Russians had invaded Afghanistan, and some Muslim fighters had risen up against the occupying army. The name given to these freedom fighters was the Mujahedin, and these were definitely *good* terrorists. They must have been extremely good, as the British and US Governments gave them billions of pounds in cash, lots of guns, and even flying lessons from the CIA, to fight the communists. The West was so supportive of these good terrorists that they were publicly praised by US President Ronald Reagan, and there is even a dedication to them in the credits of *Rambo III*. One of them was a Saudi Arabian called Osama Bin Laden.[25]

A quarter of a century later, and things have changed a bit. The IRA are now *good* terrorists. They have renounced violence and have been part of the Northern Irish Government. The Mujahedin rebranded themselves as 'al-Qaeda' and are now most certainly *bad* terrorists. They target innocent civilians and are prepared to die for their cause. The British Government is trying to stop the problem by passing draconian laws...

> *I don't think you can compare the political demands of republicanism with the political demands of this terrorist ideology we're facing now.*

> **TONY BLAIR**[26]

While the threat from al-Qaeda, and the terrorism that it inspires, is different from the threat from the IRA, does this mean that the lessons learned should be ignored? New Labour has refused to consider the lessons from the fight against Irish terrorism, for the following reasons:

1) *Al-Qaeda are prepared to sacrifice their own lives, the IRA were not*. While Islamic terrorists use suicide bombings, many IRA members sacrificed their lives in ways other than strapping explosives to themselves. One accidentally blew himself up on a bus in 1996.

2) *Al-Qaeda target civilians*. Er... So did the IRA. They bombed pubs, shopping centres and busy streets with attacks designed to cause maximum civilian deaths.

3) *The IRA gave warnings.* Actually they didn't a lot of the time, and when they did it was to claim the credit. The Omagh Bomb in 1998 had three warnings and killed 28 civilians.

4) *Al-Qaeda want to kill more than the IRA did.* Tony Blair actually said, 'I don't think the IRA would ever have set about trying to kill 3000 people'.[27] To compare numbers is a bit sick, but if Blair wants to go down that route, then 3268 died during the Irish troubles between 1968 and 1998. Islamic terrorists have killed 52 in the UK.

You'd think Blair would actually know something about solving terrorist problems, as he was Prime Minister when the Irish troubles formally ended in 1998 with the Good Friday Agreement.

> *A day like today is not a day for soundbites, really – we can leave them at home – but I feel the hand of history upon our shoulders, I really do.[28]*

John Reid uses history to make comparisons between al-Qaeda and the Nazis:

> *In the UK we are living through the most sustained period of severe threat since World War II.[29]*

To compare the threat faced from Islamic terrorism and the Nazis is tenuous, but the prize given for greatest historical distortion of all time has to go to Met Commissioner Sir Ian Blair. Just before Christmas 2006 he came out with a phrase that makes the rest of his public utterances seem calm and considered:

> *Al-Qaeda are a greater threat than the Nazis.[30]*

Over three hundred thousand Britons died in World War II fighting the Nazis, including twenty thousand civilians during the Blitz. To say that al-Qaeda are a greater threat than the Nazis is like saying that you are more scared of an ant dropping on your head than a medium-sized walrus. Can Sir Ian Blair ever face the cameras and not talk rubbish? We've seen how he tried to justify ID cards with the Ricin Plot[31] (there wasn't any…oh, never mind), and how he misled senior police over the costs of the

Brian Haw eviction.[32] But Ian Blair's greatest flight of fancy with terrorism came on 22 July 2005.

Fifteen days after the 7/7 bombings, armed police accidentally shot and killed an innocent man on his way to work. This is when the police's shoot-to-kill policy first became public, even though it had never been debated. Did the police apologise? Not quite.

JEAN CHARLES DE MENEZES: ANOTHER CASUALTY IN THE 'WAR AGAINST TERROR'

There is one basic civil liberty, which is the right to life.

TONY BLAIR, HOUSE OF COMMONS[33]

Twenty-second of July 2005. At 9.30 a.m. Jean Charles de Menezes, a Brazilian electrician, left his flat in London. He walked through the barriers and continued towards the train platform. On hearing the tube approach, he ran the last part of the way. After he entered the carriage, he was grabbed by several police officers and shot several times in the head. Even before his body was cold the misinformation started to spread.

Assistant Commissioner Andy Hayman flew into action and spent the day briefing the press. The press later ran a story that a terrorist had jumped the barrier, and that he had a big bulky coat with wires hanging out.

The same morning Sir Ian Blair wrote to the Permanent Secretary at the Home Office, John Grieve, persuading him to block an enquiry. Meanwhile it was becoming clear to officers on the ground that they had shot an innocent man.

Just after 3.30 p.m. Sir Ian Blair announced, 'This operation was directly linked to the ongoing terrorist investigation...the man was challenged and refused to obey police instructions.' In fact the only people who jumped the barrier were the police. Sir Ian then said his 'clothing and behaviour at the station added to their suspicions'.[34]

Sir Ian successfully delayed the Independent Police Complaints Commission enquiry for three days, giving time for misinformation to spread, evidence to be tampered with, and CCTV footage to 'go missing'. No one has resigned, and Tony Blair has repeatedly given Sir Ian his full support.

In order to justify the tragic accidents of the Menezes shooting, it has been explained that London was 'on edge' and everyone was extremely afraid. Of this there is no doubt. But that fear has come not just from the terrorists but from our politicians, police and media, who have systematically whipped up the fear of terrorism.

At the end of 2006 Ian Blair's rhetoric of doom reached almost Shakespearean levels.

> *The sky is dark. The terrorists seek mass casualties and are entirely indiscriminate: every community is at risk.*[35]

Why didn't he go the whole hog and come out in a cloak and a scythe?

THE POLITICS OF FEAR

Rather than calm the population and tackle the threat, the Government and police seem hell-bent on scaring the bejesus out of us. Fear is an extremely powerful political tool, and is often the first out of the New Labour toolbox.

In August 2006, John Reid gave a keynote speech at the liberal think-tank Demos in central London, where he made it clear that our freedoms had to be reduced to protect us from doom:

> *Sometimes we may have to modify some of our freedoms in the short term in order to prevent their misuse.*[36]

If Reid wants to do Nazi comparisons, so can we:

> *It is therefore permissible to restrict the rights of personal freedom.*
>
> **REICHSTAG FIRE DECREE, 27 FEBRUARY 1933**[37]

Reid said that attacks involving mass death were just around the corner, and that we give him our liberty so that he could protect us. The next day, by complete coincidence, Heathrow and other airports ground to a halt in a massive and unprecedented security operation. Armed police made a series of arrests in homes across the country in a blaze of publicity. These were the infamous 'bottle bomber' attacks (or rather attacks that didn't happen) that shook the world. Tony Blair was on holiday, John Prescott was having a bacon sarnie, so John Reid took control. But control of what? There was only conjecture and supposition about what *might* have happened. But thankfully there was more than enough conjecture to go around.[38]

For months people couldn't take any fluids at all on any planes going out of Britain. Mothers had to sip from bottles of breast milk at gunpoint to prove it wasn't Semtex. If the purpose of terrorism is to cause maximum disruption and fear with the least effort, then this was a massive success.

But even cursory inspection of the news showed that there wasn't anything immediately threatening about the situation that required this highly publicised 'terror swoop'. Some of the men who were dragged from their homes in the early hours of the morning didn't have passports. One would imagine for them to blow up planes they would first have to get through passport control. Second, none of those arrested had tickets to fly that day.[39] Again, this might have thrown a spanner in the works. While there may well have been a threat in the future, what was the purpose of shutting down several airports and causing mass panic, when the authorities knew that there could not have been an attack that day?

John Reid, meanwhile, was on a roll, and used the crisis to show that he was the hardest man in the Cabinet. He spent the rest of the summer telling the tabloids that he was in charge, and everything was under control, while simultaneously trying to scare the willies out of us.

The timing of the speech in which he advocated that our freedoms had to be 'modified' was also significant, as it was also Reid's ninety-sixth day as Home Secretary. He had been given the job after Charles Clarke was sacked in May 2006. He started as he meant to go on, and gave a series of briefings to the tabloids.

He declared that the Home Office was 'not fit for purpose', and that he would turn around the entire department in 100 days, and work 18 hours a day to do it. He then went on holiday to the South of France.[40] Three months later, his own 100-day deadline was approaching and the job was nowhere near done... And then a suspected terrorist plot passed across his desk...

The 'intelligence' for the bottle-bombing plot came from Pakistan, another country that uses torture in intelligence-gathering. The 'mastermind' was allegedly Rashid Rauf, who was arrested in Pakistan. But all terrorist charges against him were dropped in December 2006.[41] The Crown Prosecution Service in the UK said the dropping of charges against Mr Rauf in Pakistan would 'make no difference' to the case against the men charged in Britain. Their trial is set for 2008.

Later in the summer there was another raid on a house in Britain that did not make the front pages of any national newspapers. Or any pages. Two men were arrested in Windsor with the largest haul of bomb-making equipment in British history. Also found were several guns, the anarchy cookbook (three hundred pages of bomb recipes), two nuclear protection suites and a bow and arrow.[42] But there were no panicked headlines, no strutting politicians, no shut airports. The reason? Could it be anything to do with the fact that the men were not Muslim, and were in fact ex-members of the BNP? Despite the scale of the haul, the police immediately declared, 'It's not a bomb-making factory' and 'These men are not terrorists'.[43]

> *Governments need people to be frightened in order to control them. I mean if I look back just before I was born it was the Kaiser. Then after the Kaiser there was the inter-war years, then it was Hitler. Then after Hitler it was Stalin. Now it's the Muslims. And you wait and see, in a year or two it'll be the Chinese. John Reid will be sending MI5 people into every Chinese takeaway, in case Beijing is using them for propaganda.*
>
> **TONY BENN**[44]

We do not believe John Reid is a bigot, but his rhetoric is seized upon by bigots to justify their twisted cause. On 20 September 2006, John Reid went to a Muslim community in East London and made the following speech, clearly showing his great understanding of his audience.

> There is no nice way of saying this. These fanatics are looking to groom and brainwash children, including your children, for suicide bombings. Grooming them to kill themselves in order to murder others. Look for the tell-tale signs now, and talk to them before their hatred grows and you risk losing them forever. In protecting our families, we are protecting our community.[45]

He later qualified this in the *Sun*:

> I appeal to you, the Muslim community, to look for changes in your teenage sons; odd hours, dropping out of school or college, strange new friends.[46]

Just about covers most of the teenage population of Britain then.

In January 2007 history repeated itself. John Reid was again coming under attack for the Home Office still being a shambles. Even his old ally the *Sun*, like a demented dog turning on its owner, bit him in the trousers.

JOHN REID'S BRAIN IS MISSING

SUN, *25 JANUARY 2007*

Suddenly the headlines were full of another terror raid, this time in Birmingham. Like clockwork the leaks to the tabloids started immediately, and attention was diverted away from the embarrassment.

> # NINE ARRESTED OVER ALLEGED KIDNAP AND BEHEADING PLOT
>
> *TELEGRAPH, 1 FEBRUARY 2007*

> # BLAIR BLACKMAIL TERROR BID FOILED
>
> *SUN, 31 JANUARY 2007*

At the same time as terror raids were being spun to the media, he was also resurrecting the policy on 90-day pre-charge detention.

> # REID TO REVISIT TERROR DETENTIONS
>
> Home Secretary John Reid is to make another attempt to extend the 28-day limit on holding terrorism suspects without charge.

> *BBC NEWS, 1 FEBRUARY 2007*

SOFT ON TERROR

Where, you may ask, are the opposition parties all this time? The only occasion that they have slowed down New Labour's authoritarian drive is with the 90-day detention proposals in 2005. One of the reasons that the Conservatives and Liberal Democrats have been effectively neutered as an opposition on civil liberties is because of accusations by New Labour of being 'soft on terror'.

Back in 1993, a young up-and-coming Shadow Home Secretary (let's call him Tony Blair) was passionately arguing *against* restrictions on civil liberties that were being proposed by the Conservative Government.

*We want to uphold our traditional rule of law and the
principles that go with it. In attempting to balance those
competing purposes, we should engage in discussions
without accusing each other of being soft on terrorism.*

PREVENTION AND SUPPRESSION OF TERRORISM DEBATE, 9 MARCH 1993[47]

Thirteen years later, when having the same debate but from the other side, he seems to have forgotten that the phrase 'soft on terror' is not playing by the rules:

*At every stage, whether it involves antisocial behaviour,
assets recovery, the Criminal Justice Act or terrorist
legislation, the right honourable gentleman talks tough
but he votes soft.*

PRIME MINISTER'S QUESTIONS, 14 JUNE 2006[48]

Brace yourself for another Nazi comparison; this one is just too good to let slip by.

*Voice or no voice, the people can always be brought to
the bidding of the leaders. That is easy. All you have to
do is tell them they are being attacked, and denounce
the pacifists for lack of patriotism, and exposing the
country to greater danger.*

HERMAN GOERING AT THE NUREMBERG TRIALS[49]

The politics of fear is a three-way game. First you have the Government, who find it easier to control and rule when the population is scared. Second you have the senior police officers, who can do their job more easily if they have more powers. In order to get more powers they help the Government convince itself that we are all about to die, and that the only solution is to give the police more control. But the third part of the chain is the one that acts as an interface between the people in power and the public: the media. And when it comes to the losing battle between liberty and security, there is one section of the press that has worked hand-in-glove with the police and New Labour to erode our freedom in the name of fighting terror.

THE MURDOCH MANACLE

The Murdoch press, and in particular the *Sun*, has effectively become a government newssheet in the 'War Against Terror'. In addition, the relationship between Murdoch and New Labour has undermined the most basic liberty of free speech and been integral to New Labour's suppression of dissent. While not as overt as SOCPA or as blatant as stop-and-search, the *Sun* newspaper has attacked criticism of New Labour on the crucial issues of the Iraq war, terrorism and civil liberties.

It was Margaret Thatcher who first established a *quid pro quo* with the Murdoch empire in the 1980s. She gave Murdoch free rein to buy much of the British media, in return for his papers' support. When Blair became leader of the Labour Party, and transformed it into New Labour, he made sure that he snuggled up to the Murdoch machine well before the '97 election.

Julian Petley is Professor of Film and Television studies at Brunel University in West London. He specialises in the role of the press in helping to whip up moral panics.

After 9/11 the tabloids fixated upon what it calls 'fundamentalists' or 'the terrorists'. To what extent have some groups of people, such as Muslims, not just some of them but all of them, been demonised in the wake of disasters and catastrophes? There is always a search for the folk devil, the demon.

JULIAN PETLEY[50]

CSI – FOREST GATE

An event in the summer of 2006 perfectly illustrates how the politics of fear works to destroy liberty when all three sides are working in harmony: the police, the Government and the Murdoch press.

2 June, 4a.m.: two hundred and fifty police descend on two small houses in Lansdown Road, East London, but only thirty of them could fit in the property. Abdul Kahar Kalam is shot by the police as he comes down the stairs, and is taken

to hospital. His brother, Abdul Koyair, is beaten by police, arrested, and taken to Paddington Green Station. The brothers had no link to terrorism and nothing more dangerous than a bread knife was found at the scene. While the brothers are under lock and key without charge, the police get to work.[51]

3 June: even though there is supposed to be a media blackout, the *Sun* knows what's going on. 'A chemical bomb held by Islamic terrorists is primed to go off at any time...'[52]

4 June: Kahar is transferred from hospital to Paddington Green Station. The *News of the World* – the *Sun*'s Sunday sister paper – reports that one brother shot the other. The *Sunday Times* – also owned by Rupert Murdoch – quotes 'Scotland Yard sources' suggesting that the police were looking for 'a single bomb overlaid with cyanide'.[53]

5 June: the *Sun*: 'evidence was found at the raided house in Forest Gate, East London, to suggest potential links to terrorism... The informant is highly regarded and was certain what he saw with his own eyes was a chemical bomb. We are still convinced the information is 100 percent accurate.'[54]

6 June: the *Sun* reports that Kahar was shot because the officer's chemical protection gloves were too thick and he didn't feel the trigger.[55] Tony Blair chose this moment to issue a statement saying he backs the police '101 percent'.[56]

7 June: the *Sun* reports that the older brother is a criminal who took part in the anti-Islam cartoon demonstration while on day release.[57] The *Sun* and police sources agree that this link proves that the police were right to order the raid. The pair's stepbrother was indeed on that demonstration, but if you are assumed to be guilty as a relative by marriage, then John Reid is a drug dealer (his son's father-in-law was arrested for selling amphetamines).

9 June: both brothers are released without charge due to lack of evidence. The *Sun* headline sums up its views on innocent until proven guilty: '"Chemical bomb" pair free without charge'. The paper reports that one of the brothers had a juvenile criminal record, which they can only have been told about by the police. The brothers were responsible for some petty crime as teenagers, but all of that stopped when they became devout Muslims.[58]

Even with the brothers' innocence confirmed, the community up in arms, and the rest of the media bringing the police to account, the *Sun* loyally continued to smear the brothers: 'Anti-terror cops were last night trying to find out why the two brothers arrested over a suspected poison bomb plot had a £38,000 stash in their house'.[59] Except it wasn't a riddle at all – the reason (that their religion precludes them from earning interest) was given to the police two hours after the arrest.

A fortnight later, Ian Blair made it clear that the only thing that was needed was better communication.

> 'There will be other raids,' he says, 'but the lesson of Forest Gate is that we have to find new methods of engaging with the Muslim community, in particular to reassure them of the necessity and appropriateness of police actions.'[60]

This operation took place within the current limits of pre-charge detention. If the attempt to bring in 90-day detention had been successful, then the Forest Gate brothers could have been detained for three months.

At the time of writing, John Reid is looking at giving the police more powers, and he will no doubt find a loyal supporter in the *Sun*. Whenever New Labour is criticised for this slew of anti-terror laws, the solution is always the same: another anti-terror law.

ADDICTION TO LEGISLATION

> *The more corrupt the state, the more numerous the laws.*
>
> **TACITUS** [61]

> *The amount of law that's come out of New Labour is appalling; I mean it's mad to put it simply. We're now up to about thirteen thousand five hundred pages a year of new statute law. I mean it is bonkers and no society, no culture, could digest that amount of law. It's creating a land fit for lawyers and not much else.*
>
> **LORD PHILLIPS OF SUDBURY, LIBERAL DEMOCRAT PEER** [62]

Back in the early 1990s, Blair was Shadow Home Secretary opposite Michael Howard. He knew that this could be a bit of a poisoned chalice.

> *Tony Blair knew that this was New Labour's weak spot. He said that never again were they going to be made to look weak. So much of what I think 'New Labour' was about was trying to ensure that they were not outgunned by the Conservatives on this.*
>
> **IAN LOADER, PROFESSOR OF CRIMINOLOGY, OXFORD UNIVERSITY** [63]

By 1994 Blair had actually managed to overtake Michael Howard on law and order, which is rather like out-drinking Keith Richards. By the time he was leader, he had reversed the reputation that Labour were soft on crime, and his authoritarian buzz grew.

> *Law and order has always been an issue in which he has taken a deep personal interest. One reason why the*

> *Britain comes bottom of the OECD's fighting bribery*
> *league. Britain and Japan, out of 32 nations, we come*
> *bottom. Neither Britain or Japan have had any*
> *convictions or cases brought against people committing*
> *acts of bribery.*

> **MARK THOMAS**[69]

The SFO enquiry was starting to uncover evidence of bribery, and investigators were about to be granted access to Saudi royal family Swiss bank accounts,[70] when BAe Systems and Saudi Arabia piled on the pressure at No 10. The Saudis threatened to pull out of a new BAe Systems deal worth six billion pounds and the number of jobs this would cost British industry was duly released to the press. Originally it was reported that Lord Goldsmith refused to intervene to stop the enquiry.[71] However, the pressure increased, and on the 'advice' of Tony Blair, Lord Goldsmith changed his mind and announced that the investigation was being dropped.

The reason given? National security. Goldsmith decided that 'the wider public interest' 'outweighed the need to maintain the rule of law'. Nothing to do with commercial interests, then.

But a month later, Sir John Scarlett (head of MI6) publicly made it clear that national security would not be hampered by the enquiry. He had been asked to sign a dossier that confirmed this, but refused (he wasn't about to be caught by that old chestnut again).

> *What Blair and the Attorney General have effectively*
> *said is, 'There is one law for the corporations and*
> *another law for everyone else. We will ignore the law.'*
> *He's used the War on Terror again. The War on Terror*
> *has been used for every conceivable reason. They've*
> *used it to justify every piece of draconian legislation,*
> *and now they've turned around and said, 'Unless we*
> *pay bribes, al-Qaeda will get us'. That's madness.*

> **MARK THOMAS**[72]

Blair and Goldsmith desperately tried to assert that Britain gets great intelligence from the Saudis in the 'War Against Terror'. Sandy Mitchell can testify how worthless the information that comes from the Saudi Ministry of Interior can be.

The contradictions surrounding Blair's relationship with the concept of law are now the stuff of legend:

- he's trained as a lawyer (by all accounts not a very good one);
- his Cabinet is full of lawyers (Geoff Hoon, Jack Straw, Lord Goldsmith);
- he's married to a human-rights lawyer (by all accounts a very good one);
- his Government has passed more laws than any other government in history;
- he's broken several laws – including some that he introduced;
- whenever he needs a quick political fix, he passes another law.

Blair has since passed on the baton to John Reid, who's using it to smash down the basic principles of criminal justice. Fair trial? Innocent until proven guilty? John Reid doesn't do innocent. As soon as he took over the Home Office, he made it clear exactly what he thinks of the rule of law:

NEWS OF THE WORLD, *1 OCTOBER 2006*

He's asking News of the World readers...how THEY
want the laws changed to work for them. Jail sentences,
targeting of crime, young offenders, terrorism...
paedophiles – it's your call.
*   The tough-talking Scot, dubbed the McTerminator,*
wants to STOP these issues being dominated by lawyers,

> politicians and civil servants. And he'll fight to put YOU
> in the driving seat.
>   'They are too important to be left to the
> professionals,' he said. 'We need the ideas and views of
> real people, like your readers.
>   'I want to meet them in person, they can write in,
> email me via the internet. We need their help.'[73]

Some of the responses are unprintable, but one of the more liberal and sophisticated ideas he received was this:

> I am a Conservative voter but you could change that Dr
> Reid, as you are becoming my favourite MP and the one
> I would like to see be a Labour Prime Minister. You are
> the one I trust to turn this Government around and do
> what I would do in your place and restrict immigration
> to Europeans only and evict Muslims from this country.
>
> **JOHN LEWIS, SHEFFIELD**[74]

And it's not just Britain sleepwalking into a totalitarian state. Like it or not, Britain is watched – and many other countries are taking our lead.

ROUND THE WORLD

Britain was once the cradle of democracy, and exported ideas like free speech, habeas corpus, the right to protest, and the prohibition from torture. Now, New Labour is viewed with envy by governments who are emulating our 'crackdown on terror', dismantling the rights and protections of their citizens – sometimes more brutally and viciously.

There could be an entire book on how freedoms are being eroded in each of the following countries, but here is a whistle-stop tour of how liberty loses out to 'security'.

US

Where to begin? The Bush Administration has defined an act of terrorism as things that to the Government 'appear to be intended' to 'influence the policy of a government by intimidation or coercion', or 'to intimidate or coerce a civilian population'. Such ambiguous language allows for loose interpretation that might violate civil liberties and international human rights.

The Patriot Act allows non-citizens to be detained without charge and held indefinitely once charged. It also permits the Government to scrutinise people's reading habits by monitoring public library and bookstore records, without notifying the suspect. It also allows for 'sneak and peek' tactics such as physical search of property and computers, wiretapping and monitoring of email, and access to financial and educational records, without providing notification.

Zimbabwe

In February the police placed a three-month ban on protests and political rallies after what they say was anarchy during an opposition protest rally. The police say that the ban is necessary in order to maintain law and order, but others see it as an attempt to ban the opposition party.

Scotland (Yes, it's part of Britain, but this story just had to be included)

May 2005. Property developer Sally Cameron, 34, was arrested under the Prevention of Terrorism Act for walking on a cycle path to work. She was detained for four hours and charged as a terrorist. The authorities said, 'Because the woman was in a secure area which forbids people walking, it was seen as a security risk. We were following guidelines in requirements within the port security plan set up by the Government.'[75]

France

Islamophobia is nothing new in French politics. In 2005 the heavily Muslim suburbs of Paris erupted in riots after two youths died while being chased by police. At the end of 2005, 72 Muslim airport staff, most of them baggage handlers, were barred from Paris's main airport on the grounds that they posed a security threat. This came after the publication of a book by a politician of the far Right, in which he basically talked about Muslim infiltration of the French airports.[76]

Germany

A recent conference of interior ministers of federal states discussed the necessity of 'improving co-operation between the police and intelligence services, especially through sharing data on terrorists'. By using these words, they hide the fact that the database is not supposed to be one of convicted criminals but essentially a preventative list of suspects. They are proposing a 'joint anti-terror database', which is to be supplied and used by all German police forces and all 19 intelligence services on the national and federal state level. With this network, police and intelligence services will become more entwined – despite the constitution calling for a strict separation of these two kinds of state security agencies.[77]

Belgium

In Belgium the far Right Vlaams Belang nearly captured control of the Antwerp City Government in mid-October 2006 on an openly Islamophobic platform. They won about 33.5 percent of the vote. Compare that to 35 percent assembled by the socialist coalition.[78]

Holland

The Government has recently proposed to give banks and other financial-service providers access to the population register data behind the new 'citizen service number', even before the law introducing this number is passed by both houses of parliament. The Government has decided to enforce a total ban on women wearing burkhas and face veils in public, on the pretext that they endanger 'public order, security and the protection of citizens'.[79]

Italy

Has been more complicit with Extraordinary Rendition than Britain, and has actually allowed people to be kidnapped by the CIA off Italian streets. Mr Hassan was abducted on 17 February 2003, and flown out of the country from a US base north of Venice. When he finally got word through to his family last year, he told them he had been tortured with electric shocks during his detention. Unsurprisingly, Silvio Berlusconi took Blair's lead, and refused to order an enquiry.[80]

Australia

On 8 September 2005 the Prime Minister released details of a dozen new changes to Australia's 'anti-terrorism' laws:

- increased executive discretion to target individuals and organisations because of their political views;
- detention and other restrictions on liberty without any crime being charged or proved;
- new powers for the police to stop, search and demand documents without warrant.

December 2006. Allen Jasson was refused permission to board a connecting flight within Australia unless he removed a T-shirt reading 'World's #1 Terrorist' and bearing a picture of US President George W. Bush.[81]

Japan

A controversial Immigration Bureau website was recently launched, allowing informants to report the name, address or work-place of any suspicious foreigners for such reasons as 'causing a nuisance in the neighbourhood' and 'causing anxiety'.[82]

Venezuela

London Mayor Ken Livingstone recently tried to broker a deal with Venezuelan president Hugo Chavez to swap biometric technology and CCTV systems for cheap oil. According to Amnesty International, police death squads target innocent civilians, human-rights campaigners are threatened and terrorised, and the judicial system is packed with pro-Chavez stooges. 'The idea of giving a regime like this advanced biometric fingerprinting technology is astounding,' said Aleksander Boyd, a Venezuelan exile and campaigner based in London.[83]

East Asia

Human Rights Watch said that SCO (Shanghai Cooperation Organisation) member states – which include Russia, China, Kazakhstan, Kyrgyzstan, Tajikistan and Uzbekistan – have committed serious violations of human rights and humanitarian law in the name of counter-terrorism. Of particular concern are SCO members' records with respect to extraditions, Renditions, extrajudicial executions, treatment of terrorism suspects in police custody, and the treatment of religious dissidents and of ethnic minorities, among others, who peacefully advocate independence.[84]

> *Traditional civil liberties arguments are not so much wrong, just made for a different age.*
>
> **TONY BLAIR**

Chapter 9
What next?

When the people fear their government, there is tyranny;
when the government fears the people, there is liberty.

THOMAS JEFFERSON

It really is now up to you. You need to decide what country you want to live in, as Britain in ten years could be a very different place...

2017
- Disagreeing with the Government is a criminal act in itself.
- Making jokes about politicians can get you fined, and the police don't differentiate between protesting and terrorism.
- DNA is now a currency, the Government is starting to install CCTV in homes, and you are asked to produce your ID card twenty times a day – forty if you are from an ethnic minority.
- ID fraud is the biggest crime, thanks to the National Identity Register being hacked even before it went online.
- The Government regularly puts control orders on people it has convicted of future crimes, and thousands of potentially difficult children are fitted with microchips to track their whereabouts.
- The presumption of innocence does not exist, as the police and Government can decide guilt of any crime, and you can be locked up for a year before charge.

- The police are authorised to use 'harsh interrogation techniques'.

Is this what Britain will become? The best way to find out is to do absolutely nothing. Keep your head down and carry on as though you'd read that nice book about kittens instead. It's fine, honestly, you'll never suffer an injustice. The same way that all the people in this book thought it wouldn't happen to them.

Or, if you want to live in a place that is a bit different to the nightmare described above, then you might just have to get off your arse and do something.

> *Public opinion has more power than people might think.*
> *The Iraq war happened despite the massive opposition,*
> *so people say, 'Well, we didn't stop that war'. That's true.*
> *But, so far, we've stopped the next one.*
>
> **MARK THOMAS**[1]

Whenever politicians dismiss a protest, it's usually a sure sign that it's working.

Governments tend not to like it much (it's difficult to claim to be representing the silent majority when that majority is shouting its opinions at you), but we need to remind them that they are the servants of the people and not the other way around.

> *How many times did there have to be marches before*
> *Apartheid ended? How many Suffragettes were put in*
> *prison before they got the vote? All life is the struggle of*
> *people to have some rights over those who've got power.*
>
> **TONY BENN**[2]

It's not too late to do something about this, but it will require us to do something a bit more than tutting mildly while reading this book.

It's time to take back democracy.

MASS LONE DEMOS –
DEMONSTRATION GETS PERSONAL

SOCPA, having been aimed squarely at Brian Haw, requires every protest to ask for permission. Knowing this, Mark Thomas figured out an amusing, simple way to make a pointed mockery of the act: get everyone who's up for it to apply for permission for an individual protest, all at once, for the same hour-long period. In July 2006, about twelve of us arrived at Charing Cross police station, forms in hand. The police, bemused, slowly processed the queue's SOCPA forms and told them to await their permission by post. The demonstration went ahead without incident. So Mark decided to do it again the next month.

This time, several bloggers picked it up, including Rachel North. The *Guardian* ran an article. On 24 August Charing Cross was swamped by over a hundred and seventy simultaneous form-wavers. The police station ground to a standstill, but the police were generally good-natured about it. One lady brought her form in iced upon a cake. Another lady arrived claiming she was a medium who was possessed by the spirit of Winston Churchill, and tried to hold a séance. It took three hours to process the forms, and the cake came in very useful. Mark did a piece on live news, and a couple of people saw the item and ran down to join in.

Exactly a week later, the very same individual protestors showed up in Parliament Square. They were protesting for the right to protest, and about anything else on their minds. The silliness of the placards – from 'Goth Pride' to 'Every time you masturbate, God kills a Tory' – was a very British comment on the absurdity of the law.

The mass lone demos have continued since their first success. We await news from parliament on new legislation against non-energy-saving lightbulbs, poor grammar, mobile phones playing music on buses, and the dark. Alternatively, the Government may opt to bow to public pressure and legalise everything... as well as banning everything, as suggested by one of the first protestors with a keen sense of situationism. They are a great way to meet people as well, so check out Mark Thomas's website – all you need is something to say.

If 1000 people turned up, the Government might think that SOCPA was causing problems. If 10,000 people arrived for a mass lone demo, then Sir Ian Blair would be begging for SOCPA to be repealed.

> *People talk about the checks and balances of the political system; we are the checks and balances. We are the democratic process. So we should start behaving like one.*
>
> **MARK THOMAS³**

If you want your protest a little more focused, then below is a list of groups that we've come into contact with while writing this book and making the film. There are thousands more that are just a click away on the internet. But if you can't find the group you're looking for, start your own. All you need is a piece of cardboard, a stick, some sticky tape and a felt-tip pen, and you will be transformed into a lethal democratic machine. Find some other like-minded people and cause some trouble.

> *We are made wise not by the recollection of our past, but by the responsibility for our future.*
>
> **GEORGE BERNARD SHAW**

Go to the *Taking Liberties* website (www.noliberties.com) to get you started...

Amnesty International
www.amnesty.org.uk
Amnesty's campaign against torture in the 'War Against Terror' was launched on 26 June 2005. The campaign addresses the fact that some governments are using methods of interrogation and detention that amounts to torture and inhuman and degrading treatment. Visit this website to give them your support.

Article 19

www.article19.org

An international human-rights organisation which defends and promotes freedom of expression and freedom of information all over the world. The name is taken from Article 19 of the Universal Declaration of Human Rights, which states, 'Everyone has the right to freedom of opinion and expression; the right includes freedom to hold opinions without interference and to seek, receive and impart information and ideas through any media regardless of frontiers'.

ASBOwatch

www.statewatch.org/asbo/ASBOwatch.html

ASBOwatch is part of Statewatch, and monitors the use of antisocial behaviour orders.

Avaaz

www.avaaz.org

'Avaaz' means 'voice' or 'song' in several languages (including Hindi, Urdu, Farsi, Nepalese, Dari, Turkish and Bosnian), and is a community of global citizens who take action on the major issues facing the world today.

BBC Action Network

www.bbc.co.uk/dna/actionnetwork

A network that can help you change something in your local area. Get in touch with people who feel the same way, and get advice on taking action. People use this website to campaign on a variety of issues, and often there is more than one campaign on a single issue, with people arguing for and against.

Campaign Against Criminalising Communities

www.campacc.org.uk

This campaign aims to oppose all laws based on a pretext of counter-terrorism, and to lobby for the repeal of such laws as the Terrorism Act 2000, the Anti-Terrorism, Crime and Security Act

(ACTSA) 2001, and the Prevention of Terrorism Act 2005. People use this website for campaign news and information on events.

Campaign Against Arms Trade
www.caat.org.uk
This consists of a broad coalition of groups and individuals (with no formal membership structure) in the UK working to end the international arms trade through non-violent action. People use this website for information on previous campaigns and on how to get involved in the future.

Campaign for the Accountability of American Bases
www.caab.org.uk
A campaign deeply opposed to weapons of mass destruction, and nuclear weapons in particular: specifically the proposed American Missile Defense/Theater Defence Systems. This website seeks to raise public awareness, scrutiny and accountability of American bases in the UK.

Campaign for Nuclear Disarmament
www.cnduk.org
CND campaigns non-violently to rid the world of nuclear weapons and other weapons of mass destruction. People use this website for information on campaigns, events and news.

Corporate Watch UK
www.corporatewatch.org.uk
Corporate Watch is a small independent not-for-profit research and publishing group which undertakes research on the social and environmental impact of large corporations, particularly multi-nationals. People use this website for information on different industries and UK companies, DIY research guides, newsletters and mailing lists.

Downing St Says...

www.downingstsays.com

Every day the Prime Minister's official spokesman meets a small coterie of political journalists known as 'the lobby' for a topical chat, or 'briefing'.

Downing Street Says... is an unofficial site that lets you read summaries of these briefings and add your own comments.

EPetitions

http://petitions.pm.gov.uk

A UK Government site for creating petitions and delivering them directly to the Prime Minister.

Free Beagles

www.freebeagles.org

This website provides materials to introduce you to your legal rights, and to what to expect if you are unfortunate enough to run into trouble with the law. Know your rights. Often the police and others will use intimidation and ignorance to suppress those who want to change the status quo for the better. By being informed, you help yourself and your campaign.

Friends Extradited

www.friendsextradited.org

This campaign is organised by family, friends and ex-colleagues of the NatWest Three, and has already been joined by many people with no direct knowledge or contact with the men. The campaign seeks to raise the profile of this case, and gives advice to people on what they can do to get involved and contribute to the campaign.

Independent Media Center

www.indymedia.org/en

A network of collectively run media outlets, originally set up to provide grass-roots coverage of the WTO protests in Seattle. There are currently over one hundred and fifty Independent

Media Centers around the world. Each IMC is an autonomous group that has its own mission statement, manages its own finances, and makes its own decisions through its own processes. People use this website either to submit their articles, stories, and videos, and to access those submitted by others, or to get in touch with others who share their views on particular issues.

Indymedia
www.indymedia.org.uk
A network of individuals, independent and alternative media activists and organisations, offering grass-roots, non-corporate, non-commercial coverage of social and political issues, the stuff you see in the mainstream press and the stuff you don't.

IPetitions
www.ipetitions.com
IPetitions takes the power of the internet to transform society and places it in the hands of ordinary people. This website gives people the tools and community to create their own sophisticated online campaign. All you have to do is write a petition in support of your cause. IPetitions can help you gather support for your campaign from around the world.

Iraq Body Count
www.iraqbodycount.org
This is an ongoing human-security project which maintains and updates the world's only independent and comprehensive public database of media-reported civilian deaths in Iraq that have resulted from the 2003 military intervention by the US and its allies. The count includes civilian deaths caused by coalition military action and by military or paramilitary responses to the coalition presence (e.g. insurgent and terrorist attacks). It also includes excess civilian deaths caused by criminal action resulting from the breakdown in law and order which followed the coalition invasion.

Justice

www.justice.org.uk

An all-party law reform and human-rights organisation working to improve the legal system and the quality of justice.

Justice Not Vengeance

www.j-n-v.org

An anti-war group which has developed out of ARROW (Active Resistance to the Roots of War). JNV opposes the US–UK 'War Against Terror', and campaigns for a peaceful resolution of international conflicts, based on justice and equality. People use this website to get information on past, present and upcoming political events and actions.

Liberty

www.liberty-human-rights.org.uk

One of the UK's oldest human-rights and civil-liberties organisations. They lobby parliament, exposing laws that undermine civil liberties and human rights, and work with politicians to correct them. They also challenge unjust laws, by taking test cases to English and European courts.

Make it an Issue

www.makeitanissue.org.uk

Launched by the Power Inquiry in 2004, Make it an Issue's four aims are to establish clear democratic rules designed in the interests of citizens, to remove the influence of money and patronage from politics, to give people more say in the big decisions affecting the country, and to ensure power is exercised closer to the people. The website is used by people interested in joining in with debates, and giving their views on issues which are usually left to parliament.

Mark Thomas Info

www.markthomasinfo.com

As well as letting you know what Mark Thomas is up to, this is where you can find out about how to join in with mass lone demos in Parliament Square and much more.

Medact

www.medact.org

Medical Action for Global Security is a charitable organisation of health professionals concerned with the health impacts of violent conflict, poverty and environmental degradation. Since 1992, Medact has taken a lead in highlighting the health aspects of many of today's global issues, including landmines, Third World debt, climate change and refugees.

mySociety

www.mysociety.org

A charitable project which builds websites that give people simple, tangible benefits in the civic and community aspects of their lives. It also teaches the public and voluntary sectors, through demonstration, how most efficiently to use the internet to improve lives. MySociety has developed lots of the other sites here (including They Work for You, Public Whip, Write to Them, Downing St Says and Pledgebank).

Network For Peace

www.networkforpeace.org.uk

Network for Peace was set up to continue the work of the National Peace Council, one of the oldest peace organisations in the UK. Its aim is to act as a contact point for queries about peace organisations, peace education and training, actions, vigils and demonstrations, especially in times of crisis or emergency.

No2ID

www.no2id.net

No2ID is a UK-wide, non-partisan campaign opposing the Government's planned ID card and National Identity Register. It brings together individuals and organisations from all sections of the community and seeks to ensure that the case against ID cards and the database state is forcefully put forward in the media, in the corridors of power and at grass-roots level. It continues to campaign actively on all fronts for the abolition of the ID scheme and repeal of the Identity Cards Act 2006.

NUS online

www.nusonline.co.uk

NUS is one of the largest student organisations in the world, and represents the interests of around five million students in further and higher education throughout the UK.

Our World Our Say

www.ourworldoursay.org

Works to give people a voice when politicians circumvent them, particularly over world-changing issues. Through reconnecting ordinary citizens with their elected representatives and giving them a voice, it aims to give people power over their own future and invigorate the democratic process. People use this website for information on various campaigns, and on how to contact their MPs.

Parliament Square

www.parliament-square.org.uk

The website of peace protestor Brian Haw and the Parliament Square peace campaign. It asks for people to support Brian, and to get involved in defending the right to protest near parliament. People use this website for information on how to get involved and support the campaign. Or just go and visit him in front of the Houses of Parliament.

People in Common

www.peopleincommon.org

Fancy a cup of tea? Raspberry sponge? Information about SOCPA and suggestions for Parliament Square gatherings, including the famous Sunday political picnics.

Petition Online

www.petitiononline.com

International free online petition site for public petitions and responsible public advocacy. With lots of links to other interesting sites.

Plane Stupid

www.planestupid.com

This is the group that Ellen and Rose, and Malcolm Carroll, from chapter 2 belong to. Plane Stupid is a coalition of airport-area residents and environmentalists who use direct action to stop the destruction of the environment and communities caused by airport expansion and aviation.

Pledgebank

www.pledgebank.com

PledgeBank allows users to set up pledges, and then encourages other people to sign up to them. A pledge is a statement of the form, 'I will do something, if a certain number of people will help me do it'. The creator of the pledge then publicises their pledge and encourages people to sign up. One of two outcomes is possible. Either the pledge fails to get enough subscribers before it expires; in that case, everyone is contacted and told, 'Better luck next time'. But the better possibility is that a pledge attracts enough people, that they are all sent a message saying, 'Well done – now get going!'

Privacy International

www.privacyinternational.org

Privacy International is a human-rights group formed in 1990 as a watchdog on surveillance and privacy invasions by governments and corporations. It has conducted campaigns and research throughout the world on issues ranging from wiretapping and national security to ID cards, video surveillance, data matching, medical privacy and freedom of information and expression. People use this website for information on campaigns research, and networking.

Public Whip

www.publicwhip.org.uk

An independent, non-governmental project to watch members of the UK parliament, so that the public (people like us) can better understand and influence their voting patterns. All the House of Commons and House of Lords debate transcripts (collectively, *Hansard*) back to 1988 are published on the web. Public Whip has written a program to read them for you and separate out all the records of voting. This information has been added into an online database which you can access.

Reprieve

www.reprieve.org.uk

A UK charity that fights for the lives of people facing the death penalty and other human-rights violations. Clive Stafford Smith, who formed the organisation, was the first British lawyer to enter Guantanamo and is still fighting to free people from there.

Rising Tide

www.risingtide.org.uk

Another climate change website. Although we haven't really spoken much about it, this is where activism is alive and well – and needs to be.

SchNEWS

www.schnews.org.uk

Direct action and protest news with nationwide action listings, published weekly in Brighton since 1994. People use this website for news, and for information on upcoming parties and protests.

Searchlight magazine

www.searchlightmagazine.com

Searchlight is a British anti-fascist magazine, founded in 1975, which publishes exposés about racism, antisemitism and fascism in the UK. *Searchlight*'s main focus is on the British National Party (BNP), Combat 18, and other sections of the far Right, although it has also published criticism of the United Kingdom Independence Party and sections of the Conservative Party.

SmashEDO

www.smashedo.org.uk

This is an anti-arms group specifically aimed at the EDO factory in Brighton. Its Wednesday afternoon noise demos outside the factory have been incredibly successful. See the story in the film.

Space hijackers

http://www.spacehijackers.co.uk

Trouble with an anti-capital T, they describe themselves better than anyone else could: 'The Space Hijackers believe completely in the good hard work of the IMF, World Bank and WTO. We think big multinationals are brilliant, and all wear Nike thongs.'

Spy.org

www.spy.org.uk

This website aims to open up a debate about the extent to which powerful technologies such as linked CCTV camera systems, neural network facial recognition, car-numberplate recognition, multimedia image databases etc. are being applied in the UK. People use this website to lobby political parties, for information on new developments, and to take part in the debate.

Statewatch

www.statewatch.org

This is a non-profit-making voluntary group founded in 1991 comprised of lawyers, academics, journalists, researchers and community activists. Its European network of contributors is drawn from 15 countries. Statewatch encourages the publication of investigative journalism and critical research in Europe in the fields of the state, justice and home affairs, civil liberties, accountability and openness.

Stop the War Coalition

www.stopwar.org.uk

The aim of the coalition is to stop the war currently declared by the US and its allies against 'terrorism'. It condemns the attacks on New York and feels the greatest compassion for those who lost their life on 11 September 2001. But any war will simply add to the numbers of innocent dead, cause untold suffering, political and economic instability on a global scale, increase racism and result in attacks on civil liberties. Tony Benn is president of the coalition. People use the website for news and for information on how to get involved.

The Big Opt Out

www.nhsconfidentiality.org

The NHS Confidentiality campaign was set up to protect patient confidentiality and to provide a focus for patient-led opposition to the Government's NHS care records system.

They Work for You

www.theyworkforyou.com

Follow MPs' and Lords' voting records, be alerted when they speak in the Commons, or when someone discusses something you're interested in. Find your MP's contact details and see how much they spend. A non-partisan website run by a charity which aims to make it easy for people to keep tabs on their elected and unelected representatives in parliament and other assemblies.

Truthout

www.truthout.org

Full-service news agency dedicated to establishing a powerful, stable voice for independent journalism. Truthout scours the global news media for the most important stories. It covers national issues concerning foreign policy, the war in Iraq, ethics in government, voter rights, human rights and the judiciary, and features unique coverage of women, health, energy, environment and labour issues. It also alerts readers to pivotal opinion pieces appearing in major newspapers and journals.

War on Want

www.waronwant.org

A campaign saying that 'The only war worth fighting is the war on poverty'. War on Want fights poverty in developing countries in partnership and solidarity with people affected by globalisation. They campaign for workers' rights and against the root causes of global poverty, inequality and injustice. People access the website to watch the latest campaign videos, read alternative news reports, and for news on upcoming events and campaigns.

Write to Them

www.writetothem.com

Contact your Councillors, MP, MEPs, MSPs, or Northern Ireland, Welsh and London AMs for free.

Your Rights

www.yourrights.org.uk

An easily understood guide to the Human Rights Act 1998, explaining its relevance and impact in many different areas of law, ranging from rights of privacy to rights of peaceful protest. Your Rights is written by expert lawyers, but intended primarily for people who have no specialist legal knowledge.

Z

www.zmag.org

Z is an independent monthly magazine of critical thinking, dedicated to resisting injustice and defending against repression. It sees the racial, gender, class and political dimensions of personal life as fundamental to understanding and improving contemporary circumstances; and it aims to assist activist efforts for a better future.

AND FINALLY HERE'S SOME GOOD BOOKS BY OUR CONTRIBUTORS

7/7: The London Bombings, Islam and the Iraq War by Milan Rai (JNV Publications, 2006)

As Used on the Famous Nelson Mandela: Underground Adventures in the Arms and Torture Trade by Mark Thomas (Ebury Press, 2006)

Ghost Plane by Stephen Grey (C. Hurst and Co., 2006)

Lawless World by Philippe Sands (Penguin Books, 2006)

Naming The Dead by Maya Evans (JNV Publications, 2006)

One Day in July by John Tulloch (Little, Brown, 2006)

Saudi Babylon by Mark Hollingsworth, with Sandy Mitchell (Mainstream Publishing, 2005)

Notes

Introduction

1 'Security, freedom and the protection of our values', speech by the Home Secretary to DEMOS, 9 August 2006.

2 Tony Benn, interview transcript, p.1, 24 September 2006.

3 Boris Johnson, interview transcript, p.5, 28 June 2006.

4 C.S. Lewis, *God in the Dock: Essays on Theology and Ethics*, ed. Walter Hooper (Wm B. Eerdmans Publishing Co., 1970), p.292.

5 Shami Chakrabarti, interview transcript, 23 June 2006.

6 Serious Organised Crime and Police Act 2005, chapter 15, part 4, 'Public order and conduct in public places', http://www.opsi.gov.uk/acts/acts2005/50015--l.htm.

7 National ID Scheme.

8 CCTV.

9 Prevention of Terrorism Act 2005, http://www.homeoffice.gov.uk/security/terrorism-and-the-law/prevention-of-terrorism.

10 On 31 March 2003, David Blunkett, UK Home Secretary, signed an extradition treaty on behalf of the UK with his US counterpart, Attorney General John Ashcroft, which was promoted on the basis of the need for a streamlined extradition process to deal with the new global terrorist threat after 9/11; http://www.friendsextradited.org/thelaw.htm.

11 'Britain's role in CIA "torture flights" was roundly condemned yesterday by the European parliament in a scathing report which for the first time named the site of a suspected secret US detention centre in the EU – at Stare Kiejkuty in Poland': 'MEPs condemn Britain's role in torture flights', Richard Norton Taylor, 29 November 2006, http://www.guardian.co.uk/usa/story/0,,1959360,00.html.

Chapter 1

1 The Aitken Affair, *Guardian*, http://www.guardian.co.uk/aitken; Hamilton–Al Fayed libel case, *Guardian*, http://www.guardian.co.uk/hamilton; 'Mellor resigns over sex scandal', BBC, http://news.bbc.co.uk/onthisday/hi/dates/stories/september/24/newsid_2529000/2529115.stm; Jeffrey Archer, *Guardian*, http://www.guardian.co.uk/archer/0,2759,180881,00.html.

2 Labour Party Manifesto 1997, http://www.labour-party.org.uk/manifestos/1997/1997-labour-manifesto.shtml.

3   Quoted in: 'Labour "sleazier than Major's Tories"', *Daily Telegraph*, 15 July 2006, http://www.telegraph.co.uk/news/main.jhtml?xml=/news/2006/07/15/nsleaze15.xml.

4   Quoted in speech at Specialist Schools and Academies Trust Conference, 30 November 2006, http://www.pm.gov.uk/output/Page10514.asp.

5   '1997: Labour routs Tories in historic victory', BBC, http://news.bbc.co.uk/onthisday/hi/dates/stories/may/2/newsid_248 0000/2480505.stm.

6   Rachel North, interview transcript, pp.1–3, 12 June 2006.

7   Mayor's statement, 7 July 2005, http://www.london.gov.uk/mayor/mayor_statement_070705.jsp.

8   'Blair says "terror will not win"', BBC, 7 July 2005, http://news.bbc.co.uk/2/hi/uk_news/politics/4659933.stm.

9   Prime Minister's press conference, 5 August 2005, http://www.number10.gov.uk/output/Page8041.asp.

10   http://www.homeoffice.gov.uk/security/terrorism-and-the-law/terrorism-act.

11   http://www.opsi.gov.uk/acts/acts2005/20050015.htm.

12   http://www.homeoffice.gov.uk/security/terrorism-and-the-law/terrorism-act-2006.

13   Norris and McCahill, *CCTV In London* (2002), http://www.urbaneye.net/results/ue_wp6.pdf.

14   http://www.homeoffice.gov.uk/security/terrorism-and-the-law/anti-terrorism-crime-security-ac.

15   http://www.opsi.gov.uk/acts/acts2003/20030041.htm.

16   http://www.opsi.gov.uk/acts/acts2005/20050002.htm.

17   http://www.homeoffice.gov.uk/anti-social-behaviour/penalties/penalty-notices.

18   'Ex-ambassador slams Straw over torture', *Sunday Herald*, 20 February 2005, http://www.craigmurray.co.uk/archives/2005/02/sunday_herald_e.html.

19   'Britain accused over CIA's secret torture flights', *Independent*, 10 February 2005, http://www.commondreams.org/headlines05/0210-11.htm.

20   Rachel North, interview transcript, pp.7–9, 19, 21, 12 June 2006.

Chapter 2

1   '*Vanity Fair*'s Arresting Look at Blair's Britain', *Guardian*, 29 June 2006, http://www.guardian.co.uk/terrorism/story/0,,1808226,00.html.

2   'Police hold mother of three for reading "Independent" outside
    Downing Street', *Independent*, 1 July 2006. 'Blair laid bare: the
    article that may get you arrested', *Independent*, 29 June 2006,
    http://news.independent.co.uk/uk/politics/article1129827.ece.

3   Henry Porter, 'Blair's Big Brother Britain', reprinted in
    Independent, 29 June 2006.

4   Henry Porter, interview transcript, p.4, 20 June 2006.

5   Agnes Callamard, interview transcript, p.3, 20 June 2006.

6   The Bill of Rights 1689, Modern History Sources, Fordham
    University, http://www.fordham.edu/halsall/mod/
    1689billofrights.html. 'History of Free Speech', *Observer*,
    5 February 2006, observer.guardian.co.uk/freepress/story/
    0,,1702690,00.html.

7   'You Sir, are a bore', Eric Gibson, *Wall Street Journal*,
    12 September 2003.

8   The Peterloo Massacre 1819, Modern History Sourcebook,
    Fordham University, http://www.fordham.edu/halsall/mod/
    1819peterloo.html; http://www.manchesteronline.co.uk/tourist/
    history/s/64/64106_the_peterloo_massacre.html. 'Supporting the
    Civil Power', http://www.national-army-museum.ac.uk/exhibitions/
    soldiersSeahawks/page5.shtml.

9   'Chartism', http://www.spartacus.schoolnet.co.uk/CHplug.htm.
    'Chartism, Parliamentary Reform Acts',
    http://www.spartacus.schoolnet.co.uk/chartism.htm.

10 'Emancipation of Women', http://www.spartacus.schoolnet.co.uk/
    Wcat.htm. '1918 Women Act',
    http://www.spartacus.schoolnet.co.uk/W1918.htm.

11 Shami Chakrabarti, interview transcript, p.1, 23 June 2006.

12 Serious Organised Crime and Police Act 2005,
    http://www.opsi.gov.uk/acts/acts2005/50015--l.htm; Terrorism Act
    2000, http://www.opsi.gov.uk/acts/acts2000/20000011.htm;
    Prevention of Terrorism Act 2005, http://www.opsi.gov.uk/acts/
    acts2005/20050002.htm; Prevention of Terrorism Act 2006,
    http://www.opsi.gov.uk/acts/acts2006/20060011.htm.

13 Tony Benn, interview transcript, p.4, 24 September 2005.

14 John Catt, interview transcript, p.36, 17 June 2005.

15 All quotes from Walter Wolfgang, interview transcript, pp.15, 19,
    22–23, 24–26, 28–29, 45, 25 July 2006.

16 'Wolfgang highlights deeper disquiet', BBC, 29 September 2005,
    http://news.bbc.co.uk/1/hi/uk_politics/4293502.stm.

17 'Are police misusing stop and search', 23 October 2005, BBC,
    http://news.bbc.co.uk/2/hi/uk_news/4365572.stm. 'Police stop and
    search 100 people a day under new anti-terror laws', Information

Liberation, 25 January 2006, http://www.informationliberation.com/index.php?id=5440.

18 John Catt, interview transcript, 17 June 2006.

19 John Catt, interview transcript 3, p.1, 17 June 2006.

20 '"Million" march against Iraq war', BBC, 16 February 2003, http://news.bbc.co.uk/1/hi/uk/2765041.stm. 'Millions join global anti-war protests', BBC, 17 February 2003, http://news.bbc.co.uk/1/hi/world/europe/2765215.stm. 'The 45 minute claim', BBC, 13 October 2004, http://news.bbc.co.uk/1/hi/uk_politics/3466005.stm.

21 'Blair speech key quotes', BBC, 15 February 2003, http://news.bbc.co.uk/1/hi/uk_politics/2765763.stm.

22 John Kenneth Galbraith, *The Essential Galbraith*, ed. A. Williams (Houghton Mifflin, 2001), p.241.

23 'Children march against war', BBC, 20 March 2003, http://news.bbc.co.uk/1/hi/education/2867923.stm.

24 'Stop the war protests, say heads', BBC, 20 March 2003, http://news.bbc.co.uk/1/hi/education/2869147.stm.

25 'Why we've missed school to protest', BBC, 21 March 2003, http://news.bbc.co.uk/1/hi/education/2873131.stm.

26 S2S footage tape source S2SEXT044.

27 Telephone interview with Shami Chakrabarti, 13 June 2006.

28 Margaret Mead, anthropologist (1901–1978).

29 Chartism, http://www.spartacus.schoolnet.co.uk/CHplug.htm; 'Emancipation of Women', http://www.spartacus.schoolnet.co.uk/Wcat.htm. 'Jarrow crusade remembered', BBC Online Features, http://www.bbc.co.uk/wear/content/articles/2006/10/01/jarrow_crusade_route_feature.shtml; http://www.bbc.co.uk/history/british/britain_wwone/jarrow_04.shtml.

30 Henry Porter, interview transcript 1, p.2, 20 June 2006.

31 Serious Organised Crime and Police Act, http://www.opsi.gov.uk/acts/acts2005/20050015.htm#aofs.

32 Chapter 15, part 4, Public Order and Conduct in Public Places, http://www.opsi.gov.uk/acts/acts2005/50015--l.htm.

33 Section 132, 133, 136, http://www.opsi.gov.uk/acts/acts2005/50015--l.htm.

34 'A casualty of free speech', Terri Judd and Nigel Morris, *Independent*, 10 December 2005, http://www.parliament-square.org.uk/independent101205.htm. David Blunkett, when he was Home Secretary, explained the Government's case as follows: 'It is a sledgehammer to crack a nut, but he is a nut', http://www.markthomasinfo.com/nsarticles/default.asp?id=2.

35 See previous note.

36 Brian Haw, Wikipedia, http://en.wikipedia.org/wiki/Brian_Haw.
37 See previous note.
38 See note 36.
39 See note 36.
40 See note 36.
41 See note 36.
42 Brian Haw website, http://www.parliament-square.org.uk/about. Section 32: chapter 15, part 4, Public Order and Conduct in Public Places, http://www.opsi.gov.uk/acts/acts2005/ 50015--l.htm. House of Commons Procedure Committee, 3 July 2003, Question 148.
43 Brian Haw website, http://www.parliament-square.org.uk/about.
44 'Met chief risks rift with leak probe', *Daily Telegraph*, 27 May 2006, http://www.telegraph.co.uk/news/main.jhtml?xml=/news/ 2006/05/28/nmet28.xml&sSheet=/news/2006/05/28/ ixuknews.html.
45 'Defending the right to protest', All Women Count, http://www.allwomencount.net/EWC%20LAW/ parliamentarybriefingSOCA.htm.
46 Mark Thomas, interview transcript, p.24, 12 January 2007.
47 SOCPA Recent News and Analysis, Indy Media, 4 September 2006, http://www.indymedia.org.uk/en/2006/09/ 350008.html?c=on. 'Activist Convicted Under Demo Law', http://news.bbc.co.uk/1/hi/england/london/4507446.stm.
48 *Hansard*, written answers for 20 July 2006, John Reid.
49 Milan Rai, interview transcript 2, p.4, 30 May 2006.
50 Maya Evans, interview transcript, p.32, 12 June 2006.
51 'Activist convicted under demo law', BBC, 7 December 2005. http://news.bbc.co.uk/1/hi/england/london/4507446.stm. Milan Rai, interview transcript 2, p.6, 30 May 2006.
52 Maya Evans, *Naming The Dead* (JNV Publications, 2006), p.17.
53 Maya Evans, *Naming The Dead* (JNV Publications, 2006), p.18.
54 Milan Rai, interview transcript 2, p.7, 30 May 2006. 'First person to be charged … parliament protest', http://www.spy.org.uk/ parliamentprotest/2006/01/first_person_to_be_charged_wit.html.
55 Maya Evans, interview transcript, p.10, 12 June 2006.
56 Chris Atkins, interview with Geoff Hoon, 8 January 2007.
57 Milan Rai, interview transcript 2, pp.1, 9, 30 May 2006.
58 Milan Rai, interview transcript 2, p.2, 30 May 2006.
59 Maya Evans, interview transcript, p.10, 12 June 2006.
60 Maya Evans, *Naming The Dead* (JNV Publications, 2006).
61 Home Office website, All Crime for City of Westminster, April 2005–March 2006, http://www.crimestatistics.org.uk/tool/

default.asp?region=9&force=12&cdrp=107&l1=0&l2=0&l3=0&s
ub=0&v=36.

62 'Where peaceful protest can be costly', *Independent*, 10 December
2005, http://news.independent.co.uk/uk/legal/article332149.ece.

63 Maya Evans, *Naming The Dead* (JNV Publications, 2006), p.74.

64 Maya Evans, *Naming The Dead* (JNV Publications, 2006), p.76.

65 Maya Evans, *Naming The Dead* (JNV Publications, 2006), p.77.

66 Maya Evans, telephone interview with Chris Atkins, 30 January
2007.

67 'Peace campaigner fined for Whitehall protest', 12 April 2006,
Guardian, http://politics.guardian.co.uk/iraq/story/
0,,1752389,00.html. Remembrance Sunday 2005, Department of
Culture Media and Sport Archive, http://www.culture.gov.uk/
Reference_library/Press_notices/archive_2005/dcms149_05.htm.

68 Think of the Children, http://thinkofthechildren.co.uk; *The Friday
Thing*, http://www.thefridaything.co.uk.

69 Mark Thomas, interview transcript, p.26.

70 http://www.bloggerheads.com/carols. 'Tea Party Protestor', BBC,
5 April 2006, http://news.bbc.co.uk/1/hi/england/london/
4878878.stm.

71 Betty Hunter, interview transcript, p.10, 21 August 2006.

72 Palestinian Solidarity Campaign, 'Democratic right to protest
under attack', 15 June 2005, http://www.palestinecampaign.org/
psc_news.asp?d=y&id=75.

73 Betty Hunter, interview transcript, p.8, 21 August 2006.

74 Betty Hunter, interview transcript, pp.7–11, 21 August 2006.

75 Betty Hunter, interview transcript, p.11, 21 August 2006.

76 Malcolm Carroll, interview transcript, p.27, 17 October 2006.

77 Malcolm Carroll, interview transcript, p.2, 17 October 2006.

78 Plane Stupid press release, 24 September 2006,
http://www.campaignstrategy.org/campaignexamples/planestupid_
pressrelease.html.

79 Malcolm Carroll, interview transcript, p.2, 17 October 2006.

80 'Planet saved?: Why the green movement is taking to the streets',
Alice O'Keefe, *New Statesman*, 6 November 2006,
http://www.newstatesman.com/200611060014.

81 Malcolm Carroll, interview transcript, p.6, 17 October 2006.

82 Malcolm Carroll, interview transcript, p.7, 17 October 2006.

83 Nottingham Airport family transcript, pp.20–23, 13 October
2006. Malcolm Carroll, interview transcript, p.15, 17 October
2006.

84 Malcolm Carroll, interview transcript, p.27, 17 October 2006.

85 Malcolm Carroll, interview transcript, p.15, 17 October 2006.

86 Memorable quotes from *Speed*, Independent Movie Database, http://www.imdb.com/title/tt0111257/quotes.

87 Fairford Coach Action, http://www.fairfordcoachaction.org.uk.

88 Memorable quotes from *Speed*, Independent Movie Database, http://www.imdb.com/title/tt0111257/quotes.

89 'Human Rights Act victory for Fairford Coach Action', UK Indymedia, http://www.indymedia.org.uk/en/2004/12/302517.html.

90 Press release, UK Indymedia, http://www.indymedia.org.uk/en/2006/12/358271.html.

91 'A law the Stasi would have loved', Henry Porter, *Observer*, 6 November 2005, http://observer.guardian.co.uk/comment/story/0,6903,1635351,00.html.

92 'Petty excesses that add up to a major assault on our freedom', leading article, *Independent*, 10 December 2005, http://comment.independent.co.uk/leading_articles/article332105.ece.

93 John Catt, interview transcript 2, p.13, 17 June 2005.

94 Shami Chakrabarti, interview transcript, p.8.

95 Blair's 'frenzied law making: a new offence for every day spent in office', Nigel Morris, *Independent*, 16 August 2006, http://news.independent.co.uk/uk/politics/article1219484.ece.

96 Kevin Gillam, interview transcript, 29 June 2006. 'Student challenges use of terror act', BBC, 12 September 2003, http://news.bbc.co.uk/1/hi/england/london/3101886.stm. 'Police stop and search 100 people a day under new anti-terror laws', 25 January 2006, Information Liberation, http://www.informationliberation.com/index.php?id=5440.

97 Walter Wolfgang, interview transcript 1, p.37, 25 July 2006.

98 Betty Hunter, interview transcript, p.11, 21 August 2006.

99 John Catt, interview transcript 2, p.2, 17 June 2005.

100 Richard, interview transcript 1, p.17, 17 June 2006.

101 Mark Thomas, interview transcript.

102 Forward Intelligence Team, http://en.wikipedia.org/wiki/Forward_Intelligence_Team.

103 Barry Norman, interview transcript, p.8, 14 December 2006.

104 Barry Norman, interview transcript, p.9, 14 December 2006; Richard, interview transcript 1, p.30, 17 June 2006.

Chapter 3

1 Dorothy Thompson, *Ladies Home Journal*, May 1958.

2 Jerry Fishenden, interview transcript, p.7, 15 December 2006.

3 'Ministers plan Big Brother police powers', *Sunday Telegraph*, 4 February 2007, http://www.telegraph.co.uk/core/Content/

displayPrintable.jhtml?xml=/news/2007/02/04/
ncrime04.xml&site=5&page=0.

4   *An Historical Review of the Constitution and Government of
    Pennsylvania*, 1759.

5   'Support for liberties "declining"', BBC, 24 January 2007,
    http://news.bbc.co.uk/1/hi/uk/6290867.stm.

6   'Speaking cameras to tick off litterers', *Northern Echo*, 19 September
    2006, http://archive.thenorthernecho.co.uk/2006/9/19/231601.html.

7   Norris and McCahill, *CCTV In London* (2002),
    http://www.urbaneye.net/results/ue_wp6.pdf.

8   Peugeot 207 advert.

9   Sound Alert, http://www.soundalert.com/cctv2.htm.

10 'CCTV channel beamed to your home', *Daily Telegraph*,
    10 May 2006, http://www.telegraph.co.uk/news/main.jhtml?xml=/
    news/2006/05/09/ncctv09.xml&sSheet=/news/2006/05/09/
    ixuknewsnew.html.

11 'Cameras used to monitor toilets', BBC, 28 February 2005,
    http://news.bbc.co.uk/1/hi/england/lancashire/4304337.stm.

12 'Working towards identifiable feature extraction from a
    pedestrian's gait', T. Chamberlain, UTSG, January 2006.

13 'Innovative artificial intelligence system for monitoring CCTV
    footage', CCTV Core, 12 December 2006,
    http://www.cctv-core.co.uk/12-12-2006-innovative-artificial-
    intelligence-system-for-monitoring-cctv-footage.html.

14 'Olympics audio surveillance row', BBC, 26 November 2006,
    http://news.bbc.co.uk/1/hi/uk_politics/6186348.stm.

15 'You are undie surveillance', *Sun*, 29 January 2007,
    http://www.thesun.co.uk/article/0,,2-2007040610,00.html.

16 'Helmet-cam target violent crime', Silicon.com, 2 February 2007,
    http://www.silicon.com/publicsector/0,3800010403,39165619,00.
    htm.

17 Follow Us, http://www.followus.co.uk.

18 'Microchips for mentally ill planned in shake-up', *Daily
    Telegraph*, 18 January 2007, http://www.telegraph.co.uk/news/
    main.jhtml?xml=/news/2007/01/17/ncrime17.xml.

19 http://www.cctv-information.co.uk/constant3/anpr.html.

20 'Navigating future for road charges', BBC, 29 December 2005,
    http://news.bbc.co.uk/1/hi/sci/tech/4552132.stm.

21 'Road pricing: your bill is on its way', *Independent*, 23 May
    2006,
    http://motoring.independent.co.uk/features/article570624.ece.

22 'Blair goes on ID card defensive', BBC, 6 November 2006,
    http://news.bbc.co.uk/1/hi/uk_politics/6120220.stm.

23 http://www.crimereduction.gov.uk/cctv/cctvminisite4.htm.
24 'CCTV "not a crime deterrent"', BBC, 14 August 2002, http://news.bbc.co.uk/2/hi/uk_news/2192911.stm.
25 'Peeping Tom CCTV operators jailed', BBC, 13 January 2006, http://news.bbc.co.uk/2/hi/uk_news/england/merseyside/4609746.stm.
26 'Something to watch over us', BBC, 4 May 1999, http://news.bbc.co.uk/1/hi/uk/334853.stm.
27 Boris Johnson, interview transcript 2, p.16, 25 July 2006.
28 http://www.publications.parliament.uk/pa/cm200506/cmbills/009/06009.1-7.html#j001.
29 http://www.opsi.gov.uk/acts/en2003/03en44-b.htm.
30 Genewatch UK, citing NDNAD Annual Report 2002–03; Home Office 2006; *Hansard*, 24 July and 4 September 2006, http://www.genewatch.org/sub.shtml?als%5Bcid%5D=548276.
31 Genewatch UK, reply to FOI request; 8 May 2006, http://www.genewatch.org/uploads/f03c6d66a9b354535738483c1c3d49e4/AnswerFOI8May.pdf.
32 'Child database "will ruin family privacy"', *Daily Telegraph*, 23 November 2006, http://www.telegraph.co.uk/news/main.jhtml?xml=/news/2006/11/22/nchild22.xml.
33 'New tax to hit home improvements', *Daily Mail*, 8 January 2007, http://www.thisismoney.co.uk/mortgages/article.html?in_article_id=416183&in_page_id=8.
34 '"Computer says no" to Mr Blair's botched £20 bn NHS upgrade', *Daily Telegraph*, 4 June 2006, http://www.telegraph.co.uk/news/main.jhtml?xml=/news/2006/06/04/nhs04.xml.
35 All quotes from Helen Wilkinson, interview transcript, pp.3, 5, 7, p.11–12, p.14, 13 December 2006.
36 Helen Wilkinson, House of Commons debate, 16 June 2005, http://www.publications.parliament.uk/pa/cm200506/cmhansrd/cm050616/debtext/50616-35.htm.
37 *Transformational Government*, http://www.cio.gov.uk/documents/pdf/transgov/transgov-strategy.pdf.
38 'Blair rebuts Big Brother claims', *Guardian*, 15 January 2007, http://www.guardian.co.uk/uk_news/story/0,,1990939,00.html.
39 Phil Booth, interview transcript 3, p.4, 14 June 2006.
40 'Brown to sell ID card data to offset project's high cost', *Scotsman*, 7 August 2006, http://news.scotsman.com/topics.cfm?tid=428&id=1141782006.
41 Rachel North, interview transcript, p.20, 15 December 2006.
42 'The pregnancy police are watching you', *Guardian*, 4 September 2006, http://www.guardian.co.uk/women/story/0,,1864317,00.html.

43 Tony Blair, speech to Labour Party Conference 1995, http://www.theyworkforyou.com/lords/?id=2006-01-16b.427.12&s=%22instead+of+wasting+hundreds%22+id#g431.1.

44 http://www.publications.parliament.uk/pa/cm200506/cmhansrd/cm060118/debtext/60118-03.htm.

45 Speech at the Conservative Party Spring Forum, 8 April 2006, http://www.conservatives.com/tile.do?def=news.story.page&obj_id=129136.

46 'Meme, counter-meme', *Wired*, October 1994, http://www.wired.com/wired/archive/2.10/godwin.if.html.

47 http://www.preventgenocide.org/prevent/removing-facilitating-factors/IDcards/.

48 War speech, House of Commons, 3 September 1939, http://www.winstonchurchill.org/i4a/pages/index.cfm?pageid=878.

49 Lord Philips, interview transcript 1, p.26, 22 August 2006.

50 'Identity cards in Britain: past experience and policy implications', *History and Policy*, http://www.historyandpolicy.org/archive/pol-paper-print-33.html.

51 Holocaust Memorial Day, http://www.hmd.org.uk/files/1157732967-102.pdf.

52 'Sectarian violence escalates', Associated Press, 10 July 2006, http://www.wwrn.org/article.php?idd=22090&con=34&sec=46.

53 'The Stasi', CNN, http://www.cnn.com/SPECIALS/cold.war/experience/spies/spy.files/intelligence/stasi.html.

54 Henry Porter, interview transcript 1, p.18, 26 June 2006.

55 *Daily Telegraph*, 6 November 2006, http://www.number10.gov.uk/output/Page10360.asp.

56 'ID cards "wouldn't stop attacks"', BBC, 8 July 2005, http://news.bbc.co.uk/2/hi/uk_news/politics/4663155.stm.

57 Rachel North, interview transcript, p.8.

58 http://www.publications.parliament.uk/pa/cm200405/cmhansrd/cm050209/debtext/50209-03.htm.

59 Phil Booth, interview transcript 1, p.14, 14 June 2006.

60 http://www.publications.parliament.uk/pa/cm200506/cmhansrd/cm060118/debtext/60118-03.htm.

61 'ID cards will lead to "massive fraud"', *Scotsman*, 18 October 2005, http://news.scotsman.com/index.cfm?id=2103982005.

62 Jerry Fishenden, interview transcript, p.8, 15 December 2006.

63 'DVLA man helped activists', BBC, 25 October 2004, http://news.bbc.co.uk/1/hi/england/staffordshire/3951945.stm.

64 'DWP staff hit by online tax fraud,' ePolitix, 13 December 2005, http://www.epolitix.com/EN/News/200512/74432b4c-1956-49eb-8fef-a859a341bcf8.htm.

65 'Data protection charges for the sale of police data', *The Register*,
    26 April 2005, http://www.theregister.co.uk/2005/04/26/
    data_protection_charges.
66 *What Price Privacy*, 10 May 2006,
    http://www.ico.gov.uk/upload/documents/library/corporate/
    research_and_reports/what_price_privacy.pdf.
67 Jerry Fishenden, interview transcript, p.21, 15 December
    2006.
68 http://www.publications.parliament.uk/pa/cm200203/cmhansrd/
    vo031015/debtext/31015-02.htm.
69 http://www.nao.org.uk/pn/05-06/05061387.htm.
70 'Marathon runner jailed for benefit fraud', *Guardian*,
    19 January 2007, http://www.guardian.co.uk/crime/article/
    0,,1994626,00.html.
71 Ross Anderson, interview transcript, p.5, 24 August 2006.
72 Phil Booth, interview transcript, p.15, 14 June 2006.
73 Ross Anderson, interview transcript, p.17, 24 August 2006.
74 http://www.publications.parliament.uk/pa/cm200506/cmhansrd/
    vo050517/debtext/50517-06.htm.
75 Geoff Hoon, interview, 8 January 2007.
76 Simon Davies and Gus Hussein, interview transcript 1, p.11,
    22 August 2006.
77 'US imposes biometric entry demand', BBC, 26 October 2006,
    http://news.bbc.co.uk/1/hi/world/americas/6080384.stm.
78 'New, secure biometric passports in the EU strengthen security and
    data protection and facilitate travelling', EU press release,
    29 June 2006, http://europa.eu/rapid/
    pressReleasesAction.do?reference=IP/06/872&format=HTML&ag
    ed=1&language=EN&guiLanguage=en.
79 http://www.statewatch.org/news/2005/sep/03clarke.htm.
80 'Blunkett plan for ID cards for adults denounced by civil liberties
    group', *Independent*, 7 July 2003,
    http://news.independent.co.uk/uk/politics/article95056.ece.
81 'Cameras capture racist taunts of anti-riot police', *Times*,
    10 November 2005, http://www.timesonline.co.uk/tol/news/world/
    europe/article588472.ece.
82 'ID cards in other countries', BBC, 4 August 2004,
    http://news.bbc.co.uk/go/pr/fr/-/1/hi/uk_politics/3527612.stm.
83 Simon Davies and Gus Hussein, interview transcript 1, p.12,
    22 August 2006.
84 Shami Chakrabarti, 'Yet another step along a dangerous road',
    Independent, 15 January 2007, http://comment.independent.co.uk/
    commentators/article2154801.ece.

85 'Parents prepare to sue fingerprint grabbers', *The Register*, 6 October 2006, http://www.theregister.co.uk/2006/10/06/fingerprint_action.

86 'Blair haunted by his health problems', *Scotsman*, 1 October 2004, http://news.scotsman.com/topics.cfm?tid=1037&id=1145652004.

87 'William cautioned for selling cannabis', *Independent*, 13 January 1998, http://www.findarticles.com/p/articles/mi_qn4158/is_19980113/ai_n9648922.

88 'Kelly defends private school decision', *Guardian*, 8 January 2007, http://www.guardian.co.uk/pda/story/0,,1985185-Top+stories,00.html.

89 'Criminal records bureau mix-up uncovered', BBC, 21 May 2006, http://news.bbc.co.uk/1/hi/uk/5001624.stm.

90 'Tax credits still being overpaid', BBC, 25 April 2006, http://news.bbc.co.uk/1/hi/business/4939186.stm.

91 'Plundering the Public Sector', David Craig with Richard Brooks, http://www.wsws.org/articles/2006/jun2006/cons-j17.shtml.

92 'Costly CSA reforms "not working"', BBC, 29 June 2006, http://news.bbc.co.uk/1/hi/uk_politics/5130206.stm.

93 'Website to "shame" absent parents', BBC, 1 December 2006, http://news.bbc.co.uk/1/hi/uk/6166045.stm.

94 'UK court project farce continues', *ComputerWire*, 22 June 2006, http://www.computerwire.com/industries/research/?pid=9980EA5E-043F-4F3E-B712-B52FB0616ECA.

95 'Farm subsides system criticised', BBC, 24 January 2006, http://news.bbc.co.uk/1/hi/uk/4642134.stm.

96 '1.5bn squandered on government IT', *Computing*, 13 March 2003, http://www.computing.co.uk/articles/print/2069823.

97 'ID cards scheme may cost £18bn', BBC, 29 May 2005, http://news.bbc.co.uk/1/hi/uk_politics/4590817.stm.

98 All quotes from Simon Davies and Gus Hussein, interview transcript 1, pp.6, 13, 16, 23–27, 29–30, 33–37, and interview transcript 2, pp.31, 33, 22 August 2006.

99 'ID cards to costs £300 per person', *Observer*, 29 May 2005, http://observer.guardian.co.uk/politics/story/0,6903,1494944,00.html.

100 http://www.theyworkforyou.com/lords/?id=2005-11-16b.1073.9.

101 http://www.publications.parliament.uk/pa/cm200506/cmhansrd/cm060118/debtext/60118-03.htm.

102 Henry Porter, interview transcript, p.18, 20 June 2006.

103 Shami Chakrabarti, interview transcript, p.18, 23 June 2006.

104 Boris Johnson, interview transcript, p.15, 28 June 2006.

105 Clare Short, interview transcript, p.32, 20 September 2006.

106 'Parents prepared to sue fingerprint grabbers', Mark Ballard, *The Register*, 6 October 2006, http://www.theregister.co.uk/2006/10/06/fingerprint_action.

Chapter 4

1   Mouloud Sihali, interview transcript 1, pp.1, 4, 6, 8, 21 November 2006.

2   Tony Blair, 'Prevention and suppression of terrorism debate', 10 March 1993, http://www.publications.parliament.uk/pa/cm199293/cmhansrd/1993-03-10/Debate-3.html.

3   Henry Porter, interview transcript 1, p.15, 20 June 2006.

4   'Does Magna Carta mean nothing to you? Did she die in vain?!' – Twelve Angry Men/Hancock's Half Hour.

5   *Magna Carta*, The British Library, http://www.bl.uk/treasures/magnacarta/basics.html.

6   See previous note.

7   Adam Hoschild, *Bury The Chains: The British Struggle to Abolish Slavery* (Pan MacMillan, 2005), pp.48–51.

8   Brian A.W. Simpson, *In the Highest Degree Odious* (Oxford University Press, 1992).

9   See previous note.

10 Kenneth Clarke, interview transcript, p.7, 25 January 2007.

11 'Northern Ireland activates internment law', 'On This Day', BBC, http://news.bbc.co.uk/onthisday/hi/dates/stories/august/9/newsid_4071000/4071849.stm; Internment: Chronology of Events, CAIN, University of Ulster, http://cain.ulst.ac.uk/events/intern/chron.htm.

12 Michael Mansfield, interview transcript 1, p.25, 24 June 2006.

13 Northern Ireland Office, http://www.nio.gov.uk/the-agreement. Malcolm Sutton, *Index of Deaths* (CAIN, University of Ulster), http://cain.ulst.ac.uk/sutton/book/index.html#append.

14 Martin Melaugh, *Deaths Related to the Conflict, 2002–2006* (CAIN, University of Ulster), http://cain.ulst.ac.uk/sutton/chron/index.html.

15 'Terror detention law "Must Go"', BBC, 4 August 2004, http://news.bbc.co.uk/2/hi/uk_news/politics/3534274.stm.

16 'How did 7/7 change politics?', BBC, 30 June 2006, http://news.bbc.co.uk/1/hi/uk_politics/5071578.stm.

17 The Patriot Act, http://www.legal-definitions.com/civil-rights-law/patriot-act.htm?gclid=CN_8rND92okCFQm0EAodPk0R4A.

18 Anti-Terrorism Crime and Security Act 2001, http://www.homeoffice.gov.uk/security/terrorism-and-the-law/anti-terrorism-crime-security-ac.

19 Liberty press office, 30 January 2007: 'The Anti-Terror, Crime and Security Bill was introduced in late September 2001 and became law just two months later in November 2001. The average time for a bill to become an act is generally three months of consultation (when it is introduced as a white paper), then four–six months of Parliamentary scrutiny after it has been published as a Bill. Therefore many bills take roughly nine months to become an Act, give or take a few months depending on the type of bill, of course.'

20 'Q&A: Anti-Terrorism Legislation', BBC, http://news.bbc.co.uk/1/hi/uk/3197394.stm.

21 Gareth Peirce, interview transcript, p.4, 2 December 2006.

22 'Belmarsh, Britain's Guantanamo Bay?', BBC, 6 October 2004, http://news.bbc.co.uk/1/hi/magazine/3714864.stm.

23 Ian Loader, interview transcript 2, p.21, 28 September 2006.

24 'Belmarsh, Britain's Guantanamo Bay?', BBC, 6 October 2004, http://news.bbc.co.uk/1/hi/magazine/3714864.stm.

25 *Human Rights: A Broken Promise* (Amnesty International, February 2006).

26 Michael Mansfield, interview transcript, p.13, 24 June 2006.

27 'Al-Qaeda plotter jailed for life', BBC, 7 December 2006, http://news.bbc.co.uk/1/hi/uk/6123236.stm.

28 'Apart from sharing a surname, what do the Prime Minister and the Metropolitan Police Commissioner Sir Ian Blair have in common?', *Sun*, 15 November 2006.

29 Gareth Peirce, interview transcript, p.3, 2 December 2006.

30 'Britain's dark places', *Village Voice*, 7–13 January 2004, http://www.villagevoice.com/news/0401,fahim,50037,1.html; *Human Rights: A Broken Promise* (Amnesty International, February 2006).

31 'Terror detainees win Lords appeal', BBC, 16 December 2004, http://news.bbc.co.uk/1/hi/uk/4100481.stm.

32 See previous note.

33 'Terrorism Act: the real threat to the nation', *Socialist Review*, March 2005, http://www.socialistreview.org.uk/article.php?articlenumber=9281.

34 'Terror detainees win Lords appeal', BBC, 16 December 2004, http://news.bbc.co.uk/1/hi/uk/4100481.stm.

35 See previous note.

36 *States of Emergency* (Office for Democratic Institutions and Human Rights), http://www1.osce.org/odihr/13485.html.

37 Gareth Peirce, interview transcript, pp.4–5, 2 December 2006.

38 'New terrorism law fundamentally flawed', *Human Rights News*, 16 March 2005, http://hrw.org/english/docs/2005/03/15/uk10321.htm.

39 Michael Mansfield, interview transcript 1, p.12, 24 June 2006.

40 'Judge grants bail to Belmarsh detainees', *Times Online*, 10 March 2005, http://www.timesonline.co.uk/article/0,,2-1519241,00.html.

41 *Biography of Nelson Mandela*, http://www.anc.org.za/people/mandela.html.

42 Gareth Peirce, interview transcript, pp.3–4, 2 December 2006.

43 'Wood Green Ricin Plot', Wikipedia, http://en.wikipedia.org/wiki/Wood_Green_ricin_plot.

44 Peter Oborne, *The Use and Abuse of Terror* (Centre of Policy Studies, 2006), p.24, http://www.channel4.com/news/microsites/S/spinning_terror/downloads/oborne_terror.pdf.

45 Mouloud Sihali, interview transcript 1, p.14, 21 November 2006.

46 Mouloud Sihali, interview transcript 1, pp.19, 22, 21 November 2006.

47 'MI5's "torture" evidence revealed', BBC, 21 October 2005, http://news.bbc.co.uk/2/hi/uk_news/politics/4363254.stm; Mouloud Sihali, interview transcript 1, pp.19, 22, 27, 21 November 2006; 'Ricin Case Timeline', BBC, http://news.bbc.co.uk/1/hi/uk/4433459.stm.

48 'Wood Green Ricin Plot', Wikipedia, http://en.wikipedia.org/wiki/Wood_Green_ricin_plot; 'Terror police find deadly poison', BBC, 7 January 2003, http://news.bbc.co.uk/2/hi/uk_news/2636099.stm; 'UK Terror Trial Finds No Terror', George Smith PhD, Senior Fellow, GlobalSecurity.org, 11 April 2005, http://www.globalsecurity.org/org/nsn/nsn-050411.htm.

49 Peter Oborne, *The Use and Abuse of Terror* (Centre of Policy Studies, 2006), p.21.

50 *Daily Mail*, 8 January 2003.

51 'UK Terror Trial Finds No Terror', George Smith PhD, Senior Fellow, GlobalSecurity.org, 11 April 2005, http://www.globalsecurity.org/org/nsn/nsn-050411.htm.

52 'Blair warning over terror threat', BBC, 7 January 2003, http://news.bbc.co.uk/1/hi/uk_politics/2635807.stm.

53 'Europe sceptical of Iraq-Ricin link', CNN, 12 February 2003, http://www.cnn.com/2003/WORLD/meast/02/12/sprj.irq.powell.ricin/; 'UK Terror Trial Finds No Terror', George Smith PhD, Senior Fellow, GlobalSecurity.org, 11 April 2005, http://www.globalsecurity.org/org/nsn/nsn-050411.htm.

54 'Tony Blair on *Newsnight:* part two', *Guardian*, 7 February 2003, http://politics.guardian.co.uk/foreignaffairs/story/0,11538,891113,00.html.

55 General Myers made this claim on CNN's *Late Edition With Wolf Blitzer*, 30 March 2003, www.edition.cnn.com/TRANSCRIPTS/

0303/30/le.00.html; Peter Oborne, *The Use and Abuse of Terror* (Centre of Policy Studies, 2006), p.22.

56 'Ricin Case Timeline', BBC, http://news.bbc.co.uk/2/hi/uk_news/ 4433459.stm; http://www.williambowles.info/spysrus/ ricin_plot.html.

57 Jennifer and Des, interview transcript, p.25, 1 December 2006.

58 *The Politics Show*, BBC, 14 November 2004, http://news.bbc.co.uk/1/hi/programmes/politics_show/3998559.stm.

59 *Scotsman, Evening Standard, Ananova*, 14 April 2004.

60 Mououd Sihali jurors, interview transcript, 12 December 2006.

61 'Ricin Case Timeline', BBC, http://news.bbc.co.uk/2/hi/uk_news/ 4433459.stm.

62 Mouloud Sihali, interview transcript 1, p.35, 21 November 2006.

63 Mouloud Sihali, interview transcript 1, p.35; Mouloud Sihali, interview transcript 2, p.1, 21 November 2006.

64 Mouloud Sihali, interview transcript 1, p.34; Mouloud Sihali, interview transcript 2, p.1, 21 November 2006.

65 Mouloud Sihali, interview transcript 2, p.1, 21 November 2006.

66 Mouloud Sihali, interview transcript 1, p.8, 21 November 2006.

67 Mouloud Sihali, interview transcript 1, pp.1, 4, 6, 8, 21 November 2006.

68 Mouloud Sihali, interview transcript 1, p.2, 21 November 2006.

69 Mouloud Sihali, interview transcript 2, p.7, 21 November 2006.

70 Mouloud Sihali, interview transcript 2, p.13, 21 November 2006.

71 Mouloud Sihali jurors, interview transcript, p.7, 16 December 2006.

72 Michael Mansfield, interview transcript, p.24, 24 June 2006.

73 House of Commons Home Affairs, fourth report 2006, 'Background Chapter', http://www.publications.parliament.uk/pa/ cm200506/cmselect/cmhaff/910/91005.htm#note2.

74 '28 terror limit inadequate', BBC, 3 July 2006, http://news.bbc.co.uk/1/hi/uk_politics/5138294.stm.

75 Ken Luckhardt and Brenda Wall, *Organise or Starve: The History of the South African Congress of Trade Unions* (Lawrence and Wishart, 1980), http://www.anc.org.za/ancdocs/history/congress/ sactu/organsta12.html.

76 'Guildford Four released after 15 Years', 'On This Day', BBC, http://news.bbc.co.uk/onthisday/hi/dates/stories/october/19/ newsid_2490000/2490039.stm; 'Birmingham Six freed after 16 years', 'On This Day', BBC, http://news.bbc.co.uk/onthisday/hi/dates/ stories/march/14/newsid_2543000/2543613.stm.

77 Michael Mansfield, interview transcript, p.19, 24 June 2006.

78 'Ministers firm on detention charge', BBC, 7 November 2005, http://news.bbc.co.uk/1/hi/uk_politics/4411358.stm.

79   Clare Short, interview transcript, p.20, 20 September 2006.
80   'Ricin Case Timeline', BBC, http://news.bbc.co.uk/1/hi/uk/
     4433459.stm.
81   'Police urges terror rethink', BBC, 17 April 2005,
     http://news.bbc.co.uk/1/hi/uk/4451831.stm.
82   Barry Norman, interview transcript, p.15, 6 November 2006.
83   'Police urges terror rethink', BBC, 17 April 2005,
     http://news.bbc.co.uk/1/hi/uk/4451831.stm.
84   Kenneth Clarke, interview transcript, p.10, 25 January 2007.
85   'The *Sun* Says', *Sun*, 8 July 2005.
86   Peter Oborne, *The Use and Abuse of Terror* (Centre for Policy
     Studies, 2006), p.9.
87   Prime Minister's press conference, 5 August 2005,
     http://www.number10.gov.uk/output/Page8041.asp.
88   Clare Short, interview transcript, p.20, 20 September 2006.
89   Prime Minister's press conference, 5 August 2005,
     http://www.number10.gov.uk/output/Page8041.asp.
90   Michael Mansfield, interview transcript 1, 24 June 2006.
91   Counter-terrorism legislation, letter from Andy Hayman to
     Charles Clarke, 6 November 2005.
92   Peter Oborne, *The Use and Abuse of Terror* (Centre for Policy
     Studies, 2006), p.25.
93   Counter-terrorism legislation, letter from Andy Hayman to
     Charles Clarke, 6 November 2005.
94   Professor Ross Anderson, interview transcript, p.19, 24 August
     2006.
95   Counter-terrorism legislation, letter from Andy Hayman to
     Charles Clarke, 6 November 2005.
96   See previous note.
97   Michael Mansfield, interview transcript, p.20, 24 June 2006.
98   See note 95.
99   'Ministers stay firm on 90-day detention plan', Tania Branigan
     and Patrick Wintour, *Guardian*, 8 November, 2005,
     http://politics.guardian.co.uk/labour/story/0,9061,1636794,00.html;
     'Point by point: the terror debate', BBC, 9 November 2005,
     http://news.bbc.co.uk/1/hi/uk_politics/4421518.stm.
100 Kenneth Clarke, interview transcript, p.19, 25 January 2007.
101 Mark Thomas, interview transcript, p.18, 31 August 2006.
102 Tony Blair, Prevention and suppression of terrorism debate,
     10 March 1993, http://www.publications.parliament.uk/pa/
     cm199293/cmhansrd/1993-03-10/Debate-3.html.
103 'Blair facing crunch terror vote', BBC, 9 November 2005,
     http://news.bbc.co.uk/1/hi/uk_politics/4419970.stm.

104 Clare Short, interview transcript, 20 September 2006.

105 John Tulloch, interview transcript, 17 October 2006.

106 John Tulloch, interview transcript 1, p.6, 17 October 2006.

107 John Tulloch, interview transcript 1, pp.7–8, 17 October 2006.

108 John Tulloch, interview transcript 1, p.10, 17 October 2006.

109 John Tulloch, interview transcript, p.26, 17 October 2006.

110 John Tulloch, interview transcript, p.27, 17 October 2006.

111 'Blair defeated over terror laws', BBC, 9 November 2006, http://news.bbc.co.uk/1/hi/uk_politics/4422086.stm.

112 Associated Press, Bowie TV/Sky tape 466683EF05/0998.

113 'Blair facing crunch terror vote', BBC, 9 November 2005, http://news.bbc.co.uk/1/hi/uk_politics/4419970.stm.

114 'Blair loses vote', Associated Press, 11 November 2005, Bowtie TV/Sky tape 466683EF05/0998.

115 'Blair defeated on terror bill', *Guardian*, http://politics.guardian.co.uk/terrorism/story/0,15935,1637542,00.html.

116 'Sentamu criticises 90-day detention', *Guardian*, 5 February 2007, http://www.guardian.co.uk/uklatest/story/0,,-6394026,00.html.

117 http://www.quotedb.com/quotes/2283.

Chapter 5

1   Antisocial behaviour orders, Home Office, http://www.homeoffice.gov.uk/anti-social-behaviour/penalties/anti-social-behaviour-orders/.

2   'Edinburgh study of youth transitions and crime' cited in 'The War on Youth', Alice O'Keeffe, *New Statesman*, 16 October 2006.

3   Crime And Disorder Act 1998, chapter 3, http://www.opsi.gov.uk/acts/acts1998/98037--b.htm#1.

4   Antisocial Behaviour Orders, Revised Training Material Incorporating New Powers Contained in S61–66 Police Reform Act 2002 and Antisocial Behaviour Act 2003.

5   'Balance of Probabilities', Legal Definitions, http://legal-dictionary.thefreedictionary.com/Balance+of+probabilities.

6   ASBO Watch – Children, Statewatch, http://www.statewatch.org/asbo/asbowatch-children.htm.

7   See previous note.

8   See note 6.

9   See note 6.

10 See note 6.

11 See note 6.

12 See note 6.

13 'ASBO: An analysis of the last 6 years', ASBO Concern, July 2005, http://www.asboconcern.org.uk/asbodossier.pdf.

14 ASBO Watch – Children, Statewatch, http://www.statewatch.org/asbo/asbowatch-children.htm.

15 'ASBO: An analysis of the last 6 years', ASBO Concern, July 2005, http://www.asboconcern.org.uk/asbodossier.pdf.

16 ASBO Watch – Children, Statewatch, http://www.statewatch.org/asbo/asbowatch-children.htm.

17 'Half of Asbo holders breach order', BBC, 7 December 2006, http://news.bbc.co.uk/1/hi/uk_politics/6214662.stm.

18 'Teenagers see Asbos as badge of honour', *Guardian*, www.guardian.co.uk/crime/article/0,,1937030,00.html.

19 'Court rejects Asbos for airport activists', IndyMediaUK, 18 December 2006, http://www.indymedia.org.uk/en/2006/12/358491.html.

20 http://www.guardian.co.uk/crime/article/0,,1823019,00.html.

21 'Super-ASBOs to target gangsters', BBC, 12 January 2006, http://news.bbc.co.uk/1/hi/uk/6269581.stm.

22 'Child commissioner attacks baby Asbo plan', *Guardian*, http://politics.guardian.co.uk/homeaffairs/story/0,11026,1592015,00.html.

23 'We can clamp down on antisocial children before birth, says Blair', *Guardian Unlimitied*, 1 September 2006, http://politics.guardian.co.uk/homeaffairs/story/0,,1862706,00.html.

24 'Problem children target defended', BBC, http://news.bbc.co.uk/1/hi/uk_politics/5309890.stm.

25 'Sweden to compensate sterilised women', 4 March 1999, http://news.bbc.co.uk/1/hi/health/background_briefings/international/290661.

26 Prime Minister's Respect Action Plan launch speech, 10 January 2006, http://www.number10.gov.uk/output/Page8898.asp.

27 Eric Metcalfe, interview transcript 1, p.29, 23 June 2006.

28 'Summary justice needed to fight crime', *Scotsman*, 12 October 2005, http://news.scotsman.com/politics.cfm?id=2075882005; 'Penalty notices for disorder', Crimereduction.gov, http://www.crimereduction.gov.uk/policing20.htm.

29 'Take away the right to say "fuck" and you take away the right to say "fuck the government"', Lenny Bruce, *Fusion Anomaly*.

30 'Teenager fined for swear word', BBC, 20 February 2006, http://news.bbc.co.uk/1/hi/england/kent/4734350.stm; 'Swearing student's case dropped', BBC, 8 March 2006, http://news.bbc.co.uk/1/hi/england/kent/4785754.stm.

31 'Stallholders fined for offensive Blair T-shirts', *Times*, 4 July 2006, http://www.timesonline.co.uk/article/0,,2-2254574,00.html.

32 'Girl arrested over Bollocks to Blair shirt', *Horse & Hound*, 22 September 2005, http://www.horseandhound.co.uk/competitionnews/392/68779.html.

33 Phil Bennett and Jo Tacon, interview transcript, p.1, 20 August 2006.

34 Phil Bennett and Jo Tacon, interview transcript, p.5, 20 August 2006.

35 Phil Bennett and Jo Tacon, interview transcript, p.6, 20 August 2006.

36 Phil Bennett and Jo Tacon, interview transcript, p.8, 20 August 2006.

37 'Cops spot-fine Goth £80 for upsetting weapons detector', *The Register*, 6 July 2006, http://www.theregister.co.uk/2006/07/06/accursed_metal_detector/; 'Opinion: Freedom of speech does not extend to criticising the police', 3 July 2006.

38 Fixed Penalty Notices, Home Office, http://www.homeoffice.gov.uk/anti-social-behaviour/penalties/penalty-notices.

Chapter 6

1   Alex Stone, interview transcript 1, 14 June 2006.

2   Lords *Hansard* text, 16 December 2003, http://www.parliament.the-stationery-office.co.uk/pa/ld200304/ldhansrd/vo031216/text/31216-04.htm#31216-04_head3%20.

3   Geoff Hoon, interview with Chris Atkins, 13 January 2006.

4   Alex Stone, interview transcript 1, p.2, 14 June 2006.

5   Alex Stone, interview transcript 1, p.4, 14 June 2006.

6   Alex Stone, interview transcript 1, p.10, 14 June 2006.

7   'Snatched by the American Courts', Zoe Brennan, *Sunday Times*, 19 March 2006.

8   Boris Johnson, interview transcript 1, p.2, 28 June 2006.

9   'Bankers at centre of extradition test case', BBC, 27 September 2006, http://news.bbc.co.uk/1/hi/business/3658664.stm.

10 'Q and A: The Enron Case', BBC, 5 July 2006, http://news.bbc.co.uk/1/hi/business/3398913.stm.

11 David Bermingham, interview transcript, p.24, 19 June 2006.

12 David and Emma Bermingham, interview transcript, p.2, 19 June 2006.

13 'Sept. 11 suspect: "I am a Victim"', CNN, 15 February 2002, http://archives.cnn.com/2002/WORLD/europe/02/15/inv.uk.raissi/index.html.

14 Boris Johnson, interview transcript 2, p.2, 25 July 2006.

15 Extradition Treaty 2003, articles 8.2b and 8.3c.

16 Boris Johnson, interview transcript 1, p.1, 28 June 2006.

17 'Deferred Division – Extradition', David Lepper MP, 17 December 2003, http://www.publicwhip.org.uk/mp.php?id=uk.org.publicwhip/member/1454&showall=yes.

18 Sir Digby Jones, interview transcript, p.7, 15 December 2006.

19 'Q and A: Extradition and the NatWest Three', BBC, 13 July 2006, http://news.bbc.co.uk/1/hi/business/5164652.stm.

20 David Bermingham, interview transcript, p.39, 19 June 2006.

21 http://www.liberty-human-rights.org.uk/news-and-events/1-press-releases/2006/high-court-rules-to-extradite-enron-3.shtml.

22 David Bermingham, interview tape, 11 July 2006.

23 David Bermingham, interview tape, 11 July 2006.

24 Prime Minister's Questions, 12 July 2006, http://www.theyworkforyou.com/debates/?id=2006-07-12a.1382.2.

25 House of Commons *Hansard* debate, col. 1435, 12 July 2006.

26 House of Commons *Hansard* debate, col. 1438, 12 July 2006.

27 David Bermingham, speech to the press, 13 July 2006.

28 Emma Bermingham, interview transcript, p.1, 18 August 2006.

29 Boris Johnson, interview transcript 1, p.2, 28 June 2006.

Chapter 7

1 Quoted in Moazzam Begg, *Enemy Combatant: A British Muslim's Journey to Guantanamo and Back* (Free Press, 2006).

2 'Compilation Under International Law', 'Definitions of Torture', http://www.apt.ch/un/definition.shtml.

3 These appear on the UN High Commissioner for Human Rights list of special rapporteur country visits, http://www.ohchr.org/english/issues/torture/rapporteur/visits.htm.

4 Kate Allen, interview transcript, p.13, 28 June 2006.

5 Philippe Sands, interview transcript, p.3, 4 October 2006.

6 Convention against Torture and Other Cruel, Inhuman or Degrading Treatment or Punishment, New York, 10 December 1984, http://www.ohchr.org/english/countries/ratification/9.htm.

7 http://news.bbc.co.uk/2/hi/programmes/world_at_one/programme_highlights/1099405.stm.

8 Philippe Sands, interview transcript, p.1, 4 October 2006.

9 Cheney appearing on *Meet the Press* from Camp David, 16 September 2006, http://www.whitehouse.gov/vicepresident/news-speeches/speeches/vp20010916.html.

10 Philippe Sands, interview transcript, p.4, 4 October 2006.

11 Andrews Air Force Base, 5 December 2005, http://www.state.gov/secretary/rm/2005/57602.htm.

12 'Election hustings', Blackburn, April 2005, quoted on
http://www.craigmurray.co.uk/archives/2005/12/
damning_documen.html.

13 http://www.hrweb.org/legal/cat.html.

14 'Memo offered justification for use of torture', *Washington Post*,
8 June 2004, http://www.washingtonpost.com/wp-dyn/articles/
A23373-2004Jun7.html.

15 'Defining torture', *New York Times*, 27 June 2004,
http://www.nytimes.com/2004/06/27/weekinreview/27word.html?ex=1
403668800&en=cbeefa2cfb04c87f&ei=5007&partner=USERLAND.

16 All quotes from Moazzam Begg, interview transcript, p.1, pp.6–8,
16–17, 30 July 2006.

17 Philippe Sands, interview transcript, p.12, 4 October 2006.

18 Philippe Sands, interview transcript, p.4, 4 October 2006.

19 'The Swamp', *Chicago Tribune*, 18 April 2006,
http://newsblogs.chicagotribune.com/news_theswamp/2006/04/
posted_by_mark__1.html.

20 'British government defends conditions at Guantanamo',
18 January 2002, Word Socialist Website, http://www.wsws.org/
articles/2002/jan2002/tali-j18.shtml.

21 All quotes from White House press release, 17 July 2003,
http://www.whitehouse.gov/news/releases/2003/07/20030717-9.html.

22 Philippe Sands, interview transcript, p.9, 4 October 2006.

23 All quotes from Moazamm Begg, interview transcript, p.23.

24 Kate Allen, interview transcript, p.11, 28 June 2006.

25 June 2005, http://www.globalpolicy.org/ngos/credib/2005/
0606right.htm.

26 'UK minister condemns Guantanamo', BBC, 12 September 2006,
http://news.bbc.co.uk/1/hi/uk_politics/5340104.stm.

27 Early Day Motions, House of Commons, 8 January 2007,
http://www.publications.parliament.uk/pa/cm/cmedm/
70119e01.htm.

28 'Guantanamo unacceptable – Beckett', BBC, 12 October 2006,
http://news.bbc.co.uk/1/hi/uk_politics/6044588.stm.

29 'Attorney General calls for Guantanamo to close', *Observer*,
7 May 2007, http://observer.guardian.co.uk/politics/story/
0,,1769383,00.html.

30 See previous note.

31 *People's Daily Online*, 22 June 2006,
http://english.peopledaily.com.cn/200606/22/eng20060622_27628
9.html.

32 'WMD may never be found – Blair', 6 July 2004,
http://news.bbc.co.uk/1/hi/uk_politics/3869293.stm.

33 'Cheney confirms waterboarding', 26 October 2006, http://seattletimes.nwsource.com/html/nationworld/2003323549_cheney26.html?syndication=rss.

34 All quotes from Amani Deghayes, interview transcript, pp.21–25, 16 December 2006.

35 Geoff Hoon, interview with Chris Atkins, 8 January 2007.

36 http://www.unis.unvienna.org/unis/pressrels/2005/unisinf116.html.

37 Kate Allen, interview transcript, p.11, 28 June 2006.

38 Philippe Sands, interview transcript, p.16, 4 October 2006.

39 13 June 2006, http://news.bbc.co.uk/2/hi/americas/5069230.stm.

40 'Halliburton given $30m to expand Guantanamo Bay', http://www.commondreams.org/headlines05/0618-06.htm.

41 http://www4.army.mil/ocpa/read.php?story_id_key=7988.

42 Philippe Sands, interview transcript, p.8, 4 October 2006.

43 'Blair knew of Abu Ghraib jail abuse, says MP', *Western Mail*, 19 November 2004.

44 'Europe aided CIA flights', BBC, 7 June 2006, http://news.bbc.co.uk/1/hi/world/europe/5054426.stm.

45 'Rendition: Blair in quotes', BBC, 7 December 2005, http://news.bbc.co.uk/2/hi/uk_news/politics/4627360.stm.

46 Philippe Sands, interview transcript, p.29, 4 October 2006.

47 'Rendition: Blair in quotes', BBC, 7 December 2005, http://news.bbc.co.uk/2/hi/uk_news/politics/4627360.stm.

48 Kate Allen, interview transcript, p.10, 28 June 2006.

49 *Daily Politics Show*, BBC2, 7 June 2006, http://politics.guardian.co.uk/foreignaffairs/story/0,,1792623,00.html.

50 Philippe Sands, interview transcript, p.32, 4 October 2006.

51 'Should Tony Blair apply for a Green Card?', *First Post*, http://www.thefirstpost.co.uk/print.php?menuID=1&subID=1010.

52 Shami Chakrabarti, interview transcript, p.17, 23 June 2006.

53 http://press.homeoffice.gov.uk/Speeches/10-05-sp-euro-parliament.

54 http://www.legalaffairs.org/issues/March-April-2006/review_Arimatsu_marapr06.msp.

55 'Torture evidence inadmissible in UK courts, Lords rules', *Guardian*, 8 December 2005, http://politics.guardian.co.uk/terrorism/story/0,15935,1662107,00.html.

56 Michael Mansfield, interview transcript, p.16, 24 June 2006.

57 All quotes from Sandy Mitchell, interview transcript, pp.2–28, 31 July 2006.

58 All quotes from Jim Cottle and Mary Martini, interview transcript, p.5, 24 September 2006.

59 Kate Allen, interview transcript, pp.13–14, 28 June 2006.

60   Memorandum for the President, 25 January 2002,
     http://www2.gwu.edu/~nsarchiv/NSAEBB/NSAEBB127/
     02.01.25.pdf.
61   3 April 2006, http://www.mod.uk/DefenceInternet/DefenceNews/
     DefencePolicyAndBusiness/ReidAddressesRusiOn20thcenturyRules
     21stcenturyConflict.htm.

Chapter 8

1   Rachel North, interview transcript, pp.17–21, 12 June 2006.
2   'The Hand of History', *New Statesman*, 29 September 2003,
     http://www.newstatesman.com/200309290040.
3   Crispin Black, interview transcript, p.15.
4   'Plans for Iraq attack began on 9/11', CBS, 4 September 2002,
     http://www.cbsnews.com/stories/2002/09/04/september11/
     main520830.shtml.
5   'How Labour has subverted British Intelligence', *Spectator*,
     16 August 2003, http://findarticles.com/p/articles/mi_qa3724/
     is_200308/ai_n9266615.
6   Prime Minister's address to the nation, 20 March 2003,
     http://www.number-10.gov.uk/output/Page3322.asp.
7   Prime Minister's Questions, 9 March 2005,
     http://www.publications.parliament.uk/
     pa/cm200405/cmhansrd/cm050309/debtext/50309-03.htm.
8   'BA Flight 223 delayed again', BBC, 4 January 2004,
     http://news.bbc.co.uk/1/hi/uk/3367551.stm; 'Blair authorised
     terror alert troops', BBC, 17 February 2003, http://news.bbc.co.uk/
     1/hi/uk/2747677.stm.
9   'New row on legality of Iraq war', Third World Network,
     28 March 2005, http://www.twnside.org.sg/title2/gtrends48.htm.
10   'Lacking biolabs, trailers carried case for war', *Washington Post*,
     12 April 2006, http://www.truthout.org/cgi-bin/artman/exec/
     view.cgi/59/19024.
11   'Analysis: Blair heading to war', BBC, 13 March 2003,
     http://news.bbc.co.uk/2/hi/uk_news/politics/2847155.stm.
12   'Falconer "piled on pressure" to make Iraq war legal', *Times*,
     27 March 2005, http://www.timesonline.co.uk/article/0,,2087-
     1543505,00.html.
13   'Lord Goldsmith's legal advice and the Iraq war', *Guardian*,
     27 April 2005, http://www.guardian.co.uk/Iraq/Story/
     0,,1471664,00.html.
14   'Bush calls end to "major combat"', CNN, 2 May 2003,
     http://www.cnn.com/2003/WORLD/meast/05/01/sprj.irq.main/.

15 News briefing, 22 August 2006, http://www.defenselink.mil/
Transcripts/Transcript.aspx?TranscriptID=3697.

16 Mark Thomas, interview transcript 2, p.6, 12 January 2007.

17 http://www.theyworkforyou.com/debates/?id=2005-07-
11a.565.0&s=terrorism+speaker%3A10047#g565.1.

18 'PM warned of heightened terror risks', *Guardian*, 11 September
2003, http://www.guardian.co.uk/alqaida/story/
0,12469,1040159,00.html.

19 'Reid rejects 7 July enquiry calls', BBC, 12 May 2006,
http://news.bbc.co.uk/2/hi/uk_news/politics/4760709.stm.

20 Rachel North, interview transcript, p.13.

21 Muslim leaders, *Guardian*, 12 August 2006,
http://www.guardian.co.uk/terrorism/story/0,,1843114,00.html;
Joint Terrorism Analysis Centre, *Guardian*, 19 July 2005,
http://www.guardian.co.uk/attackonlondon/story/0,16132,153172
9,00.html; Sadiq Khan (included with Muslim leaders), BBC,
12 August 2006, http://news.bbc.co.uk/1/hi/uk/4787119.stm;
International Institute for Strategic Studies, BBC, 19 October
2004, http://news.bbc.co.uk/1/hi/world/middle_east/3756650.stm,
David Cameron, *Scotsman*, 19 December 2006,
http://news.scotsman.com/topics.cfm?tid=1&id=1880782006; US
National Intelligence Estimate (US Intelligence Agencies);
http://www.dni.gov/press_releases/Declassified_NIE_Key_Judgment
s.pdf; Foreign Policy in Focus, http://www.fpif.org/fpiftxt/467;
Martin Bell, *Guardian*, 10 August 2006;
http://commentisfree.guardian.co.uk/martin_bell/2006/08/
connecting_the_dots.html; the JIC, *Daily Telegraph*, 12 September
2003, http://www.telegraph.co.uk/news/main.jhtml?xml=/news/
2003/09/12/ndoss12.xml&sSheet=/news/2003/09/12/
ixnewstop.html; Home Affairs and Foreign Office, *Times*, 10 July
2005; http://www.timesonline.co.uk/tol/news/uk/article542420.ece;
Michael Scheuer (22-year CIA veteran and former head of the
CIA's bin Laden unit); Frontline, http://www.pbs.org/wgbh/pages/
frontline/shows/front/interviews/scheuer.html; Professor Robert
Pape, University of Chicago, http://www.antiwar.com/scheuer/
?articleid=6286; Juan Cole (Middle East expert), Salon,
http://dir.salon.com/story/news/feature/2005/07/08/blowback/
index.html; Chatham House, http://image.guardian.co.uk/sys-files/
Politics/documents/2005/07/18/Chathamreport.pdf; 79 percent of
Londoners, CND press release, http://www.cnduk.org/pages/press/
190504.html, two thirds of British people, *Guardian*, 19 July 2005,
http://www.guardian.co.uk/attackonlondon/story/
0,16132,1531387,00.html; EU Counter Terrorism Group,

Channel 4 News, 25 September 2006, http://www.channel4.com/news/special-reports/special-reports-storypage.jsp?id=3391.

22 http://www.opsi.gov.uk/Acts/acts2000/20000011.htm.

23 'The Operator, *Guardian*', 2 March 2002, http://www.guardian.co.uk/Northern_Ireland/Story/0,2763,659705,00.html.

24 'Gandhi will be my inspiration, says Brown', *Guardian*, 19 January 2007, http://politics.guardian.co.uk/labourleadership/story/0,,1994151,00.html.

25 'Frankenstein the CIA created', *Guardian*, 17 January 1999, http://www.guardian.co.uk/yemen/Story/0,2763,209260,00.html.

26 'IRA are not al-Qaeda says Blair', BBC, 26 July 2005, http://news.bbc.co.uk/2/hi/uk_news/northern_ireland/4718223.stm.

27 See previous note.

28 Belfast, 8 April 1998, http://news.bbc.co.uk/2/hi/uk_news/politics/3750847.stm.

29 'We must use science to defeat al-Qaeda', *Daily Telegraph*, 2 November 2006, http://www.telegraph.co.uk/news/main.jhtml?xml=/news/2006/11/01/ureid4001.xml.

30 'Al-Qaeda a greater threat than Nazis', *Daily Telegraph*, 24 December 2006, http://www.telegraph.co.uk/news/main.jhtml?xml=/news/2006/12/22/ublair122.xml.

31 'Police chief urges terror rethink', BBC, 17 April 2005, http://news.bbc.co.uk/2/hi/uk_news/4451831.stm.

32 'Mayor of London blog', 28 May 2006, http://www.mayor-of-london.co.uk/blog/2006/05/.

33 Tony Blair House of Commons *Hansard* debates, 9 March 2005, part 3, http://www.publications.parliament.uk/pa/cm200405/cmhansrd/cm050309/debtext/50309-03.htm#50309-03_spmin13.

34 'Met Chief tried to stop shooting enquiry', *Guardian*, 18 August 2005, http://politics.guardian.co.uk/terrorism/story/0,15935,1551416,00.html. 'Met Chief kept in dark over De Menezes', *Guardian*, 19 February 2007, http://www.guardian.co.uk/menezes/story/0,,2016279,00.html.

35 'UK still target, warns Met Chief', BBC, 16 November 2005, http://news.bbc.co.uk/2/hi/uk_news/4443638.stm.

36 'Sometimes we may have to modify some of our freedoms', *Guardian*, 11 August 2006, http://politics.guardian.co.uk/terrorism/story/0,,1842285,00.html.

37 http://en.allexperts.com/e/r/re/reichstag_fire_decree.htm.

38 'Papers pore over "bomb plot"', BBC, 11 August 2006, http://news.bbc.co.uk/2/hi/uk_news/4782397.stm.

39 'New facts emerge in terror plot', *New York Times*, 28 August 2006, http://www.blairwatch.co.uk/node/1327.

40 'Reid takes a holiday as Home Office flounders', *Daily Telegraph*, 27 May 2006, http://www.telegraph.co.uk/news/main.jhtml?xml=/news/2006/05/28/nho28.xml.

41 'UK plot terror charge dropped', BBC, 13 December 2006, http://news.bbc.co.uk/1/hi/world/south_asia/6175427.stm.

42 'Ex BNP man wanted to shoot PM', BBC, 13 February 2007, http://news.bbc.co.uk/1/hi/england/lancashire/6357261.stm.

43 'Ex-BNP man held in bomb swoop', *Burnley Citizen*, 2 October 2006, http://www.burnleycitizen.co.uk/news/newsheadlines/display.var.947927.0.exbnp_man_held_in_bomb_swoop.php.

44 Tony Benn, interview transcript, p.1, 24 September 2006.

45 'Home Secretary calls for unity in meeting with Muslim group', Home Office, 20 September 2006, http://security.homeoffice.gov.uk/news-publications/news-speeches/424848.

46 'Muslims must shop extremists', *Sun*, 19 September 2006, http://www.thesun.co.uk/article/0,,2-2006430384,00.html.

47 http://www.publications.parliament.uk/pa/cm199394/cmhansrd/1994-03-09/Debate-3.html.

48 http://www.publications.parliament.uk/pa/cm200506/cmhansrd/cm060614/debtext/60614-0477.htm.

49 http://www.snopes.com/quotes/goering.htm.

50 Julian Petley, interview transcript 2, p.8.

51 'Man shot in anti-terrorism raid', BBC, 2 June 2006, http://news.bbc.co.uk/2/hi/uk_news/5040022.stm.

52 'Police in toxic bomb hunt', *Sun*, http://www.thesun.co.uk/article/0,,2-2006250638,00.html.

53 'Cyanide fear triggered terror raid', *Times*, http://www.timesonline.co.uk/tol/news/uk/crime/article671509.ece.

54 'Stooge sketched bomb', *Sun*, http://www.thesun.co.uk/article/0,,2-2006250747,00.html.

55 'Gun cops blame gloves', *Sun*, http://www.thesun.co.uk/article/0,,2-2006260117,00.html.

56 'Don't inhibit police, Blair says', BBC, 14 June 2006, http://news.bbc.co.uk/2/hi/uk_news/politics/5079696.stm.

57 'Bomb brother in hate protest', *Sun*, 7 June 2006, pp.1, 9.

58 'Bomb pair not charged', *Sun*, 10 June 2006.

59 'Raid brothers' £38k stash', *Sun*, 15 June 2006, http://www.thesun.co.uk/article/0,,2-2006270627,2.html.

60 'Anti-terror raid intelligence was credible, says Met chief', *Daily Telegraph*, 30 June 2006, http://www.telegraph.co.uk/news/main.jhtml?xml=/news/2006/06/30/nterr30.xml&sSheet=/news/2006/06/30/ixuknews.html.

61 *Concise Oxford Dictionary of Quotations*.

62 Lord Phillips, interview transcript 1, p.16.

63 Ian Loader, interview transcript 1, p.5, 28 September 2006.

64 Ian Loader, interview transcript 1, p.9, 28 September 2006.

65 Prime Minister's speeches 2002, 'I have always said...',
    http://www.number10.gov.uk/output/Page1726.asp.

66 Ian Loader, interview transcript 1, p.15, 28 September 2006.

67 C.S. Lewis, *God in the Dock: Essays on Theology and Ethics*, ed.
    Walter Hooper (Wm B. Eerdmans Publishing Co., 1970).

68 'Saudi defence deal probe ditched', BBC, 15 December 2006,
    http://news.bbc.co.uk/1/hi/business/6181949.stm.

69 Mark Thomas, interview transcript 1, p.34, 12 January 2007.

70 'Saudi threat to scrap security ties shook number 10', *Financial
    Times*, 31 January 2007, http://www.ft.com/cms/s/85eeec12-b167-
    11db-b901-0000779e2340.html.

71 'Saudi arms deal enquiry closes in on secret papers', *Guardian*,
    http://www.guardian.co.uk/armstrade/story/0,,1952407,00.html.

72 Mark Thomas, interview transcript 1, p.36.

73 'The McTerminator', *News of the World*, 1 October 2006,
    http://www.newsoftheworld.co.uk/reid.shtml.

74 'Dear John...', *News of the World*,
    http://www.newsoftheworld.co.uk/reiderswrite.shtml.

75 'Two wheels: good. Two legs: terrorist suspect', *Times*, 17 October
    2005, http://women.timesonline.co.uk/article/0,,17909-
    1829289,00.html.

76 'Paris airport bars 72 employees', BBC, 2 November 2006,
    http://news.bbc.co.uk/1/hi/world/europe/6108574.stm.

77 'Ministers of the Interior adopt two-part anti-terror database',
    Heise, 5 September 2006, http://www.heise.de/english/newsticker/
    news/77728.

78 'Poll gains for Belgium's far right', BBC, 9 October 2006,
    http://news.bbc.co.uk/1/hi/world/europe/6032331.stm.

79 'Dutch unveil toughest face in Europe', *Times*, 13 October 2005,
    http://www.timesonline.co.uk/tol/news/world/europe/
    article577915.ece.

80 'Italian judge orders first rendition trial of CIA agents', *Times*,
    16 February 2007, http://www.timesonline.co.uk/tol/news/world/
    europe/article1395637.ece.

81 Parliament of Australia, http://www.aph.gov.au/library/intguide/
    LAW/TerrorismLaws.htm. 'Banned for a George Bush T-shirt',
    news.com.au, 14 December 2006, http://www.news.com.au/story/
    0,23599,20925632-38200,00.html.

82 'Japan website irks illegal aliens', *Asia Media*, 7 May 2004,
    http://www.asiamedia.ucla.edu/article.asp?parentid=11031.

83 'Ken's Big Brother deal with death squad President', *Evening Standard*, 14 September 2006, http://www.findarticles.com/p/articles/mi_qn4153/is_20060914/ai_n16739749.
84 'Eurasia: uphold human rights in combating terrorism', Human Rights Watch, http://hrw.org/english/docs/2006/06/14/eca13545.htm.

Chapter 9

1 Mark Thomas, interview transcript 2, p.8, 12 January 2007.
2 Tony Benn, interview transcript, p.9, 24 September 2006.
3 Mark Thomas, interview transcript 2, p.10, 12 January 2007.